MERCHANTS
SAILORS
& PIRATES
IN THE ROMAN WORLD

MERCHANTS
SAILORS
& PIRATES
IN THE ROMAN WORLD

Nicholas K. Rauh

with illustrations by
Herbert D. Rauh

TEMPUS

To Lorraine and Anna

First published 2003

PUBLISHED IN THE UNITED KINGDOM BY:
Tempus Publishing Ltd
The Mill, Brimscombe Port
Stroud, Gloucestershire GL5 2QG

PUBLISHED IN THE UNITED STATES OF AMERICA BY:
Tempus Publishing Inc.
2 Cumberland Street
Charleston, SC 29401

British Library Cataloguing in Publication Data.
A catalogue record for this book is available from the British Library.

ISBN 0 7524 2542 0

Typesetting and origination by Tempus Publishing.
Printed in Great Britain by Midway Colour Print, Wiltshire.

Contents

Acknowledgements

Humanists in other disciplines have difficulty recognising the basic fact that archaeologists do not work alone. Much of the information presented in this book represents the results of collective field efforts by the Rough Cilicia Archaeological Survey Team, reaped to my immediate benefit and twisted in some degree to my needs. The ideas thus formulated would not have been possible without the cooperation and hard work of my teammates and collaborators, LuAnn Wandsnider, Rhys Townsend, Michael Hoff, Matthew Dillon, Sancar Ozaner, Hulya Caner, Mette Korsholm, Richard Rothaus Kathleen Slane, Jennifer Tobin and Stephen Tracy. I am deeply indebted as well to the Turkish authorities responsible for authorising and for facilitating our research these many years, Dr Alpay Pasinli, M. Aykut Özet, Levent Vardar and Aliyeh Usta at the T.C. General Directorate for Monuments and Museums in Ankara, and Dr Ismail Karamut and staff of the Alanya Archaeological Museum. I also need to thank our legion of intrepid service representatives, Gülcan Demir, Nursel Uçkan, Funda Unal, Berrin Taymaz, Canan Dökmeci, Mehmet Sener, Unal Demirer and Ilknur Subasi. In Athens I remain forever grateful for the support and encouragement I have received from directors, past and present, of the American School of Classical Studies in Athens and the École Française d'Athènes, including the late William Coulsen, Stephen Tracy, Roland Étienne and Dominique Mulliez. I must also thank Bob Bridges, ASCSA school secretary, for bailing me out of one jam after another these past score years. At Delos I am mindful of the warm hospitality that I have always received from the epimelete of the island, Panagiotis Hatzidakis, and the guardians, Iannis Grammatikis and Panagiotis Alexiou. At Kinet Hüyük Marie Henriette Gates, Charles Gates, and the late Toni Cross have offered insight, opportunity and friendship throughout my career. At Isthmia, Tim Gregory and Richard Rothaus pushed me into pottery research. At Purdue, Bernard Engel and Larry Theller introduced me to the science of GIS; Darryl Granger and Ken Ridgeway that of geomorphology. John Yellen at the National Science Foundation has proven one of our strongest supporters, offering advice and encouragement that has brought certain clarity to our research. My mentor, Henry Boren, read an earlier version of this manuscript and offered many useful insights. Through his writings and through past conversations, Marcus Rediker profoundly influenced my way of thinking. In the manner of pirates I plunder his ideas, if not his very words. My father, Herb Rauh, performed feats with the illustrations. Robert Hohlfelder, Maria Pilali, Lindley Vann, Sam Wolff, Philip de Souza, Hervé Duchêne and J.Y. Empereur have all contributed in significant ways. At Tempus Publishing , Michelle Burns and Alex Cameron induced a considerable degree of polish to the manuscript. To one and all, I express heartfelt gratitude. Last but not least, I wish to thank John Lund and Elizabeth Lyding Will for the support and encouragement they have offered me these past several years. Without their help the best of what this manuscript has to offer would simply not be present. While I am certain that the people above mentioned will in many ways find this manuscript troublesome and on many points will want to disagree, I would be remiss were I to fail to acknowledge the profound effect that each has had on this project.

1

Historical introduction
and patterns of Mediterranean trade

The Athenian demos always more or less resembles a ship without a
captain. In such a ship when fear of wind gusts or the danger of
storm induces sailors to be sensible and to attend to the orders of the
captain, they do so admirably. However, once things are calm, sailors
grow overconfident and begin to express contempt for their
superiors and to quarrel with one another. The crew can no longer
agree on anything; some want to continue the voyage, while others
want the helmsman to steer to port. Some begin to let out the sheets
while others obstruct them and argue that the sails be taken in. Not
only does this spectacle of disagreement and confusion strike anyone
who watches it as disgraceful, but the state of affairs raises the spectre
of danger to everyone else on board. Often after escaping the perils
of the widest seas and fiercest storms, sailors will needlessly
shipwreck themselves within arm's reach of the shore.

Polybius, *History of Rome*, 6.44.1–7

As the ancient historian Polybius (second century BC) observes, the wooden
decks of cargo vessels plying the Mediterranean Sea harboured pervasive social
tensions that could disrupt the smooth operation of Roman trade. Merchants,
sailors and pirates lived and worked in close proximity to one another, taking
advantage of each other's professional skills, talents and resources. Each in turn
ran the risk of abuse, exploitation and violence at the hands of others. The inter-
relationships of these professionals formed the basis of an important maritime
subculture that spurred the development of commercial society at the dawn of
imperial Rome. The purpose of this book is to reconstruct this subculture from
its textual and material remains, to describe its work places, to explore its mainsprings, to define its relationship to wider Mediterranean society, and to identify
its contributions to the development of mainstream Graeco-Roman culture. To
a large degree, the violence acted out on the decks of ancient merchant vessels

was symptomatic of much broader social tensions marking the close of one era and the beginning of another. Between 167 and 67 BC the Hellenistic era of the Mediterranean world system came to an end and the Roman era began. Put in context, the emergence of piracy at this decisive juncture found its place among several defining crises of the times. As will be seen, maritime labourers played an integral role in the working out of an evolving social process. Through collectivist effort, egalitarian behaviour and acts of rebellion, merchants, sailors and pirates obtained for themselves a more legitimate place in Mediterranean society. To understand the historical significance of this transition and the part played by the maritime culture therein, historical developments of the late Hellenistic era need to be seen in context.

The decline of the Hellenistic world order (323–62 BC)

The last two centuries BC form an excellent vantage point from which to explore this emerging maritime society (**1**). These centuries marked a world in transition as the Roman West and the Hellenistic East converged, painfully for the most part, to form a cohesive Mediterranean world culture. Each half of the picture, Hellenistic Greek and Roman West, collided with the force of tectonic gravity, propelled largely by the military actions of Rome. While the setting for most of these developments was invariably the eastern Mediterranean seaboard, there is little doubt that the initiative came from

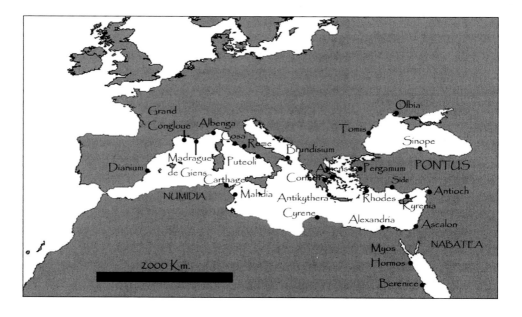

1 *Mediterranean, major towns and shipwrecks*

Rome. The political landscape of the eastern Mediterranean in 167 BC requires some elaboration.

Following the conquest of the Persian Empire by Alexander the Great in 323 BC, the eastern Mediterranean world had evolved into a competing array of dynastic principalities, independent maritime states and confederacies of loosely aligned cities. Succeeding Alexander's line in Macedonia were the Antigonids (269–166 BC), who relied on that region's rugged natural defences and its yeoman soldiers to impose their will on the cities of mainland Greece. Directly to the east, the Attalids of Pergamum (260–133) became the dominant power among the cities of what had formerly been known as Ionia (Greek cities along the Aegean coast of Anatolia). Known chiefly for their industry, craftsmanship and artistry, the Attalids survived one assault after another in their mountain-top citadel high above the Caicus River.

Along the south coast of Anatolia and the coastal lands of Syria, Phoenicia and Palestine, the Seleucids of Syria (301-62) exerted their influence with an unwieldy field army of 80,000 mercenaries and numerous garrison forces. Seleucid success was funded by its control of the luxury trade extending halfway across the globe to India and China, and by the worth of its craft production – its widely circulating, blacked-slipped fineware, its purple dyed textiles, its glass and metal production. The core region of the Seleucid empire was fortified by garrison colonies, its capital city, Antioch, was one of the most bustling of the world, its thousands of royal slaves produced priceless tapestries and other goods desired throughout the seas.

With maritime domains in Cyprus, Crete, the Cyclades and eastern North Africa, the Ptolemaic dynasty of Egypt (301–27) sustained a naval empire buttressed by contingents from smaller maritime states. First among these were the naval communities of the island of Rhodes, whose well-trained fleet of 100-plus warships enabled the Rhodians to assume moral ascendancy in the international defence of maritime trade. In tandem Egypt and Rhodes set high cultural standards for the rest of the world. From the colossal statue that lay fallen in its harbour to its wine trade, to its many diplomats and intellectuals who ranged across the Mediterranean, the Rhodians played a leading part in advancing Greek cultural heritage in this age. The beneficiary of these advancements, invariably, was Ptolemaic Alexandria, the capital of the empire housing the remains of Alexander the Great himself. A burgeoning metropolis that eventually attained a million inhabitants, Alexandria was the greatest international city of its day. Its sweeping harbours, broad avenues and magnificent public monuments withstood all comparison. Its centres of science and learning set the pace for the entire world. As a centre of international trade it was the world's greatest emporium. Its wharves dazzled with goods arriving from four continents, its market places were awash with a diverse array of languages and racial features. It was, in short, the most cosmopolitan centre of its day. Although militarily weakened and heading towards decline by the late second century BC, the Ptolemaic dynasts of the Lagid line enjoyed the benefit of what their predecessors had created long after their navies ceased to play a decisive role in world affairs. Several lesser principalities such as those of the kings of Pontus (particularly Mithradates VI, c.115–62 BC), Bithynia (Nicomedes IV 94–74), Cappadocia, the Celtic chieftains of Galatia (settled in the Phrygian highlands), and further removed, the kings of Armenia were ranged along the frontiers of these empires, inextricably mired in border wars among one another, and lending their military, financial and marriage support to one great power after another.

The complexity of dynastic relationships and the speed with which forces could be mobilised and transported throughout the eastern Mediterranean theatre managed to keep the weight of these competing empires in a state of equilibrium, at least until the era of Roman intervention in Greece (215–146 BC). Federated leagues of smaller Greek polities, the Aetolians to the north of the Gulf of Corinth, the Achaeans to the south (headquartered at Corinth), and independent states such as Athens and Sparta (still dangerous, although only vestiges of their Classical selves), added to the mix. Unless firmly united – a rare event, to say the least – weaker states such as these generally could do little more than lend their support to the political initiatives of the great powers, while exercising care to avoid exploitation and/or outright subjection.

Momentum lay in the hands of competing rulers, and each dynasty saw its moment in the sun. After intimidating the Aegean world for decades, the Antigonids finally pushed their neighbouring Greek states to the brink, compelling them to summon the aid of the battle-hardened legions of Roman Republican Italy. Having finally rid themselves of the Carthaginian nemesis, Hannibal, Roman forces twice bludgeoned Antigonid rivals (200–198, 172–167 BC). The dynasty was ultimately deposed and their subjects reduced to the status of a Roman protectorate (148 BC). Next came the turn of the Seleucids. Having extended his dynasty's sway to the banks of the Indus in the east and to the Hellespont in the west, Antiochus III of Syria (223–187 BC) helplessly watched as the generals who had previously subdued Hannibal at Zama decimated his field army on the plains of Magnesia (188 BC). In the wake of this debacle, Antiochus was forced to accept a humiliating peace that essentially eliminated Seleucid authority west of Syria once and for all.

Next came Rhodes and the Attalids of Pergamum. After inviting Rome eastwards to reduce Philip V of Macedonia, these two powers assumed a more equivocal stance during Rome's subsequent conflict with Philip's son Perseus (172–167 BC). Independently, these powers attempted to mediate a peace between Rome and Perseus at an anxious moment during the Roman offensive in the Macedonian highlands. Rome ultimately prevailed and its senatorial aristocracy suddenly turned on its former allies with hostile intent. Rhodes was forced to beg for a new treaty of friendship, even as its mainland territories, particularly the cities of Lycia, declared their independence, backed by the threat of Roman intervention. From then on Rhodes assumed a quieter, far less conspicuous role in international affairs, dutifully complying with the requests of its western ally.

Having expanded their empire as far as Pamphylia through collaboration with Rome, the Attalids endured similar humiliation for undercutting Rome's offensive against Perseus. With the Roman aristocracy menacingly looking on, Attalid subject territories, one after another, declared their independence (166 BC). Like Rhodes the dynasts at Pergamum were helpless to resist. As far as the oligarchs that dominated the Roman Senate were concerned, the times called for the dismemberment of empires, friend and foe alike. In 133 BC, the last of the line, Attalus III, posthumously relinquished his kingdom and its valuable treasury to the protection of the Roman people. Apparently, this was the only means his advisers could devise to prevent the outbreak of civil war because the king left no legitimate heir. By 129 BC Roman legions were dispatched to crush a rag-tag rebellion instigated by his illegitimate son, Aristonicus, and to reduce the former kingdom, like Macedonia, to Roman provincial rule. In much the same way that Rome had acquired that rugged highland region of the northern Aegean, rich in timber and metals, they now assumed control over the coastal lands of Aegean Anatolia.

By the end of the second century BC, the Seleucids and the Ptolemies were all that remained from the glorious days of Alexander's marshals. However, these realms were likewise consumed by dynastic dissensions, by the seething ethnic hostility of subject peoples, and by repeated civil wars. Throughout the period in question the Seleucid realm of Syria remained embroiled in a perpetual cycle of violence, enduring incessant civil wars among competing dynastic interests, rebellions among its Aramaean and Jewish inhabitants (not least of which, the revolt of the Maccabees, 150–141 BC), and the breaking away of Phoenician maritime states such as Tyre, Sidon, Beirut and Ascalon. Watched carefully by Roman observers, by 142 BC, competing Seleucid pretenders were reduced by the cycle of violence to little more than warlords and pirate chiefs.

Long recognised as the weakest of the successor states, the Ptolemies did their best to remain on the good side of Rome, not to mention their own surly populace in Alexandria. In 96 BC, after a particularly violent dynastic dispute, the pretender Ptolemy Apion (116–96 BC) followed the example of Attalus III and ceded his territory of Cyrene to Rome. At the time senatorial leaders were too consumed with crises in Italy to notice. Trapped in the emerging power vacuum of the eastern Mediterranean, by the 80s BC, the Ptolemies abjectly yielded command of the sea-lanes of the eastern Mediterranean, crucial to its grain trade, to the bands of Cilician pirates (**2**).

By 100 BC the most powerful Hellenistic state, the kingdom of Pontus, was the one farthest removed from the threat of Rome. The great king, Mithradates VI Eupator, busily constructed an empire that exploited the abundant resources

2   *Mithradates VI Eupator, King of Pontus, c.115-62 BC. Based on a bust in the Louvre*

of the Black Sea region, its grain, timber, maritime supplies and fish. Simultaneously, he worked to enhance his standing among both traditional Hellenic states and renegade elements alike. By the beginning of the first century BC, Mithradates was viewed throughout the region as the last bulwark to Roman domination. From his isolated capital on the Black Sea, he funded and encouraged rebellion against Rome throughout the Mediterranean. Soon he found loose partners in anti-Roman animus among Illyrian and Thracian tribal elements that marauded along the borders of Macedonia (116–112 BC), among renegade nomads of Numidia (Jugurtha, 112–104), among mutinous Italian armies during the Social War (90–84 BC), among rebellious slaves who followed the Capuan gladiator Spartacus (73–71 BC), among the notorious Cilician pirates (75–67 BC), and among renegade Roman legions in Spain (Q. Sertorius, 75–72 BC). Only after eliminating one by one each of these sources of resistance were the Romans finally able to concentrate on the destruction of Mithradates himself (62 BC).

The emergence of Roman hegemony (264–64 BC)

In the West a similar dynamic had played itself out between Rome and Carthage. Through three momentous conflicts (264–242; 218–201; 148–146 BC) Rome reduced the once extensive maritime empire of this Phoenician city to ruin, ultimately sacking and destroying the city of Carthage and reducing its population to slavery in 146 BC. By the end of the second century BC, Rome reigned supreme throughout the west. Its Republican government controlled an interlocking network of allied Italian city-states (totalling perhaps 5 million people), and ruled several subject provinces, including Sicily, Sardinia-Corsica, the two Spains, Lusitania, Africa (formerly Carthage), Numidia, Mauretania, Liguria, Cisalpine and parts of Transalpine Gaul, Macedonia, Thrace, Achaia and Asia. It drew support as well from a number of allied states beyond Italy, including Massilia, Rhodes and Athens. Rome was able to project military strength in any direction and, if need be, to deploy armies in several Mediterranean theatres at once.

The city itself was dominated by a sophisticated senatorial aristocracy, at the core of which stood a score or more of patrician and consular plebeian families, proud, ancient, even arrogant, and closely knit through intermarriage. Names such as the Fabii Maximi, the Cornelii Scipiones, the Claudii Marcelli, the Aemilii Pauli and the Sempronii Gracchi had opened the doors to Mediterranean conquest. By the second century, however, these aristocrats were outnumbered in the senate by scores of new members, Roman citizens from formerly allied cities in neighbouring Latium, Etruria and Campania. The political struggle that this situation entailed was one of several emerging sources of tension during the Late Republican era (133-27 BC). The subtle transition from Roman wars of conquest to wars for provincial maintenance taxed the resolve of Roman legionaries and threatened to weaken the oligarchy's ability to administer its empire and thereby retain its revenues. Massive slave revolts in Sicily and Italy exposed additional dangers to the Republican social fabric, offering fresh indications that the commercial economy taking root in Italy had progressed too rapidly (136–130, 105–100, 73–71 BC). Political agitators such as the Gracchi and Saturninus (133–121, 104–100 BC) clamoured, meanwhile, for fresh allotments of state land to replenish the ranks of Roman citizen-soldiers. Such concessions as were achieved were paid for invariably in demagogic lives.

Eventually legionaries from Italian allied states began to demand benefits commensurate with their long-term military service, including political enfranchisement at Rome. Passions mounted as Rome's senatorial oligarchy resorted to intrigue and assassination to stem the tide on so many fronts. By 90 BC the Republic collapsed into civil war between Rome and its long-standing allies of the peninsula, the same allies that had displayed such firm resolve against Hannibal and had helped Rome to build its far-flung Mediterranean empire. By 88 BC King Mithradates of Pontus chose this moment of weakness to invade the province of Asia, expelling Roman military authorities offshore to Rhodes, inciting widespread popular uprisings across the Aegean to mainland Athens, and massacring Roman and Italian inhabitants throughout the region. The Roman trading post at Delos was particularly singled out for conflagration. Amid this orgy of chaos and violence, even the seemingly obvious matter of addressing the threat of the Pontic invasion could not be resolved without violence. Supporters of C. Marius (cos. 107, 104–100 BC) and L. Cornelius Sulla (cos. 88 BC) fought in the streets of Rome for the right to command this expedition, igniting conflagrations and engaging in violent purges of one another's street factions.

Ultimately, the faction of Sulla prevailed, supported by the mercenary aspirations of his standing field army. Assigned to the command in Asia, Sulla promptly expelled the forces of Mithradates from Greece, sacked Athens and Thebes, and compelled the Pontic king to withdraw to his homeland. Harshly punishing the inhabitants of the province of Asia for their betrayal of Roman authority, Sulla then turned his attention back to Italy where he quickly rooted out the remaining elements of Marian and Italian rebellion. Through harsh dictatorship (81–79 BC), Sulla restored order to the empire, but his reliance on brute force, proscriptions and confiscations of property prolonged the era of violence by several decades. Having buttressed his establishment through the forced settlement of 23 legions on confiscated land, Sulla the Dictator thus set a new and dangerous precedent for the use of private armies in Roman political domination. It was a lesson quickly learned by his successors, Cn. Pompeius Magnus, M. Licinius Crassus (consuls together in 70 and 55 BC), and the eventual dictator, Julius Caesar.

Those who opposed Sulla's edicts were proscribed, their names placed on death lists, with bounties placed on their heads. Their lands were confiscated and their progeny deprived of citizenship. Hundreds fled to the provinces of Spain where a renegade Marian general, Q. Sertorius, offered the hope of continuing resistance (78–72 BC). Though loyal to the ideals of the Republic, Sertorius' desperate circumstances led him to contract distasteful alliances with long-term Roman foes – King Mithradates and the emerging Cilician pirates (75 BC). Constantly on the run against legionary forces dispatched by the central government at Rome, this was the only means at Sertorius' disposal to delay inevitable defeat and annihilation.

By the late 70s BC, the Roman Mediterranean world was caught in the grip of asymmetrical conflicts ranging from the arid plateau of Spain to the jagged coasts of the Bay of Pamphylia and the damp forested coastlands of Pontus. Disparate elements of the resistance, highly unlikely bedfellows under usual circumstances, co-ordinated efforts as much as humanly possible to pin Roman forces down in distant theatres of the sea. If Rome had a weakness, it was at sea, which it never really benefited from and hence failed to maintain a navy. Rome had always conquered with its armies; naval affairs were adjunct to a land strategy. Like the Hellenistic dynasts of the previous era, Roman authorities tended to rely on the conscription of naval contingents from allied states with long experience at sea. Rome's failure to sustain a standing navy, accordingly, left the burgeoning maritime trade of Roman Italy, Sicily and Spain exceedingly vulnerable to attack. At the very moment that Roman trade was becoming ascendant in the Mediterranean, Roman security for its maritime commerce was extremely limited and cumbersome to mobilise. The irony, if not the inexplicable reality of this development, is that a moment of such widespread political and military instability was precisely the moment at which Roman trade attained its peak throughout the Mediterranean.

The Mediterranean sea-lanes: wind, currents and trade routes

Since most of the region's population was situated within relatively close proximity of the sea, city states, kingdoms and confederacies throughout the Mediterranean depended entirely on the sea-lanes of maritime transport for food and supplies. The sea was the great highway to the Graeco-Roman world, its lifeblood, its interior lake. In a world sustained by trade conducted in sailing vessels, fundamental environmental features, such as winds, currents and geography, determined the outcome of world affairs.

Enclosed at each end by straits, nine miles wide at the west (Gibraltar) and less than a mile wide at the east (the Bosporus), the Mediterranean is ideally suited for seafaring. The surrounding topography, particularly the moun-tainous north coasts of the Mediterranean, invited sea travel by furnishing an abundance of coastal breezes, sheltered coves and deep-water ports. Though it could bristle with dangers and offer surprises, the Mediterranean in no way confronted humankind with the range of extremes one encounters in the world's great oceans – the surging tides, the driving currents, the violent storms, the freezing waters, and the vast, limitless voids of oceanic space. In essence, the Mediterranean's warm climate, calm winds and land-locked character made it an ideal basin for maritime trade.

As Pryor notes (1988: 12), navigation under oars and sail was always strongly influenced, if not actually controlled, by the set of the currents and tides, the patterns of prevailing winds, the configuration of the coasts and the contours of localised meteorological phenomena. Approximately 2,200 miles long (from Gibraltar to Syria) and never more than 500 miles wide (from Massilia to Carthage), the Mediterranean together with the Black Sea furnishes some 1,158,300 square miles of seagoing terrain (Bradford 1971: 28). Formed during the Tertiary period from a much larger expanse of water, the sea occupies a depression between the continental masses of Africa and Eurasia (Morton 2001: 13). The African shield is gradually moving northwards, thrusting up and buckling the accumulated sediments on the sea floor to form mountains. At the same time the Arabian shield has driven north-westwardly toward the Black Sea. The heavy mass of the Black Sea in essence forms a barrier to this movement, diverting much of the force of the plate movement in a counter-clockwise motion along the northern coast of Anatolia and downwards into the Aegean. Alpine orogeny resulting from tectonic collisions throughout the basin formed mountain chains along all borders of the Mediterranean except the south-east. These mountains powerfully influence the winds and currents of the sea.

Prevailing currents

Cut off from the stronger currents of the oceans and set within a warm latitude, the Mediterranean experiences very high levels of evaporation and corresponding salinity. Of the 115,400 cubic metres of water that evaporate from the Mediterranean every minute only a little over 25 per cent is replaced by precipitation and by the outflow of rivers (the Rhône, the Po, the Nile and the Black Sea river basins).[1] This massive net loss of water explains the force of the inflow from the two chief access channels, the Strait of Gibraltar in the west and the Hellespont/Bosporus passages in the north-east. The flow of water into the Mediterranean from these two channels, in turn, strongly affects the anticlockwise direction of currents in the sea, and with that ancient navigation.

As noted above, at its narrowest point, the Strait of Gibraltar is only 9 miles wide (Bradford 1971: 33), promoting an influx of colder, less saline Atlantic water into the Mediterranean with a surface current of approximately 6 knots. Beneath the surface current denser, more saline water runs out into the Atlantic, forming a constant exchange between the inland sea and the ocean beyond. The volume of inflowing water is controlled not only by the narrowness of the strait but also by a submarine ledge linking Spain to North Africa (Bradford 1971: 36; Pryor 1988: 13). Since at its deepest point the strait is little more than 300m deep and in places a great deal shallower, the strait admits a relatively low volume of water at any one time.

In the Hellespont/Bosporus breach, waters flowing into the Mediterranean from the Black Sea (which stands a few centimetres higher in altitude) are carried in the upper surface currents while smaller quantities of water leaving the Mediterranean form a deeper undercurrent. This passageway is far more constrained than that at Gibraltar. The depth of the water at the Bosporus sill is only 37m and at the Hellespont more like 70m. At their narrowest the Bosporus is less than 800m wide and the Hellespont less than 1,500m. (Morton 2001: 42). Despite the significant depths (1,000m) and the heavy faulting of the intervening Propontus, the shallowness and narrowness of the passageways work to induce a considerable surface current, ranging from 4 to 7 knots in the Bosporus and from

3 to 5 knots in the Hellespont. Recessed bays along the shores occasionally disrupt the steady flow of the current, causing standing eddies to develop. In addition, the rotation of the earth contributes a considerable degree of irregularity through its 'coriolis effect'. The force of the earth's rotation causes a slight displacement of the waters of the upper current towards one shore and of the waters of the lower current towards the opposite shore. At times the submerged northward current actually appears on the surface of the strait.

The inflow of less dense water through these passageways helps to determine the force of the currents of the Mediterranean Sea as a whole. The inflow of surface waters in the Strait of Gibraltar alone offsets approximately 70 per cent of the total amount of water lost from the Mediterranean Sea through evaporation, setting in motion a sea-wide current of approximately 3 knots. This main current follows a relatively unobstructed path eastwards across the southern part of the Mediterranean, between the shores of Africa to the south and Sardinia, Sicily, Crete and the extremities of Italy and Greece to the north. From Egypt this current turns northward along the east coast of the Mediterranean and westward along the south coast of Asia Minor. The highly irregular coastline of southern Europe inevitably hampers the completion of this counter-clockwise circulation of surface waters. However, even along these shores, around the Aegean, Ionian, Adriatic and Tyrrhenian Seas, the anti-clockwise motion of the waters invariably sustains its course (Morton 2001: 39).

The chief exception to this simple pattern occurs in the Gulf of Sirte bordering Libya, where the eastward trending current strikes against the projecting head of Cyrenaica in eastern Libya and is deflected southward and westward in a clockwise motion back toward Tunisia.[2] In a few other localities as well submerged topography combines with tidal influences to disturb the course of the prevailing anticlockwise current. For example, (Bradford 1971: 32) a submerged land bridge extending beneath the channel between Sicily and Malta, 72km wide and nowhere deeper than 180m, tends to separate Mediterranean sea flow into two separate, slowly counter clockwise swirling currents. Despite the general absence of tides, moreover, the moon's gravitational pull exhibits significant influence in areas of shallow water, such as the coast of North Africa, where the spring or maximum range of tides can sometimes attain crests of 1.5m, and the Strait of Messina, where currents in opposite directions and considerable turbulence in the form of eddies and whirlpools are commonplace.[3] Similar tidal effects exist in the northern reaches of the Adriatic and the Gulf of Corinth (Morton 2001: 45). Elsewhere, regions exhibiting submerged coastal orogeny, such as the island-choked Aegean and the eastern Adriatic with its many fjords, tend to deflect the prevailing current in various directions, provoking erratic, unpredictable movements of surface water in areas of close proximity. The minimal 5km passage from Mykonos to Delos could easily confound ancient navigators and their modern counterparts by its contrary winds and currents. Ancient seafarers had no choice but to study the movements of these currents and to learn the eccentricities of both these and the winds in order successfully to perform their work within this environment. The variability of Mediterranean surface currents placed a premium on the services of pilots whenever cargo masters sailed in unfamiliar waters.

The prevailing winds

The comparative absence of tides means that atmospheric winds have far greater effect on the Mediterranean Sea than they do on any ocean (Bradford 1971: 37). The winds themselves are influenced by the unique geographical features of the Mediterranean basin, by the fact, for example, that the sea is surrounded on all sides except the south-east by mountains, as well as by the tendency of the climate to keep the water relatively warm (Bradford 1971: 33). In broader terms the prevailing winds of the Mediterranean are influenced by massive intercontinental systems of air pressure far beyond the horizons of the ancient navigator – over the Atlantic far to the west and central Asia to the east.[4] In the most general terms, fronts and pressure cells track in a roughly easterly direction across the Mediterranean basin. Interacting with effects of the warm water of the sea and the cold highlands of the mountains surrounding it, these cells produce complex and variable localised weather systems. During summer when an Atlantic subtropical high centred over the Azores dominates conditions in the west, maritime air from the Atlantic enters the Mediterranean in a generally clockwise turning motion from the north, giving the region its prevailing northerly and north-westerly winds. Simultaneously, the influence of the prevailing Indo–Persian monsoon low over Pakistan during summer can extend as far as Asia Minor and Saharan Africa, inducing prevailingly anticlockwise north-easterlies across the breadth of Anatolia, from the Bosporus to the Bay of Iskenderun. Trapped between the effects of converging weather systems, the Ionian Sea was particularly susceptible to complex, changeable and often inclement weather.

Clear skies, great heat, and drought generally characterise the Mediterranean summer as the sun stands high in the sky and the high pressure ridge over the Azores blocks the incursion of cooler and wetter airstreams from the Atlantic. In the eastern Mediterranean the prevailing northerly winds of summer blow steadily across the Aegean and out into the Mediterranean clear to the coasts of Libya, Egypt, Palestine and Syria. These are the *meltemi*, the famous Etesian winds of antiquity that blow steadily from May to September. According to Roman sources, the force of Etesians blew so steadily that they could bring voyages from Egypt to Rome to a virtual halt for weeks on end.

During winter months North Atlantic low-pressure and Mongolian high-pressure systems move southward from arctic regions to dominate

Mediterranean weather patterns. From late September westerly airstreams and depressions from the Atlantic enter the Mediterranean, attracted by the low relief and moist air of the sea basin. Since the Mediterranean is virtually an enclosed sea and its waters circulate and mix with those of the oceans very gradually, the surface layers retain a constant and unusually high temperature all year round. During winter this leads to rising currents of warm air and consequently to the development of low pressure across the whole Mediterranean basin. In the western Mediterranean the North Atlantic low generates depressions that track eastwards, setting up a whole series of localised storms. In the east the Mongolian high generates anticlockwise wind patterns that traverse the north Aegean and spill into the Mediterranean as north-westerly to north-easterly gusts. The one variation from the general pattern of prevailing northerlies arises with the Scirocco, or the ancient *Notos*, a hot wind of great strength generating dust storms along the entire southern coast of the Mediterranean. Prevailing southerly winds in the Mediterranean tend to be hot and dusty and readily absorb moisture as they cross the sea. Often arriving with clouds or haze at the southern coast of Europe, these violent, dangerous winds were of little use to ancient navigators.

The winter winds of the Mediterranean typically exhibit tremendous variability in their direction and duration and substantial precipitation (Morton 2001: 48). Occasionally high-pressure cells block winter depressions sweeping across the Mediterranean over the landmasses to the east. In these instances the depressions can linger stormily, their winds remaining relatively constant, above the deep recesses of the northern Mediterranean − the Tyrrhenian, the Adriatic, and the Aegean Seas. The limited manoeuvrability and effectiveness of ancient sailing vessels at commanding these conditions inevitably restricted winter voyages to short excursions across enclosed waters.

Given the comparative absence of tides, the winds of any season can exert tremendous influence on the surface waters of the Mediterranean (Bradford 1971: 37). Not only do surface currents yield to the direction of the prevailing wind, but the absence of a tidal range causes breaking seas to develop rapidly. A sudden electric storm lasting no more than half an hour can change the existing pattern of the sea's surface, generating swells that can continue for many hours.

The natural routes of trade

Together with the winds and the currents, Mediterranean coastal topography helped to shape the patterns of ancient navigation. Like the currents and the winds, the topography tends to divide the sea into unequal halves, north and south. The northern coasts of the Mediterranean were relatively kind to ancient seamen. The relief profiles are high, providing good landmarks that are easily observable from far out at sea. During inclement weather numerous bays and sheltered beaches furnished refuge in the lee of the land. In addition, the sea bottom generally drops away quickly, providing deep water and safe navigation while close to land. Although offshore reefs, hidden shoals, and submerged rocks posed significant dangers, by and large, the northern coast tended to present a more welcoming aspect to ships powered by oars or sails (Pryor 1988: 21). The close proximity of several large islands offering refuge during bad weather, facilities for repairs, and trading opportunities, yielded further advantage to navigation along the northern Mediterranean coast. From west to east, the Balearics, Corsica, Sardinia, Sicily, Corfu, the Ionian Islands, Crete, Euboea, the Aegean Islands, Rhodes and Cyprus all offered crucial way-stations for mariners seeking to navigate open waters from one landmass to the next.

In contrast to the north Mediterranean coast, the North African shore enjoyed a poor reputation for sailing (Pryor 1988: 20). The islands in the south of the Mediterranean were small and poorly populated, offering significantly less advantage than those in the north. From Mauretania eastward to Carthage the coast exhibits shallow reefs and islands running far out to sea. The Tunisian promontory beyond Carthage displays cliffs, islands and reefs all the way to Cape Bon. With few natural deep-water anchorages, most of the ports along this coast were artificial creations, the results of effectively placed moles, and laboriously dredged river mouths and coastal lagoons. Accordingly, the entire western coast of North Africa was a graveyard for ancient shipping, a dangerous lee shore to the prevailing northerly winds of the sea. Further east the Libyan coast posed similar dangers. Essentially as far as Alexandria in Egypt the coastline presented ancient mariners with low featureless terrain. Hidden sandbars and quicksands could extend as far as twelve miles out to sea. For ships driven southward by northerly storms, this coast was implacably hostile. As the recorded voyages of St Paul and the fourth-century AD bishop Synesius make clear (noted below), the Etesian winds whipped up considerable swells along this coast and were potentially catastrophic to sail-propelled merchant vessels (Pryor 1988: 22–23). The region was nevertheless rich with agriculture. Along the western shores of Libya and Tunisia a number of settlements such as Leptis Magna, Leptis Minor, Thapsus, Hadrumentum, Utica and Hippo Regius survived Carthage's fall to produce substantial quantities of wine, oil, fish sauce and grain. Equally important, they served as the maritime depots to an overland caravan trade that made its way across the Sahara to central Africa, returning with exotic animals for Roman games, ebony, ivory, gold, gems and slaves. Despite the destruction of the great emporium of Carthage in 146 BC, therefore, Roman private development of the region quietly progressed, with veterans' colonies and large private estates harnessing the best of the lands that had formerly sustained the most powerful classical maritime empire of the west.

The eastern Mediterranean forms an approximate middle ground where the environmental forces of the Mediterranean converge. The prevailing current surges northwards, even as the prevailing winds blow south. Topographically the sandy wastelands of the African desert yield to the moister coastal ridges of Palestine, Lebanon and Syria. These features rendered the eastern Mediterranean a crucial axis to the ancient maritime navigation. This point of confluence for winds and tides became most important as voyages proceeded from places such as Alexandria to points north and west. For sea voyages from northern Mediterranean regions to points south, ships' captains could rely on the prevailing winds to make relatively straight trajectories from landfall to landfall across the sea. From southern Gaul the seas lay open towards the Balearics, Sardinia and Carthage. From the west coast of Italy, Sicily was easily accessible. From the mouth of the River Po, a straightforward run down the Adriatic propelled cargo vessels to the Peloponnese, Corinth, Crete, Rhodes and Cyprus. Ships navigating the Ionian Sea to Crete, Egypt or Palestine cruised easily before the Etesians. Even ships embarking on longer voyages from Massilia or Puteoli to Egypt, Palestine or Syria could count on winds from astern or port stern quarter to convey them to their destinations.[5] However, the technological limitations of ancient cargo ships prevented navigators from taking the same routes in reverse. In the case of sailing ships, poor upwind performance, the fear of lee shores, and the need for refuge in inclement weather remained critical considerations (Pryor 1988: 37). Cargo ships attempting to pursue return routes from south to north or east to west generally proved incapable of overcoming the obstacle of adverse winds on the open sea.

To sail against the winds during the peak summer sailing season, commercial transports had no choice but to rely on a more circuitous route that clawed around the coasts of Palestine, Phoenicia, Syria and south Anatolia with the assistance of the currents and the diurnal land and sea breezes (Pryor 1988: 90). In some places extending as far as 30km out to sea, localised land and sea breezes of the mountainous coasts of the Mediterranean result from the differing rates at which land and sea gain heat during the day and cool during the night (Morton 2001: 51–3). As significant differences in air pressure occur between land and sea, a circular pattern of up-draughts and down-draughts develops, land breezes blowing from the mountains to the sea during the daylight hours and sea breezes blowing the other way at night. In mountainous coastal regions these diurnal winds are sufficiently strong to propel the course of sailing vessels cruising close to shore. Particularly in enclosed bays such as the Bay of Pamphylia where the Tauros Mountains form a broad, semicircular wall around the sea, these diurnal breezes can actually prevail over the northerly winds (Morton 2001: 53). During the peak of summer sailing, the slow coastal winds of Palestine, Phoenicia, Syria and southern Anatolia served as thrusters to ancient navigation, furnishing a less efficient but far safer alternative to voyages in the open sea (**3**).

Geographical and meteorological conditions combined, therefore, with the technological limitations of ancient cargo ships to promote certain narrow and

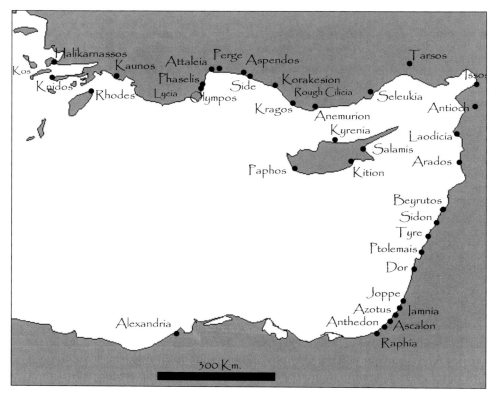

3 *Eastern Mediterranean, various harbors and pirate sites labelled*

well-defined sea-lanes for ships navigating the Mediterranean Sea. These trunk routes ranged generally along the chains of the northern islands and coasts (Pryor 1988: 37). Traffic easily moved in a north–south and west–east flow across the open waters of the Mediterranean. Voyaging in these directions, navigators generally attempted to sail from landfall to landfall. Intermediary islands between the north and south and west and east coasts of the Mediterranean offered important way-stations beyond coastal horizons. Navigators naturally set their bearings for these maritime nodes. As a result, shipping tended to cluster at pivotal way-stations such as the Balearic Islands, Corsica and Sardinia, Sicily, Crete, Rhodes and Cyprus, particularly when the winds were fierce. It was the torturously slow passages northwards and westwards from Alexandria to Rome that determine the locations of numerous eastern Mediterranean ports of call. In the arid regions of southern Palestine, small roadsteads such as Raphia, Anthedon, Ascalon (Ashkelon), Azotus (Ashdod), Iamnia (Yabhneh), Jaffa (Joppe), Dor and Ptolemais (Akko), offered shelter as well as 'trail heads' to the caravan trade to Nabataea and beyond (Patai 1998: 136f.). By the end of the second century BC, the Hasmonaean rulers of Judaea seized control of most of these emporia, obtaining important revenues from the traffic that circulated among them. Traders from ports such as Ascalon, Anthedon, Azotus and Iamnia came to enjoy important contacts, for example, with Roman and Italian traders converging at the duty-free emporium of Delos.

Further north, the proximity of the Lebanese mountains and their cedar harvests had long favoured the Phoenician harbours of Tyre, Sidon, Byblos, Berytos, Byblos, Tripolis and Arados. By the mid-second century BC several of these famous cities availed themselves of the anarchy induced by Seleucid civil wars to reclaim their autonomy, reopening contacts with the caravan traders of Mesopotamia, and reasserting their place as transit centres for luxury goods from the east (Grainger 1991: 129f.). Merchant houses from these ports were likewise extremely prominent at Delos. Harbour construction in these sandy places was generally minimal but sophisticated. Archaeological analysis of the remains of the harbours at Tyre and Sidon, for example, indicate that they were the earliest to construct harbour moles with sluice gates strategically placed to enable the naturally northward-surging current to clear their artificial basins of sand and alluvium (**4**).[6]

From Berytos and Arados vessels plying the coastal route had the option of sailing westward astride the wind to the lee coast of Cyprus or northward to the Syrian ports of Laodiceia, Alexandria, and Issos, Tarsos, Soli and Seleucia in eastern (flat) Cilicia (Grainger 1990). A number of harbours along southern Cyprus – Salamis, Kitium, Kurion and Paphos to name the most celebrated –

4 *Sidonian coin of 385 BC.* Based on illustration in Frost 1963: fig. 91

offered refuge to traffic making its way towards the Aegean and beyond. With favourable winds, cargo vessels could attempt the open sea route from western Cyprus to Rhodes, Kos or Crete; however, in the face of fierce northerlies, shipping would cross over to Anemurion on the rugged coast of Rough Cilicia and continue the coastal grind along the Bay of Pamphylia. A number of small, fortified roadsteads, such as Korakesion, Hamaxia and Selinus, offered havens along the remote eastern shores of this bay. At its centre stood the large urban centres of Pamphylia, Side, Aspendos, Perge and Attaleia. Enclosed by moles and imposing fortifications, the shallow harbour of Side with its docking capacity of 25–30 vessels became a favourite haunt of pirates.[7] So too did Phaselis in eastern Lycia, with its heavily fortified promontory and its wide harbour street connecting long arcing strands to either side, and Olympos, with its dredged river harbour and its fiery jets of gas in the hills above.[8] Despite their failure to honour maritime law, these harbours offered mariners strategic landfalls on the western side of the bay. Cilician pirates converted these havens into strategic choke points as they came to dominate these waters (5).

Rounding the southern peaks and promontories of Lycia ancient merchant vessels sailed head on into the force of the Etesian winds in the Aegean. With so many cargo ships seeking shelter for indeterminable periods of time, a cluster of layover points emerged precisely at this juncture: most prominently Rhodes, with its deep harbours, its massive quays and warehouses, and its strong fortifications. Equally useful havens existed at Kaunos with its sheltered lagoon harbour, at Knidos with its sheltered triple harbour conveniently located at the end of the Datça peninsula, Kos, a large island like Rhodes set further into the Aegean, and Halikarnassos on the lee shore of the last Anatolian headland before turning into the face of the Aegean winds. The growing importance of these harbours in this era testifies to the expanding volume of Mediterranean trade.

Once a vessel entered the Aegean, the voyage had to be made into the teeth of the Etesians (Pryor 1988: 90). Whether a ship followed the western Greek coasts or the eastern Anatolian coast, contrary winds and choppy seas exacerbated the dangers of rocky reef-strewn coasts and offshore islands. Along the Anatolian coast the chief maritime centres of 'Asia', Miletus and Ephesus, offered some assistance with their river-dredged harbours and neatly arranged, colonnaded squares. Numerous smaller harbours situated themselves along the Erythraean peninsula and points northward to facilitate northward/southward movement of trade. Cargo vessels making their way to the Black Sea found the current from the Hellespont through the Bosporus an additional obstacle. Beyond this lay the distant but essential lands of the Black Sea basin, a source of crucial products such as fish, grain, timber and maritime supplies. Colchis, situated at the easternmost edge of this basin, served as the outlet to an important overland route for the silk trade of China. The combination of raw materials and eastern luxury goods kept centres of the Black Sea trade, such as

5   *View of the southern harbour of Alanya. In the distance, the canyon of the modern Dim Çay or river*

Sinope and Trapezos, quietly bustling. The incorporation of so many resources into a virtual monopoly by King Mithradates VI (112–64 BC) of Pontus enabled that dynast to become a potent, if destabilising, force in late Hellenistic politics. By posing as the 'last defender' of Hellenic civilisation, Mithradates resisted Roman expansion for several decades from his mountainous territory in northeast Anatolia. The long reach of his diplomacy in 88 BC enabled him to incite anti-Roman violence in distant theatres, as noted above. To obtain intelligence about his Roman adversaries, Mithradates allegedly relied on gossip acquired from merchants sailing regularly in and out of his port at Sinope. From the exaggerated yarns of mariners, Mithradates learned of distant political events such as the rebellion of Rome's Italian allies in 90 BC and the provincial uprising of the renegade Roman general, Q. Sertorius, in Spain in 77 BC. Though never a great admiral, Mithradates recognised the advantages of cultivating the Mediterranean maritime population even as Rome did not.

Westward-trending traffic from the Dodecanese would find the force of the Etesians blunted to some degree by the availability of shelter along lee shores of numerous islands as well as by the variability of local winds and currents. Most essential in this direction was the duty-free emporium at Delos, celebrated for its Sanctuary of Apollo. Though a speck of land with minimal docking facilities, Delos emerged as one of the greatest trading centres of the world in this era due largely to the influx of wealthy traders from Rome. The Athenian magistrates and merchants who supervised this market place furnished it with an important link to the Piraeus, accessible via the lee shores of several intervening islands. The movement of goods in and out of Delos and the Piraeus enabled Athens to resume its formerly dominant position in the Aegean, at least until the moment when its populace broke with Rome in 87

BC. Despite their proximity, the Athenians appear to have learned nothing from the example of Corinth. For centuries the linchpin to traffic between the Aegean and Italy, with suitable harbours (Kenchriai and Lechaion) to either side of the isthmus, the maritime population of Corinth, much like that of Carthage, defied Rome in 148–146 BC and saw its community destroyed. Although trade across the isthmus continued, archaeological evidence indicates that it did so in private Roman hands.

From Crete or Corinth to Sicily, winds on the starboard beam had the potential to facilitate passage, but they might very easily swing to the west and drive a ship back on its path. In the western Mediterranean the passage through the Sicilian channel likewise had to be made against both current and prevailing winds. In the western waters sloppy, yet busily prosperous warehouse centres were emerging throughout Italy. For example, the cluttered, surprisingly cosmopolitan port of Puteoli, with its narrow, potsherd-littered lanes and its stone-paved Via Appia resounded to the sound of wagons and pack animals hauling their cargoes to Rome. Smaller ports – Ostia at the mouth of the Tiber (the future greatness of which remained impeded by shoals at the river's mouth) (**colour plate 13**), Cosa in Etruria, Antium in Latium, Neapolis, Pompeii and Caieta in Campania, Velia in Lucania, Tarentum in Calabria, and Brundisium in Apulia – served as homes to internationally powerful merchant families and as loading centres for tons of wine and oil produced at numerous estates of the Italian interior. The last mentioned emporium, Brundisium, is specifically described (Zon. 8.7) as a fine harbour, 'with an approach and landing place of such character for traffic with Illyricum and Greece that vessels would sometimes come to land and put out to sea wafted by the same breeze.' Slightly inland in Campania, Capua offered a bustling marketplace for the produce of an exceedingly rich agricultural region. It was arguably also the craft production centre of all Italy, capable of manufacturing crude but strong farm implements, finely profiled, black slipped ceramic wares, dyed linens, unguents, perfumes, and a wide range of bronze furnishings. Syracuse, on the opposite facing shore of Sicily, still held first place as the urban and cultural centre of 'Greek' civilisation in the west, despite its sacking and plundering at the hands of the Romans in 211 BC. Despite spoliation of its once celebrated monuments and artwork, the famed porticoed streets and warehouses of the city's broad-rimmed harbour and the majestic heights of its citadel and residential districts at Plemmyrium and Achradina were soon restored. By the 130s BC the inhabitants of Syracuse prospered again, a direct result of the influence and activity of infiltrating Roman businessmen, financiers and tax collectors.

Along the rich, rolling coasts of Etruria, Latium, Campania in the west and Apulia, Umbria, and Picenum on the Adriatic, quiet, ordered, highly efficient agricultural estates generated ambitious quantities of wine and oil for export. The high-collared, spike-toed fragments of large, solidly built amphorae by which Italian traders transported these commodities so thoroughly saturate the archaeological remains of Sicily, Sardinia, Spain, and France (not to mention Aegean Delos) that they serve as a barometer of Roman economic muscle-flexing.[9] In addition, prized herds of cattle generated meat, leather and sinew; and in the mountainous interior, armed slave gangs drove flocks of sheep and goats along remote sheep paths, nurturing their stock to produce additional stores of wool and animal by-products (**6**).

Most labourers employed in these industries were slaves, the spoils of military conquests. By conservative estimates the Roman Republican establishment by 146 BC had relocated a quarter of a million war prisoners from the peripheries of the Mediterranean to Italy. By their very numbers these slave labourers posed an immediate and present danger to the security of Italian farm communities. Given the rapid expansion of this population the Roman establishment found itself incapable of addressing issues of security, a responsibility the slaveholders themselves frequently proved incapable of assuming. The results were predictable: repeated slave uprisings plagued the farming regions of Italy and Sicily throughout the era. A revolt in 136 BC culminated in the creation of an independent slave kingdom in highland Sicily organised by an ingenious slave of Syrian origin who assumed the Seleucid dynastic name Antiochus. His revolt resonated as far away as the slave-driven mines of Attica, the workshops at Delos and the craft centres and farms of Pergamum. A second, equally widespread revolt occurred in Sicily and south Italy in 105 BC, and a Thracian gladiator named Spartacus in 72 incited a third, truly destabilising revolt (Bradley 1989).

Rome remained the focus and ultimate arbiter of these emerging conflicts, as burgeoning capital to the Mediterranean world. Despite the arrogance exhibited by its aristocracy and the dread that it inspired, the city proper presented a strangely half-finished appearance to the world, almost as if the Romans had been too preoccupied with world conquest to bother with urban repair. Crammed into the hills around a former eddy of the River Tiber, the populace spilled beyond the confines of the city's massive defensive walls. At

6 *Two coastal craft at the entrance to Rome's harbour. Third century AD relief found in the Catacomb of Praetextatus, Rome*

29

the end of the Hannibalic War (218-201 BC) this settlement consisting already of several hundred thousand people enjoyed only two paved streets. Mud or dust coated the grimy walls of storefronts and residences; large animals drifted about narrow alleyways; access to water and sewage disposal was primitive (**7**).

During the middle decades of the second century BC, the Senate tried to improve conditions through an intensive public building programme, constructing aqueducts and drainage canals, granaries and dock works, porticoed thoroughfares giving access to enclosed market areas and basilicas for business assemblies. The infusion of public monies (derived from conquest) into the local economy generated ancillary activity in housing construction, clothing and food distribution. Skilled labour was increasingly imported. The town gradually began to take on the appearance of a capital. Districts of dazzling shops, such as the Velabrum near the Forum Boarium, the Tabernae

7 *Porticus Margaritaria at Rome. Artistic illustration of upper reach of the Via Sacra, looking North toward the Forum. The Porticus Margaritaria is on the left*

Argentariae in the Forum, and the Porticus Margaritaria along the Summa Via Sacra, catered to the new found wealth of the Roman elite. Rome's military successes and international importance were gradually converting the metropolis into a western Babylon, the nerve centre for Mediterranean financial operations and public corporations, adopted home to droves of slave workers, craftsmen and artisans, and the final destination for quantities of eastern luxury goods. Albeit uneven, the pace of immigration and urban development kept resources far below demand. Thousands of gainfully employed inhabitants sought shelter in rickety, squalid, multi-storey wooden-framed structures. Thousands more who were homeless slept in the streets beneath projecting structural overhangs or in the din of all-night taverns.[10] Despite inadequate housing, poor sanitation, and squalid, overcrowded streets, immigrants kept coming – Greeks with various prized skills, destitute Roman and Italian farmers, either tired of their austere agricultural existence or were financially overburdened. These and others flocked to the city lured by the prospect of wage-labour employment in the sprawling construction trade, along with train after train of captured prisoners in chains. By the late first century BC a conservative estimate has 60 per cent of the city's 800,000 to 1 million inhabitants arising from slave origins (Brunt 1987). Many of the earliest inscribed private memorials of this 'Latin' city survive, in fact, in Greek.

Although Roman Italy formed the nerve centre and likely final destination of most maritime traffic of this era, the sea-lanes extended westward to additional destinations in Gaul and Spain. Voyages around the south-west tip of Sardinia and northward through the Gulf to Massilia were likely to be hard and long. A better route lay along coast of Italy and west to Liguria. Ships sailing against the winds would pursue the more laborious coastal routes. Traffic from Italy to Spain for example would take the route along north Italy, Liguria and the south Gallic coast, relying on land and sea breezes to propel it slowly along. The open sea route via Sicily or Sardinia to the Balearic Islands that was commonly used as the return route from Spain to Italy could easily blow a merchant vessel to the shores of North Africa.

In lieu of civil disturbances the inhabitants of settlements in these regions faced a grimmer prospect of confrontation with non-pacified peoples of the 'wilderness' – Ligurians, Gauls and Celt-Iberians. The celebrated port of Massilia (Marseille) quietly plied its trade with the hinterland settlements of Gaul, furnishing the main gateway to a bustling barge traffic that serviced the continent's vast untapped interior. Archaeological investigation has demonstrated that millions of amphorae of Italian wine made their way past Massilia up the Rhône to the Gallic hinterland regions of the Loire, the Seine and the Saône (Tchernia 1986: 68f.). According to Diodorus of Sicily (5.26.3), Italian wines were so prized by the warrior elements of Gaul that they readily swapped male prisoners for amphorae of wine on a one-to-one ratio. Along the coast of Spain several Graeco-Roman communities, including Emporium,

Tarraco, Sucro and Carthago Nova, served as gateways to the mineral wealth of that region's hinterland. During the period in question, Roman state contractors reportedly committed 40,000 slave labourers to the extraction of various ores, particularly silver, 'bringing into the Roman treasury a daily revenue of 25,000 drachmas' (perhaps the equivalent of £600,000 today), as the second-century BC Greek historian, Polybius, affirms (34.9.8). These slave labourers endured the harshest working conditions of their time. 'The slaves engaged in the operation of the mines . . . are physically destroyed,' records Diodorus (5.38.1), 'their bodies worn down from working in the mine shafts both day and night. Many die because of the excessive maltreatment they suffer. They are given no rest or break from their toil, but rather are forced by the whiplashes of their overseers to endure the most dreadful of hardships; thus do they wear out their lives in misery.' Since the Hannibalic War the Romans had devoted decades of military effort to pacifying the defiant, hardy natives of the peninsula's rugged interior. Rebellions were frequent and treachery and brutality measured out in proportion by both sides.[11] When Roman senatorial authority collapsed in chaos during the 80s and 70s BC, a renegade general, Q. Sertorius, aided and abetted by Roman refugees and their contacts back in Italy, was able to channel this native hostility into peninsula-wide rebellion, forming an independent realm, a Roman republic in exile, as it were. Maritime diplomacy enabled him by 75 BC to forge alliances with King Mithradates of Pontus and the pirates of Cilicia. According to Cicero (*Verr.* 2.4.21), Sertorius' chief port, Dianium, emerged as a notorious pirate hole, the western destination in a pirate round that originated in Phaselis in Lycia.

The orator's insistence on this point confirms the general sailing patterns thus described. For open-sea sailing the advantage of the Mediterranean obviously lay in its enclosed character. Provided sufficient water and supplies were put on board, a sailing vessel could allow itself to be blown for days across the open sea, relying on its sails to its best advantage to maintain a relatively accurate heading toward its intended direction. Eventually, a vessel propelled by favourable or unfavourable winds would reach the opposite shore. Owing to the mechanical limitations of the ancient cargo vessel's navigational equipment, landfall could occur far from one's intended location. This distance would have to be made up; however, there was little risk of drifting endlessly in open seas. The combined conditions of the Mediterranean maritime environment and the technological limitations of their sailing machines explain, therefore, not only where the ancient mariners predominantly sailed, but how and why. Using predictable sea-lanes Roman merchants and sailors worked to forge maritime connections that criss-crossed the Mediterranean linking disparate peoples and cultures to available resources that otherwise lay hidden beyond the horizon of the sea.

2

Cities in the path of Roman economic expansion

During the course of the period in question (167–67 BC), Roman trade expanded across the Mediterranean in the wake of Roman arms, in essence expelling competing goods and maritime communities from its midst. From west to east a steady progress is discernible. By 146 BC Rome had destroyed Carthage and Corinth and compelled maritime labourers at those localities to migrate eastwards. By 84 BC Roman mercantile elements firmly controlled Aegean maritime centres. By 67 BC they had penetrated eastern Mediterranean sea-lanes formerly dominated by Rhodes as Roman navies eradicated sources of piracy. By 48/7 BC Roman forces confronted the surviving maritime elements head-on in Alexandria. The purpose of this chapter is to characterise these endangered loci of maritime culture by describing their features, by identifying the motives to maritime resistance to Rome, and by determining whether anti-Roman attitudes were communicated generationally from one community to the next.

Carthage

Although a disastrous sequence of wars against Rome had by 201 BC deprived Carthage of its overseas empire, this rich commercial city was by every indication experiencing a renaissance at the beginning of the period in question (**colour plate 2**). According to the terms of the peace of 201, Rome required that Carthage cede the last of its overseas territories, pay substantial war indemnities, furnish large quantities of grain to feed the burgeoning population of Rome as well as its armies overseas, and reduce its military establishment to purely defensive levels. The Carthaginians reluctantly eliminated their once sizeable elephant corps and reduced their navy to a coastal squadron of ten warships. To meet their obligations, the Carthaginians had little choice but to harness the potential of their agricultural hinterland and mercantile trade. In fact, between 200 and 171 BC this maritime 'republic' met its commitments with relative ease, going as far as offering to pay the entire ten-year indemnity in one lump sum and on more than one occasion furnishing grain to Roman armies at cost (*Liv.* 43.6). Such was the economic vitality of Carthage just prior to its destruction in 146 BC. During visits to this maritime community, Roman observers such as Cato the Elder were struck by the well ordered character of its vineyards stretching across the landscape, as well as by the hustle and bustle of its commercial harbour.[1] Carthaginian traders, the notorious *guggae*, were familiar figures at Rome; Plautus in his play *Poenulus* portrays one clad like his slaves in a tunic and with rings in his ears, pretending quite falsely not to comprehend any language other than his own (Lancel 1995: 405-6). Carthaginian amphorae of the second century, particularly the torpedo-shaped Mana C, conveyed North African wine, oil and garum throughout the Mediterranean, showing up in significant quantities not only in Sicily, Sardinia and Spain, but as far removed as the island emporium of Delos. Other goods dispatched from Carthage include wild animals for the games held in Rome, hides, wool, metal (tin and silver), salted meats and farm produce (wax and honey, fruit and vegetables). In short, twice defeated by Rome, the Carthaginians had by every indication refocused their energies to maximum effect on production, development and trade (Lancel 1995: 144, 172).

Under the continued guidance of an oligarchy of mercantile families, Carthage by 167 BC had seen the expansion of domestic quarters along the south slope of their acropolis (the hill of Byrsa) as well as along the 'suburban' plateau to the north of the harbour, known as the Megarid. Excavations conducted in the past two decades by teams from Tunisia, Germany, France, England and the United States, with the support of UNESCO, indicate that the timing of this expansion coincides with the last years of the Hellenistic city's existence. On the south slopes of the Byrsa acropolis, solid-walled domestic quarters reveal artisan shops and the abundant cisterns on ground floors deemed necessary to sustain the occupants of densely packed multistorey tenements or *insulae*, much as the second-century AD Roman historian, Appian, describes.[2] These areas most probably housed the labouring elements that had come to influence affairs in the city at this time. During his visit in 157 BC Cato the Elder was struck by the extent to which 'the city had grown in the strength of its defences and in the size of its population during the short time since its defeat by Publius Scipio' (App. *Lib.* 69). The city teemed with artisans and manual labourers whose livelihoods were centred around the port. As a Carthaginian ambassador complained to the Roman commander at the outset of the siege in 149 BC (App. *Lib.* 85), 'it is impracticable for our people, a countless number of whom get their living by the sea, to pick up and move inland.' This, however, was the order of the Roman Senate, delivered by Roman consuls with an armed host in that year. Prior to revealing this secret instruction, the consuls had requested the former lords of north-western Africa to yield their weaponry as a token of submission. Reluctantly, the Carthaginians surrendered 200,000 panoplies of armour and 2,000 pieces of 'artillery' from their armouries in the city. On learning the Roman Senate's further demand that the population abandon its maritime location and move its residence to a location 15km inland, the populace rebelled and prepared its defence (Polyb. 36.6.7; Lancel 1995: 413). The artisan population wasted little time converting 'all the sacred places, the temples and every other wide and open space into workshops' to produce more arms. 'Men and women worked together day and night on a fixed schedule, without pause, taking their food by turns. Each day they made 100 shields, 300 swords, 1,000 missiles for catapults, 500 darts and spears and as many catapults as they could.'[3] The desperation of a maritime population under siege reveals itself through predictable behaviour. To levy necessary manpower, Carthaginian authorities proclaimed freedom to all the slaves (App. *Lib*. 93). With the maritime population up in arms, any provocation was liable to send it into a frenzy. When one politician was found to enjoy marriage ties with Numidian princes allied with Rome, the mob immediately assaulted him in the assembly, beating him to death with truncheons torn from benches close at hand (App. *Lib*. 111).

Ultimately, whatever slim hope the Carthaginian populace held rested in the strength of the city's defences. The whole of this community had been enclosed within a massive 'triple defence' of moat, palisade and fortification wall some 23km in length. The innermost line of defence exhibited towers four storeys tall every 60m. Beneath the ramparts stood barracks and stables sufficient to house 24,000 troops, 300 elephants, and 4,000 horses (App. *Lib*. 95). The strength of these defences stymied Roman siege efforts for three years (149–146 BC). However, it was the massive construction programme of the city's enclosed harbours that gave the population its greatest recourse. Along the shore the perimeter walls enclosed a virtually impregnable maritime facility combining a long rectangular harbour for merchant shipping and a circular inner harbour for the war fleet, referred to by the sources as the *Cothon*. As described by Appian (*Pun*. 96) these installations set contemporary standards of maritime organisation and security:

The harbours had communication with each other, and a common entrance from the sea seventy feet wide, which could be closed with iron chains. The first port was for merchant vessels, and here were collected all kinds of ships' tackle. Within the second port was an island and great quays set at intervals around both the harbour and the island. These embankments were full of shipyards which had the capacity for 220 warships. In addition to these were magazines for their tackle and furniture. Two Ionic columns stood in front of each dock, giving the appearance of a continuous portico to both the harbour and the island. On the island stood the admiral's house, from which the trumpeter gave signals, the herald delivered orders, and the admiral himself overlooked everything. The island lay near the entrance to the harbour and rose to a considerable height, so that the admiral could observe what was going on at sea. Anyone approaching by water, meanwhile, could not get any clear view of what took place within. Not even incoming merchants could see the docks at once, for a double wall enclosed them. There were even gates by which merchant vessels could pass from the first port to the city without traversing the dockyards.

Recent archaeological exploration by British and American teams has confirmed the general outline of this description. British excavations on the island and along the shore of the circular lagoon of the former Cothon have revealed, for example, foundations of quays along their perimeter dating probably to the late Punic era as well as a series of graving docks and winter berthings in the form of ramps. These formed an ensemble of 30 docks arranged symmetrically in a slightly fan-shaped manner on either side of an axis formed by the central open area of an elongated hexagonal shape. On the short south side of this would have stood a watch tower, quite possibly the fleet commander's building mentioned by Appian.[4] Limited excavation along the north bank of the perimeter shore of the harbour revealed five additional ramps, 40m. in length. An extrapolation based on the average width of the ramps reveals that some 135 to 140 docks must have existed over the whole of the perimeter, and that together with those of the islet, the military harbour conceivably accommodated a total of 165–170 docks, for a total of 170–180 vessels, or a fleet whose number of units approaches that indicated by Appian (Lancel 1995: 178). Archaeological evidence indicating that the use of this complex continued right to the moment of the city's destruction in 146 BC, if not beyond, raises important questions about Roman motives for destroying the city.[5]

The mercantile harbour had experienced similar efforts at development during the last century of Carthaginian existence. Massive dredging operations had converted soggy lagoon-bottom land into an enclosed rectangular basin, the stone-constructed entrance to which remains visible today as a half-submerged platform known as Falbe's quadrilateral.[6] Appian asserts (*Lib.* 123) that this was used as a vast platform for manoeuvres, unloading and storage; its southern tip acted as a pier head furnishing a wind break to the harbour entrance (Lancel 1995: 180). Inside the harbour, the basin would have been fairly cramped and shallow (with a depth of approximately 2.5m). The rectangular port offered around seven hectares of docking space (Lancel 1995: 181). These sheltered basins were too small to accommodate the full strength of Carthage's military and merchant marines; rather, they were used as repair facilities and as havens where vessels could be removed during inclement weather. Outside the defensive walls, the city relied on a series of sheltered beaches and roadsteads for mooring purposes.[7] This pattern remained extremely common throughout the seas.

Numerous archaeological indicators point, therefore, to decided urban development and expansion in the early second century BC, particularly in the area of military installations – the solid defensive wall around the community, with its living quarters and supply depots, and the famous interior harbour of the navy (Lancel 1995: 156f.; 404f.). This development, archaeologically indicated as reaching its peak in the period in question, stands at odds with the assertions of the literary sources that the Carthaginians had eliminated their elephant corps and had reduced its navy to a squadron of ten in accordance with the terms of 201 BC. On the other hand, the apparent willingness of the Carthaginian oligarchy to submit to the orders of the Roman Senate, surrendering first 300 of their children as hostages and then their abundant armament, confirms the unpreparedness of the Carthaginian population for war. On learning of the further Roman order that they relocate their community inland, hysterical Carthaginians reportedly visited the empty ship sheds of the military harbour and the spacious stables of their defensive walls, lamenting their previous decision to surrender their military equipment to perfidious Rome (App. *Lib.* 92). When combined with the archaeological evidence, these accounts would seem to indicate that building complexes, such as the perimeter walls and the military harbour, had been constructed in anticipation of some future conflict but that the resources they were designed to house were as yet unavailable when this war began (Lancel 1995: 182). The Romans had apparently arrived at a similar conclusion. In his history of the siege of Carthage, Appian expressed these very concerns in a speech delivered by the Roman military commander, L. Marcius Censorinus (cos. 149 BC). Rebutting the entreaties of Carthaginian ambassadors sent by the community to his camp in Utica, he questioned the purpose behind the construction of such massive defences (*Lib.* 88): 'If you still yearn for dominion and bear ill-will towards us who took it away from you, and are merely waiting for your opportunity to reclaim it, then of course you have need of this city, this great harbour and its dockyards, and these walls built to shelter a large army . . . Do not pretend, however, that you are grieved for your temples, your hearths, your forum and your tombs. For we have no desire to harm your tombs: you may come and make offerings there, and sacrifices in your temples as often as you like . . . Anyone with sense knows, however, that you do not sacrifice to your shipyards, nor do you make offerings to your walls.' The siege of Carthage amounted to a pre-emptive strike.

For three years the urban population resisted the Romans. In the end, the besieging army managed to storm the harbour, securing control of the forum, and then slashed and burned their way through the tenement district up the slope to surround the citadel on Byrsa. Exhausted and famished, the defenders surrendered their women and children, some 50,000 in all, to the safety of Roman enslavement. Even the Carthaginian commander, Hasdrubal, managed to sneak away and begged for his life at the foot of the newly-commissioned

Roman commander, P. Scipio Aemilianus (cos. 147 BC). Like her predecessor, Queen Dido, the wife of Carthage's last general publicly reviled her husband from the walls of the temple of the Phoenician goddess Tanit on the acropolis. Slaying her children, she threw their remains and then herself into the fire. Romans and Carthaginians alike watched in horror at this final act in the city's carnage. Apart from the grizzly account preserved by Appian, the remains of mass burials, bones from hundreds of victims, have been exposed on the south slopes of Byrsa (Lancel 1995: 149). So perished Carthage, one of the greatest ports of its day. With its destruction the Mediterranean maritime community lost one of its principal havens from this period of turmoil.

Corinth

Straddling the narrow isthmus that connected central Greece with the Peloponnese, Corinth with its defensive circuit of around 16km, its twin harbours, the Lechaion on the Gulf of Corinth and Kenchreai on the Saronic Gulf, had for centuries served as a maritime bridge to east/west trade across the region (**8**).[8] As Strabo observes (8.6.20 (378)):

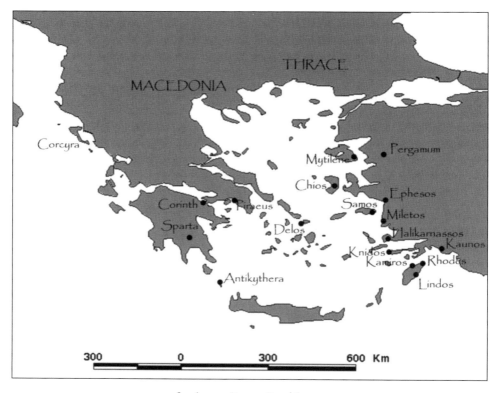

8   Aegean sites mentioned in text

Corinth was called wealthy because of its commerce. Since it is situated on the isthmus and is master of two harbours, one of which leads straight to Asia and the other to Italy, it makes easy the exchange of merchandise from two regions otherwise quite distant from one another. And just as in early times the strait of Sicily was not easy to navigate, so also the high seas and particularly the sea beyond Cape Malea were difficult because of the contrary winds. Hence the proverb, 'but when you double Malea, forget your home'. At any rate Corinth was a welcome alternative for the merchants both from Italy and from Asia who preferred to avoid the voyage to Malea and to land their cargoes here.

The remains of Lechaion stand 3km north of ancient Corinth (**9**). Formerly joined to the city by double long walls (fashioned after the Long Walls of Athens) and a broad paved avenue, the largest paved road in all of ancient Greece, the Lechaion harbour occupied an area of around 10ha, making it one of the largest harbours in all of Greece. Unfortunately, the site has received minimal archaeological investigation, leaving chronological aspects of its development difficult to determine. Surviving details indicate that the remains visible today reflect the stature of the harbour during its later life as the western harbour to the Roman colony, Laus Julia Corinthiensis, founded by Julius Caesar and Augustus.[9] In some ways the design of the harbour appears to resemble that of the harbour at Carthage. Two outer harbours protected by moles lay on the shore and communicated with a spacious inner harbour through a narrow channel bordered by stone jetties (**colour plate 32**). In the middle of the western half of the inner harbour stands the masonry core of a Roman monument, oddly recalling the coning tower of the island facility of Cothon harbour at Carthage. The prominent mounds of sand near the shore were probably heaped up by Roman engineers during repeated dredging operations. On a mound of dredged material to the east of the harbour, the remains of a large rectangular fire pit are visible, used possibly to create dense columns of smoke intended to be visible far out to sea (Rothaus 1995: 297). For all practical purposes these fire pits, two more of which are likewise visible on the island of Delos, functioned as ancient lighthouses.[10] Again, it is difficult to determine the degree to which this layout at Lechaion accurately preserves the state of the harbour in 146 BC. The ancient sources certainly indicate that prior to the destruction of Corinth, the Lechaion exhibited ship sheds as well as sanctuaries to Poseidon and Aphrodite.[11] (**10**)

The remains of Kenchreai, the harbour situated at the opposite Saronic Gulf – end of the isthmus – stand some 11km east of the centre of ancient Corinth and 4km south of the celebrated Isthmian Sanctuary of Poseidon. Nearby to the north lies the Saronic mouth to the modern Corinth canal, and during Antiquity the eastern end of the *diolkos*, a paved causeway approximately 4m

9 *View of the Lechaion Road at Corinth*

Interior Basin   Entrance

10   View of Lechaion from the Acrocorinth

wide, constructed in the sixth century BC to haul warships and unladed cargo ships across the isthmus from one gulf to the other. The process of dragging ships 11km on small cradles whose deep wheel ruts some 1.5m apart are still visible on the pavement, doubtless required the labour of scores of teams of oxen, similarly large gangs of labourers, and numerous muleteers and wagoners. Although poorly recorded by our sources, the *diolkos* appears to have functioned more or less continually until the ninth century AD, and helped to give Corinth its strategic importance in maritime trade (**11**).[12]

Kenchriai presents itself as a triangular alluvial plain about 600m deep facing a broad straight beach *c.*500m long[13] (**colour plate 3** & **4a**). Along the north side of the valley is a steep bluff extending east beyond the beach. In the cove formed by the beach and the bluff the remains of moles point to the existence of the ancient harbour approximately 250m in diameter. Excavations conducted by a team from the University of Chicago along the north and south ends of the harbour indicate that the ancient Greek harbour probably lies buried beneath the alluvial plain. In addition, local tectonic disturbances combined with a slight rise in sea level since ancient times have lowered the remains in relation to the sea by 2m, submerging the two moles that extend from the north and the south-west ends of the cove. Remains of warehouse facilities extend along the southern and northern perimeters of the harbour, some of these dated to the fourth century BC. Along the south end of the harbour lie the remains of a small pier; along the northern bluff stand those of a broad quay (**12**).

11 View of excavated portion of the diolkos, *near the modern canal, on the Corinthian Gulf side of the Isthmus*

12 View of excavated remains of the basilica at Kenchriai

Attempts have been made to identify several of the surviving remains with complexes made famous by ancient literary sources, for example, the ruins sitting on the southern pier, displaying a sunken apsidal structure with mosaic floor and a fountain, and beside that the remains of a temple cellar. The excavators want to associate these remains with the Sanctuary of Isis mentioned by Apuleius' *Metamorphosis* (10.35) as the location where the novel's hero, Lucius, returned to human form. More significantly, in the apsidal basin the excavators found the remains of over 45kg of *opus sectile* glass dating to 370 AD. These glass panels, the largest around 1m by 2m, are made of a type of plaster and coloured glass cut and placed to form designs and representational pictures, including one of the most vivid representations of a maritime town to survive from Antiquity.[14] Damaged by earthquakes in 365 and 375 AD and perhaps damaged further during the Avar invasions at the end of the sixth century AD, Kenchreai survived, nevertheless, as a modest fishing port to modern times.

Corinth's position, at the maritime crossroads of east/west trade, as well as at the head of the land bridge connecting the Peloponnese to central Greece, had from earliest times enabled its population to assume status as one of the great cities of the Aegean. Although its population suffered severely during warfare at the outset of the fourth century BC, Corinth had experienced resurgence during the Hellenistic era, first as the headquarters of Philip II's short-lived League of Corinth (338 BC), then as the leading city of the Achaian League. For more than a century its acropolis, the heavily fortified, well watered Acrocorinth (**colour plate 5**), was recognised by Macedonian dynasts as one of three strategic 'choke points' for all land movement in Greece. With the advent of Roman intervention in the Aegean, Corinth assumed increasing importance both as the nominal capital of the Achaian League and as a pivotal production centre for burgeoning Italian markets, where among other goods, Corinthian bronzes were prized in Cicero's time (*Verr.* 2.4.1). Like Carthage, by the time in question, Corinth was susceptible to public demonstrations by its labouring population. In 146 BC, the Greek historian Polybius described the Corinthian populace as an urban mob of artisans and manual labourers, hooting and jeering at Roman ambassadors sent to reason with them. 'For never had there been collected such a pack of artisans and manual labourers. All the towns, indeed were in a drivelling state, but the malady was universal and most fiercely felt at Corinth' (Polyb. 38.12.2-11).

Like the inhabitants of Carthage, the maritime population at Corinth in 148 BC was passionately anti-Roman. Incited by widespread indebtedness among landholders and urban dwellers alike (Cass. Dio 32.26.5), and taking their cue from conflicts raging simultaneously in Carthage and Macedonia, elements of Achaian leadership persuaded the league assembly to declare war on their inveterate foe, Sparta, knowing full well that their aggression would not be countenanced by Rome. Despite repeated Roman attempts to mediate, the league assembly, dominated by urban dwellers of Corinth proper, violently accosted the Roman envoys, provoking war. The leading instigator, a general named Critolaus, whipped the mob into a frenzy through his proposed abolitions of debts and debtor imprisonment and his call for forced contributions from the rich, including money and military conscription of slaves (Polyb. 38.11.8-11). 'As a result of his appeals to the rabble,' continues Polybius, 'everything he said was accepted as true and the people (*plethos*) were ready to do anything he ordered, incapable as they were of taking thought for the future, and enticed by the bait of present favour and ease . . . By dealing freely and systematically in such phrases Critolaus continued to excite and irritate the mob (*ochlos*).'

When the Roman legions arrived from Macedonia and Italy, the rapidly organised forces of Achaia proved no match. Once the city was seized, the Roman commander, L. Mummius, ordered the entire Achaian population to assemble. The inhabitants of Corinth proper were singled out and sold into slavery; the city's land was confiscated, its walls dismantled, its monuments destroyed, and its priceless treasures – statues, paintings, ornaments having accumulated over several centuries – confiscated and publicly auctioned (Zon. 9.31; Strabo 8.6.23 (381)). Sources record the callous disregard of Roman victors for their spoils, including the sight of Roman soldiers playings games of knucklebones on gameboards improvised from priceless Corinthian paintings.[15]

As with Carthage, however, the archaeological evidence demonstrates the existence of 'squatters' dwelling in the ruins of Corinth during the century of the city's abandonment.[16] Doubtless, Greek and Roman proprietors who purchased and/or rented the land confiscated by Mummius continued to use the site and its harbours for mercantile purposes. The maritime population that had once dominated affairs of Achaia and played so important a role in maritime trade, however, was either reduced to slavery or forced to find another port of call.[17]

Athens and the Piraeus

Naturally, the destruction of Carthage and Corinth in 146 BC sent shock waves throughout the Mediterranean world. It also caused a sudden realignment of trade networks, not to mention the displacement of numerous maritime distributors and workers throughout the region. The resilience of this working element inevitably led to adjustments. For example, the transshippers of Corinth relocated their warehouses to Athens, sustained by its great harbour at the Piraeus, one of the major emporia of the late Hellenistic world. They also relocated to Delos, an island protectorate of Athens rapidly emerging as the most brilliant trading centre of the era. Both port cities aligned their fates with Rome and prospered in the decades following 146 BC.

As a maritime community the polity of Athens had long been favoured by the proximity of its impregnable harbour, the Piraeus, approximately 8km south-west of the city (Garland 1987) (**colour plate 30**). For centuries an urban population in its own right, the Piraeus occupied the spacious peninsula of Akte, the rocky hill of Mounychia to the east, the lower ground in between the two, and a small tongue of land called Eetioneia to the west. The irregularities of the coastline created three natural harbours: the great commercial harbour on the west, known as the Kantharos, and two smaller round harbours, Zea and Mounychia (**colour plate 7**), situated along the south shore below Akte and Mounychia. The last two mentioned shelters functioned primarily as naval harbours. Formed from the erosion of the limestone of the Akte peninsula and the hill of Mounychia as well as of softer rocks and sedimentary material between these two points, the Mounychia and Zea harbours display distinctly oval shapes with headlands stretching across their mouths from either side, leaving a relatively narrow gap for winds and waves to penetrate (Morton 109, 126f.). With harbours essentially facing east, south and west, the Piraeus offered wind-driven cargo ships maximum accessibility, regardless of the direction of the prevailing winds. The docking facilities of the main harbour, the Kantharos, ranked second only to those of Alexandria, and the city, designed on a grid plan by the famous Milesian architect, Hippodamus, furnished its maritime population with a welter of warehouses, taverns, inns and brothels.[18] The Piraeus boasted two *agorae* – the emporium in the Kantharos and the Hippodameia at the city centre, somewhere west of modern Mounychia (Paus. 1.1.3). Two theatres exploited the slope of Mounychia (the larger theatre, west of Mounychia, used occasionally for meetings of the assembly, the smaller one, constructed in the second century BC, west of Zea harbour: Thuc. 8.93.1). Municipal facilities also included a *bouleuterion*, and a generals' staff headquarters (*strategion*: *IG* 2^2 1035.43–44), thus duplicating many of the urban facilities of the city of Athens itself.

Commerce transpired primarily in the great harbour of Kantharos. On its east side stood the emporium with its broad open display area, the *deigma*, framed by a line of *stoae* of which slight traces survive. Inscribed boundary stones indicate the area's public designation. In 1959 at the northern end of this area excavators encountered five bronze statues of exceptional quality from the Archaic and classical periods, along with several other fragments of sculpture. Found in what was identified as the remains of an ancient warehouse, these larger-than-life bronzes include two statues of Artemis, one of Apollo, and one of Athena. An Athenian coin found in context and dated to 87/6 BC furnishes the date of the warehouse's destruction. The statues had apparently been placed in the harbour warehouse prior to the siege of the Piraeus by the Roman general, L. Cornelius Sulla, in 87/6 BC. Conceivably, the statues were sacred images plundered from Delos along with other treasures by Archelaus, the naval commander dispatched by King Mithradates of Pontus, and Aristion, the tyrant of Athens, when they assaulted the island in 87 BC. Transported to the Piraeus, the statues were buried during the destruction of their storehouse during Sulla's siege. Hidden from the view of Sulla's plundering Roman soldiers, they were lost and forgotten until modern times.[19] Their discovery furnishes a revealing snapshot of the violence that beset Athenian territories at this time.

To either side of the emporium extended some 94 military ship sheds (*neosoikoi*)[20] (**13**). Much like today, berthing existed along three sides of the harbour from the emporium on the east past a small sheltered inlet known as the *Kophos*, or the Blind Harbour, to the north, to the shore of Eetioneia on the west. Like the entrances to the military harbours, Zea and Mounychia, the mouth of the Kantharos was protected by fortification walls constructed on projecting moles that narrowed the entrance sufficiently to allow for it to be closed by suspended iron chains. The smaller oval harbours of Zea and Mounychia sheltered the naval arm of the Athenian polity, particularly Zea

13 *View of the excavated remains of the ship shed in Zea Harbour*

where inscriptions record the existence of 196 ship sheds and a further 82 in Mounychia, more than enough to accommodate an Athenian warfleet of 283 ships at this time.[21] Excavated remains of some of the sheds are visible at various points in each harbour. An inscription dated to the latter half of the fourth century BC (*IG* 2^2 1668), found up-slope on Mounychia, furnishes detailed specifications for the construction of a great *skeuotheke*, or arsenal, for the storage of equipment. The architect Philon fashioned this long rectangular structure into three adjoining halls separated lengthwise by colonnades. This magnificent building was likewise destroyed by Sulla during the siege of 87/6 BC.

The whole of the Piraeus, from Eetioneia in the west to the Akte in the south-east, was enclosed within a massive curtain wall, the construction of which spanned several centuries (Garland 1987: 163–9) (**colour plate 6**). At the height of the fifth-century BC Athenian empire, the fortified community of the Piraeus had been connected to the defences of Athens proper by massive Long Walls, three parallel defences approximately 200m apart that furnished a protected corridor between the Piraeus and the inland city. During times of siege this fortified strip of land enabled the inland community to receive provisions from the granaries in the Piraeus and to maintain control of its naval empire. It also harboured refugees from the exposed farmlands of Attica. When grain ships from Egypt brought the plague to Athens in 430 BC, it was particularly among the refugees squatting in tent settlements within the Long Walls that the pestilence wreaked its toll (Thuc. 2.47–54). Dismantled by Sparta at the end of the Peloponnesian War, the fortunes of the Long Walls appear to have declined during the era of Macedonian domination. At the time of Sulla's siege, they clearly lay in ruins. In 87 BC, Sulla conducted separate, simultaneous sieges against Athens and the Piraeus, repeatedly intercepting traffic between the two communities, and constructing huge mounds and towers with blocks scavenged from abandoned remnants of the Long Walls (Habicht 1997: 310).

Despite the availability of this material, Sulla found the defences of the Piraeus impregnable. According to Appian (*Mith.* 30), the walls manned by Archelaus' army stood some 18m tall and were solidly constructed of large ashlar blocks. Scaffolds, stairways and projecting towers extended along their length at close intervals. The gargantuan character of Sulla's siege efforts underscores the imposing stature of these defences (App. *Mith.* 30; Plut. *Sull.* 12–14). After a futile attempt to storm the walls with ladders, Sulla 'retired exhausted to Eleusis and Megara where he built engines for a new attack and formed a plan for besieging the Piraeus with a mound. Machines and equipment of all kinds, iron, catapults and everything of that sort, were supplied by Thebes. He constructed additional siege engines from the wood he obtained by cutting down the grove of the Academy. He also demolished the Long Walls and used the stones, timber and earth for building the mound.' Repairs attested by inscriptions demonstrate that the maintenance of the Piraeus walls was an expensive and complicated task.

Although the bulk of these fortifications remain hidden beneath the streets of the modern, very dense city of Piraeus, short lengths of the walls have been exposed at various points. The principal gate (the Asty), allowing access for the road to Athens, stood just to the west of the point where the Long Wall joined the circuit wall of the Piraeus. Another gate stood a little farther east within the area enclosed by the Long Walls. It was here that Sulla's siege efforts were the fiercest (App. *Mith.* 36-7) (**14**) .[22]

> Sulla pounded the wall with rams erected on the top of the mounds until part of it fell down. Then he hastened to burn the neighbouring tower and discharged a large number of fire-bearing missiles against it, while ordering that his bravest soldiers mount the ladders. Both sides fought bravely but the tower was burned. Another small part of the wall was thrown down also, against which Sulla at once stationed a guard post. Having now undermined a section of the wall so that it was only sustained by wooden beams, he placed a large quantity of sulphur, hemp and pitch under it and set fire to the whole at once. The walls fell, now here, now there, carrying defenders down with them. This great and unexpected crash demoralised the forces guarding the walls everywhere . . . Archaelaus brought up new forces, however, to replace those discouraged and supported the attack continually with fresh troops cheering and urging them on . . . Eventually growing exhausted, Sulla sounded the retreat. Archelaus forthwith repaired the damage to his wall by night, protecting many parts of it with lunettes toward the interior. The following day Sulla set about to storm these with his entire army, thinking that they were still moist and wet because they were newly constructed. However, the need to work in a narrow space exposed his troops to missiles from above, both in front and on the flank, as usually happens in attacking crescent-shaped fortifications, and they were soon demoralised. With that, Sulla abandoned all hope of taking the Piraeus by assault and established a siege around it in order to reduce it by famine.

Excavations at the gate beside the northern Long Wall actually revealed small semicircular courses of block resembling the lunette walls described above. Archelaus defended the Piraeus with the army he had brought from Asia Minor, reportedly a significantly larger force than the one brought by Sulla. According to Appian (*Mith.* 31) Archelaus even went so far as to arm and to man the battlements with his rowers, 'knowing that everything was at stake'. The maritime population of the Piraeus likewise contributed to the defence, as Appian's account of Sulla's violent behaviour on seizing the harbour in 86 BC makes clear (*Mith.* 41): 'Sulla set fire to the Piraeus for having given him

14 *View of remains of the Piraeus walls in the vicinity of the gate stormed by Sulla in 87 BC*

more trouble than the city of Athens itself, sparing neither the arsenal or the naval yard nor any of its famous buildings.' Apart from the priceless find of statuary noted above, one of the best indicators of the intensity of the fighting has surfaced in the form of numerous coin hoards, hidden by their owners at the time of the siege and never reclaimed. Undoubtedly they represent merely a small fraction of Athenian valuables buried at this time.[23]

Throughout its history the Piraeus formed a melting pot of Mediterranean cultures. Inscribed dedications recovered in the Piraeus demonstrate that it was one of the earliest places in the Aegean for the assimilation of Near Eastern cults including those of Anatolian Bendis, Kybele, Zeus Sabazios, Syrian Aphrodite Ourania, Sidonian Baal, Egyptian Isis and Sarapis, and Libyan Zeus Ammon (Garland 1987: 101f.). Its bustling harbour exhibited a highly cosmopolitan character. For reasons that seem unclear, this highly diverse, maritime element invariably opposed Roman expansion. In fact, the siege of the Piraeus provides the best example of the animosity exhibited by maritime populations toward Rome. No state had received more benefit from its dealings with the Roman Republic than Athens. For more than a century the Athenians had remained firmly aligned with Rome – against Philip II of Macedonia in 215 and 200 BC, against Antiochus III of Syria in 192, and against Perseus of Macedonia in 172 BC. Due to this unwavering support the Roman Senate rewarded the Athenians with grants of territory throughout the Aegean, most prominently the island of Delos and its celebrated Sanctuary of Apollo. The Roman Senate ceded this island sanctuary on condition that the Athenians allow it to remain a 'free port', that is exempt from all tariffs on goods passing in transit through the island's emporium. As the importance of this duty-free harbour grew, Athenian officials who monitored its trade and the many Piraeus-based mercantile houses that serviced it prospered in direct proportion.[24] Evidence of the close relationship between Athenian trade and that of Delos is perhaps best demonstrated by the remarkably similar distribution ratios of transport amphorae that have been recovered in the American excavations at the Athenian Agora and at the French operations at Delos. These indicate a pronounced shift in trading patterns that favoured Athens during the period in question. Commercially and economically, while Rhodes became increasingly isolated, Athens, Delos, Kos, Knidos and Chios had by 88 BC all become closely aligned with Rome.[25]

Although the cleruchy of lower class settlers dispatched to Delos by the Athenian government appears quickly to have faltered and returned, this failure was most likely a result of the rapid development of an emerging international trading community on that island, than it was a reflection of any failure on the Athenians' part. The influx of wealthy merchants from Italy and the Near East placed such high demand on the necessities of life – building supplies, lodgings, food and beverages – that underclass Athenian colonists could not afford to remain. Athenian administrators of the island likewise appear to have yielded certain aspects of their authority in order to accommodate the demands of the newly installed and highly influential foreign community. Administrative staff positions were reduced, and several subtle indicators reveal that the foreign residents were allowed to acquire property and to express some vague sense of home rule, perhaps as separate and partially autonomous ethnic enclaves (Rauh 1993: 1–53). Apart from these limitations, however, the economy of Athens and the Piraeus appear to have benefited from their direct association with Delian trade. Several prominent mercantile families, especially families who dwelt in the Piraeus, rose to prominence in the Areopagus as well as in the Athenian administrative offices directly associated with Delian trade. Athenian supervision of Delian commerce appears to have enabled the city to set uniform trading standards for the Aegean region as a whole, echoing their behaviour during the height of their classical empire. The newly commissioned series of Athenian silver tetradrachms became the standard medium of exchange throughout the Aegean, causing other states engaged in the Delian trading network, such as Kos and Knidos, to adjust the weights of their currencies accordingly.[26] Changes in the volumes of Koan and Knidian transport amphorae, combined with epigraphically recorded Athenian administrative reforms of weights and standards both in Athens and at Delos, indicate that the Athenians once again imposed their own system of measurement on the wider Aegean world. Athenian dedications honouring Rome, Roman magistrates, and Hellenistic dynasts such as Ptolemy Euergetes II of Egypt, John Hyrcanus of Israel, and Mithradates VI of Pontus, demonstrate as well the degree to which Athens assumed increasing importance in international affairs, perhaps a mediating influence at that.

By 88 BC, however, none of this commercial success was sufficient to dispel the surging undercurrent of popular antipathy against Rome. According to historical sources, however much an elite group of commercial families prospered from diplomatic and commercial co-operation at Rome, the vast majority of Athenians endured poverty, insolvency and restrained political expression during this time. The ability of the populace even to vent its frustration with the local state of affairs appears to have been stifled by those in charge. Some attributes of Roman authority likely to provoke resentment, such as the speaker's podium erected in the Agora for the ceremonial visits of Roman dignitaries, were merely symbolic irritations. Others were more reflective of the Roman tendency to secure its interests in the East by buttressing the property rights and political ascendancy of limited elites. Unlike Hellenistic kings of the preceding era, who had for decades maintained their influence in Greek urban communities by deftly playing wealthy land-holding elements and wage-labouring urbanites one against the other (in the latter instance by giving philanthropic subsidies to the poor), the Roman Senate tended by and large to entrust local governance to property-holding gentries alone.

In Athens prevailing tensions between the pro-Roman elite and the urban masses remained suppressed until the outbreak of the Mithradatic War (88 BC).[27] Repeated slave rebellions, in 133 and 103 BC, particularly the virulent, costly rebellion that erupted at the silver mines at Laurion in the latter instance, put the population on edge (Habicht 1997: 292). Between 91/90 and 89/88 BC one of the wealthiest, pro-Roman sympathisers, Medeios son of Medeios, scion to a prominent mercantile house in the Piraeus, took the unconstitutional step of assuming three consecutive terms as eponymous archon.[28] His government likewise cancelled the celebration of the Pythias, a costly but very popular ceremonial procession (90/89 BC). Despite striking coins displaying the symbol of Roma in 90/89 and 89/88 BC, the pro-Roman oligarchy was clearly losing its grip on Athenian popular sentiment. The king's early successes in Asia Minor during the winter of 88 BC – his expulsion of Roman forces from the provinces of Asia and Cilicia, his capture of several Roman commanders, and his incitement of massacres of Roman residents throughout the provinces – emboldened democratic elements to challenge Athenian authority at home. The oligarchy responded by cancelling religious festivals, by shutting down the courts, by closing the theatres, lecture halls, and public gymnasia, and by appealing to the Roman Senate for assistance.[29] One member of the opposition, a peripatetic philosopher named Athenion, undercut Medeios' authority by sailing directly to the camp of Mithradates to negotiate with the king. Letters from the Mithradates, dispatched by Athenion in his name, proclaimed the king's willingness to restore Athenian democracy, to annul all debts, and to lavish the Athenian people with subsidies.[30] Returning to Athens

15 *View of remains of defensive walls in Keramikos, where Sulla broke through in 87 BC*

in early Spring displaying a ring given to him by the king, Athenion was greeted by a crowd of citizens and foreigners. He rode into town on a litter and was fêted at the mansion of a merchant known to have profited from Delian trade (Athen. 5.212d). Several politicians whom Athenion nominated for the archonships in 88/7 likewise hailed from families with known Delian interests (Habicht 1997: 303). To such a degree had Rome lost its support in the city. With seemingly broad-based support, Athenion imposed a reign of terror (**15**).

A feeble assault on Delos in 87, commissioned and disastrously conducted by a second philosopher named Apellicon, seems to have marked Athenion's undoing. When Archelaus' marine forces arrived in the Piraeus, flush with the plunder of his successful storming of Delos, Athenion's ascendancy yielded to that of a third philosopher named Aristion. An Athenian citizen of Tean origin, Aristion substituted ruthlessness and violence for Athenion's inept demagoguery. While preparing for war in 87/6, he appears to have struck a great deal of currency, including gold staters possibly derived from the treasure seized at Delos the previous year (Habicht 1997: 310). During Sulla's siege of Athens, Aristion disdainfully taunted the Roman general from the city walls, showering particular abuse on Sulla's wife, Caecilia Metella, who had sought refuge with her husband from enemies at Rome (Plut. *Sull.* 13). At the same time he cruelly suppressed any and all entreaties for moderation from within, reserving particular violence for Athenian aristocrats.[31] Ultimately, Sulla stormed the gates at the Kerameikos and unleashed his legionaries on helpless citizens. 'He ordered an indiscriminate massacre not sparing women and children. For he was angry that the Athenians had joined the barbarians so suddenly without cause and had displayed such violent animosity toward himself.'[32] Aristion and his supporters retreated to the Acropolis where they resisted a few months longer before finally succumbing to starvation and surrender. Following the opinion of the contemporary philosopher Poseidonius (*c*.135–50 BC), neither Appian (*Mith.* 28) nor Plutarch (*Sull.* 13) have anything positive to say about the rag-tag collection of philosophers who had encouraged the Athenian populace to ruin. 'They dwelt in mean hired flats, dressed in rags' and were otherwise 'obscure, and poverty-stricken, wearing the garb of philosophy as a matter of necessity and railing bitterly against the rich and powerful, thus winning themselves a reputation, not for despising riches and power, but for envying them' (App. *Mith.* 28). By and large, men such as these furnished the brains of the maritime mob.

Sulla plundered what little he could of Athens, seizing columns from the unfinished Temple of Olympian Zeus, the library amassed by Apellicon, and numerous works of art, such as a famous painting by the fifth-century BC artist, Zeuxis.[33] This last-mentioned work of art was lost at sea when the cargo ship bearing it and other treasures to Rome went down in the waters off Cape Malea (Plin. *NH* 36.54). The literary record of this shipwreck has long raised suspicions about actual wrecks, dated to this era and found to be laden with priceless art works, especially those of the Antikythera wreck and the wreck off Cape Mahdia in Tunisia.[34] As for Athens, poverty stricken and much reduced in population, Sulla relinquished the city's independence, for what this was worth. For many months the surviving population existed on the philanthropy of resident Romans such as Cicero's good friend, T. Pomponius Atticus (Corn. Nep. *Att.* 2). Eventually it regained its rights even to Delos. However, the days of its resurgent mercantile empire were finished. Thoroughly destroyed and gutted by Roman troops, the Piraeus was reduced to a small, defenceless community clustered around its three ancient harbours (Strabo 9.1.15 (396); cf. 14.2.9 (654)).

Delos

An unlikely locale for a major emporium of the Mediterranean, Delos was but a sliver of land at the centre of the Cyclades, measuring at its greatest a mere 5km north–south by 1.3km east–west. The island nevertheless emerged as an important trading centre at the end of the second century BC. Long venerated as the birthplace of the god Apollo, the island's sanctuary and community were controlled for much of their history by Athens (478–314 BC). Obtaining its independence during the period of Macedonian hegemony, the Delian community prospered as a nerve centre of the Aegean grain trade and as a focus of religious pilgrimages from throughout the eastern Mediterranean (Reger 1994). Hellenistic dynasts such as Antigonus Gonatas, Philip V of Macedonia and Ptolemy VI Euergetes of Egypt consciously advertised their arrival on the political scene by embellishing the borders of the ancient sanctuary with majestic marble porticoes decked with self-congratulatory statuary. The sanctuary and its priests furnished an important node of communications to these dynasts, particularly during its annual festival for Apollo. For example, on the eve of his war with Rome King Perseus of Macedonia used the occasion of this festival to broadcast his offer of asylum in Macedonia to insolvent debtors throughout the Greek world (Livy 42.13.9). Much like the island republic of Rhodes, the priests of Delian Apollo miscalculated their international importance at the outbreak of Rome's war with Perseus (172–167 BC). Failure to prohibit Macedonian inspired piratical raids from issuing from their harbour, even as Roman ambassadors watched in anger, undermined the community's credibility, not to mention Roman patience. At the war's conclusion the Roman Senate expelled the island's native population and ceded the island and its sanctuary to Athens, as noted above, with the proviso that trade at its harbour enjoy *ateleia*, exemption from all tariffs on goods passing through the harbour in transit (Rauh 1993: 2).

Within thirty years of this decision, Delos emerged as the distribution centre of a broad trans-Mediterranean trade network. Judging from the remains of housing and commercial facilities, its volume of trade expanded enormously and its population, mostly traders from outside the Aegean basin, burgeoned to an unprecedented level. The influx of new residents and new activities provoked a building boom of extraordinary proportions. Delos' sanctuary attained a popularity and importance unmatched in the Hellenistic world, though in this period its renown owed more to its increasing association with trade.

Excavations conducted since 1873 by the French School of Archaeology in Athens have exposed a sizable portion of the remains of ancient Delos. In his *Guide de Délos* the great explorer of the past half-century, Philippe Bruneau, divided the site into seven 'neighbourhoods' (**colour plate 31**). These include the Sanctuary of Apollo itself, situated on a small plain behind the main port; the domestic quarters of the Sacred Lake and the Theatre district, which border the sanctuary to the north and south respectively; the quarter of the Inopos, situated slightly to the north and east of the Theatre District in the gorge cut by the drainage of the Inopos; the highland district of the Terrace of the Foreign Gods and Mount Kynthos (112m in altitude), and two outlying neighbourhoods, the Stadium Quarter at the north-east point of the island and the Bay of Fourni to the south.

Unlike the other harbours considered in this chapter, the port facilities of Delos remained completely unprotected by defensive walls and vulnerable to naval assaults. This lack of security seemingly testifies to the rapid character of

16 *The Agora of Theophrastos at Delos, looking west*

the development of this emporium. In addition, the bulk of the docking facilities were constructed in relatively shallow waters along the island's west coast, near the sanctuary. With little relief terrain, these facilities were exposed to the full force of highly unpredictable winds. Three natural coves offered deeper water and better protection, depending on wind direction, namely Ghourna, at the north-east corner of the island facing east; Skardhana, slightly to the north of the Sacred Harbour, facing west; and Fourni, approximately 1.5km south of the Sacred Harbour, facing south west. However, none of these were sufficiently close to the island's commercial centres to function as anything more than service harbours to their adjoining neighbourhoods. Merchants voyaging to Delos conducted their business in or near the Sacred Harbour, with the result that a considerable array of maritime facilities were crammed into a relatively narrow band of coast in that vicinity (**colour plate 11**).

The one pre-existing agora of Delos, the Tetragonal or Delian Agora (the enclosed square to the south-east of the Sanctuary of Apollo), proved too small and too distant from the harbour to accommodate the emerging commerce of the new emporium (**16**). Accordingly, Athenian authorities and arriving merchants from Italy hastily constructed two new agorae on makeshift terrain reclaimed from the sea through landfill. A statue dedication discovered *in situ* in the flat, open, unpaved square directly to the north of the Sacred Harbour marks the location of the Agora of Theophrastos, constructed

55

by the Athenian administrator of the island in 126/5 BC. Surrounded on three sides by shrines, monuments and commercial structures, its most notable feature was a large covered meeting hall (the Hypostyle Hall) (**colour plate 17**). Constructed during the last years of the third century BC, this building utilised 24 Doric columns and 20 Ionic columns to support a massive roof with a central clerestory.

At the opposite south end of the Sacred Harbour, a similar landfill operation, completed probably in conjunction with that of the Agora of Theophrastos, created space for the so-called Agora of the Compitaliastai. This paved open square, roughly 60m by 32m, accommodated the business dealings of the resident Italian community at Delos. Porticoes leading to the Sanctuary of Apollo framed the square on the north side while shops and offices flanked it along its east and south. Two distinctive monuments constructed of marble, one round and the other square and step-like, stood at its centre, both apparently dedicated by Italian religious fraternities to Herakles. To the west of these, the agora was apparently left undeveloped, its pavement extending to the edge of the quay. Based on surviving structural remains, the shops on the east and south sides of this square housed offices for Italian groupings such as the *trapezitai* (bankers), the *ploizomenoi* (shippers), and the *oinopolai* (wine dealers). The façades of these buildings were set off by shallow colonnades and overhanging second-storey apartments. Based on surviving setting holes in the flat gneiss paving stones of the square, poles standing before these buildings supported awnings that extended toward the interior space of the square. Like the Agora of Theophrastos, the Agora of the Compitaliastai exhibited a significant array of altars, statues, smallish temples, and a dozen or more marble votive offerings dedicated to the gods of trade at this emporium, particularly Apollo, Hermes, Herakles and Poseidon. Given the superior depth of the Sacred Harbour at this point, it has long been assumed that this was the principal point of debarcation to the sanctuary (Rauh 1993: 75f.) (**17**).

South of the Sacred Harbour the remains of a vast row of contiguous quays, warehouses, and associated business structures extend nearly 1500m along the strand. This district, referred to as the 'Commercial Harbour', was apparently separated from the residential neighbourhoods to its east by a narrow (roughly 2–3m wide), paved road commonly known as 'Road Five' (**colour plate 10**). Some archaeologists have suggested that this road served not only as the main avenue between the Commercial Harbour and the town, but also as a line of demarcation separating the commercial district of the emporium from the residential neighbourhoods to its east (Rauh 1993: 85). Constructed on reclaimed land like the agoras mentioned above, the warehouse district of the Commercial Harbour was developed presumably to facilitate Delian transit commerce, with Road Five functioning as a customs boundary. The arrangement of the warehouses of this region presents a generally cluttered effect. Each building complex borders directly upon the shore with its own quay and/or

17 *View of warehouse remains on the shore of Commercial Harbour at Delos. Boats in the distanced are moored in the Sacred Harbour*

docking facility. Each is generally separated from the one to either side by a narrow alleyway running at right angles to the shore. Each complex, in other words, appears to have been constructed independently by a separate proprietary firm acting on its own initiative. Small finds discovered within several of these complexes, including Warehouses Alpha, Beta and Gamma directly to the south of the Agora of the Compitaliastai, and the Warehouses of the Bathtub and the Columns, further to the south, indicate that they functioned as Roman commercial complexes during the height of the island's international trade (**18**).

Standing near the southern end of the 'Commercial Harbour', the remains of the Warehouse of the Columns offer potentially the most illuminating example of a Roman warehouse to survive from this era (**colour plate 8**). This large two-storey structure (60 (50m) bordered directly onto the sea at so-called 'Quay Five'. The warehouse utilised a fairly common design of this region on a vastly extended scale. It incorporated some ten independent exterior shops on the quay, an interior arrangement of a central peristyle court combined with two auxiliary courts, eighteen adjoining ground-floor rooms and equally spacious first-floor living quarters. Freedom of movement was undoubtedly the chief feature this building had to offer. A series of internal transverse passageways were kept wide and straight to permit easy conveyance of bulk commodities throughout the building. Directly behind the exterior shops facing the harbour, a long, straight corridor (1.65m wide) ran parallel to

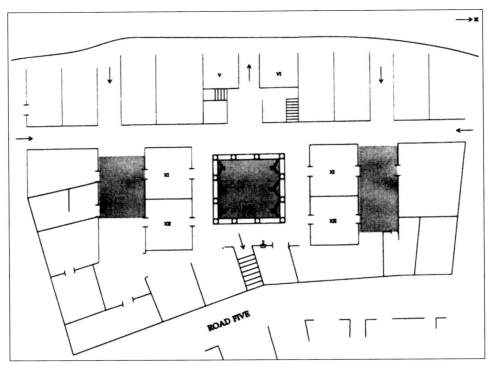

18 *Plan of the Warehouse of the Columns.* Drawn by John Cassidy

the shore along the entire length of the building (57m). This allowed for the circulation of bulk commodities not only back and forth between the exterior quay and the courtyards, but also laterally from one courtyard to the next. In addition, the four internal rooms which isolate the three courtyards had aligned doorways on their northern and southern walls, thus providing two additional means of lateral communication within the building. Each granite column in the central courtyard on the north and south sides of the peristyle exhibits two setting holes, 55 to 60cm above the stylobate and aligned in an axis tangential to that of the colonnade itself (**colour plate 9**). These holes probably supported two-legged, wooden table stands which could be erected and removed as needed, thus functioning potentially as merchandising displays.

Since the colonnades on the east and west sides of the courtyard lacked these settings, the arrangement of the setting holes demonstrates the direction in which goods apparently circulated inside the building. Traffic of goods appears to have flowed in from the sides, moving from ships on the quay to the two outer courtyards via side doors. It then progressed toward the peristyle of the central coutyard through the aligned doorways of the four interior rooms. Within the peristyle goods would be displayed for sale on the tables erected between the columns of the northern and southern colonnades. After purchase, presumably by auction, the merchandise would be removed through the large central doorway back to the quay for shipment abroad, or, conversely, into town via the stairway at the rear of the central courtyard. Although the rooms on the first floor display a greater degree of refinement, they too were integrated into the overall plan of the complex. The configuration suggests that the activities of both floors and, indeed, of the entire complex were complementary and, thus, conducted by a single proprietary firm. The building's small finds and wall paintings confirm that the Warehouse of the Columns was a Roman establishment.[35] Among other finds an internal altar dedicated to the Italian household deities, the Lares, stood against the back wall of the central, ground floor courtyard. Above the altar, French excavators discovered wall paintings depicting the preliminary proceedings of a gladiatorial spectacle, including a combat between *paegniarii* and a *venatio*, or animal hunt. The features and material remains of the Warehouse of the Columns are decidedly in keeping, therefore, with the requirements of a Roman trading establishment. Cut short in their bloom by destruction in 88 and 69 BC, the excavated remains of the international emporium at Delos conserve the clearest, most detailed example of a Roman commercial centre to survive from the period of the Roman conquest of the Mediterranean. Offering as they do varied insight into the character of maritime society at the dawn of the Roman era, the archaeological remains of this emporium will require repeated visits in the chapters that follow.

19 *View of the transverse corridor in the Warehouse of the Columns at Delos*

Having considered in the broadest possible terms the topographical remains of this emporium, the general outline of Delian trade requires some description. Strabo (14.5.2 (669)) reports that the port at Delos rose to great height with the destruction of Corinth (146 BC) when the *emporoi* transferred their business to the island. He also states that the location of Delos, midway across the Aegean, made it a convenient port of call for those wishing to sail from Italy and Greece to the Roman province of Asia. Delos' position straddling these trade routes became particularly important following the bequest of the kingdom of Pergamum by King Attalus III to Rome in 133 BC.[36] Though Delian inscriptions rarely elucidate these matters explicitly, it is probably safe to assume that with the passage of the *lex Sempronia de provincia Asia* in 123 BC, formally establishing the tax-collecting procedure for the province, Delos emerged as an important way-station for a host of Roman *publicani* and associated professionals passing to and from the province.

Passing observations by other sources lend weight to Strabo's assertion. Pausanias describes Delos at this time as the trading station of all of Greece (3.23.3-6); Festus (122 M.) goes so far as to call it the greatest emporium on the planet (*maximum emporium totius orbis terrarum*). Pliny (*NH* 34.9) concurs that the *mercatus in Delo* was the most frequented of the world (*concelebrante toto orbe*) and adds that it was a great place to acquire luxury products, including highly prized Delian bronze statues, couch fixtures and balances. Cicero (*Rosc. Amer.* 133) likewise raved about these wares. This said, the main reason for Delos' popularity at this juncture would appear to have been its commerce in slaves. While describing the rise of Cilician piracy in the late second century, Strabo reports that the pirates furnished Delos with a black market commerce in slaves as the other powers of the Mediterranean looked away (14.5.2 (669)):

> The exportation of slaves induced the Cilician pirates most of all to engage in their evil business, since it proved most profitable. For not only were the slaves easily captured, but the market, which was large and loaded with cash, was not very far away. I mean Delos, which could take in and ship out tens of thousands of slaves [muriadas] in a single day. From this arose the proverb, 'Merchant, sail in and unload your ship, your cargo is already sold.' The slave trade arose after the Romans became rich from the destruction of Carthage and Corinth and began to make use of numerous household slaves. Seeing easy profit in this, large numbers of pirates emerged to accommodate the demand and handled both the kidnapping of prisoners and the sale of them at Delos. The kings of both Cyprus and Egypt [i.e. the Ptolemies] co-operated with them in this because they were enemies to the Seleucids. Since the Rhodians were equally unfriendly, they too looked the other way. As a result, the pirates, posing as slave dealers, went about their evil business unchecked.

Strabo's account is significant for a number of reasons, not least because it provides the only explicit testimony for the island's emerging importance as a centre of a trans-Mediterranean slave trade. According to Strabo, the merchants (and pirates) at Delos engaged in the trans-shipment of prisoners from the eastern Mediterranean, particularly from Cilicia and Syria, to the agricultural estates, mines, shops and households of the Roman west. Strabo's testimony appears to dovetail in this regard with other evidence for the slave trade, including the evidence for chaotic political conditions in the eastern Mediterranean and that for occurrence of slave revolts in Sicily, Italy, Greece and Asia Minor in the 130s and 100s BC (Rauh 1993: 52). As noted earlier, the collapse of the Seleucid realm of Syria ushered in a protracted period of anarchy in the Near East, during which time the sources report that competing ethnic groups in Syria and Palestine – Hellenistic Greek colonies, Phoenician merchant communities along the coast, the Jewish inhabitants of Judaea, and Arab tribes in the hinterlands – conducted repeated slave raids against one another. More specifically, a dynastic dispute between Seleucid pretenders, Demetrius II and Diodotus Tryphon (146–138 BC), appears to have encouraged Cilician piracy, and this, in turn, accelerated the trans-shipment of prisoners to Delos after 139 BC.[37] Within a few years, simultaneous slave revolts erupted in Sicily, Italy, Attica, Delos and Asia Minor.[38]

The fact that Delos is one of only five places mentioned in connection with these uprisings suggests that the difficulties on the island were significant. While this in itself fails to confirm the existence of a Delian slave trade, further correlations arise with the arrival dates of several eastern Mediterranean trading associations on the island. A Delian ephebic dedication of 119/8 BC furnishes possibly the best demonstration of this Near Eastern immigration: more than half of the ninety-one recorded ephebes exhibited eastern Mediterranean origins, such as Patara, Knidos, Halikarnassos and Mallus in southern Asia Minor, Salamis and Karpasia in Cyprus, Antioch, Arados, Hierapolis, Laodiceia and Apamaea in Syria, Berytos, Sidon and Tyre in Phoenicia, Ptolemais and Anthedon in Palestine, and Alexandria in Egypt (Rauh 1993: 46). Some of the merchant elements of Delos, such as the Poseidoniasts of Berytos, whose city was destoyed in 145 BC, the Samaritans of Gerizim, whose homeland was severely ravaged by John Hyrcanus in 120–110, and the banking house of Philostratos of Ascalon, whose city had likewise submitted to Hasmonean rule by the time of his arrival in 106/5 BC, may actually have taken up residence at Delos as small exile communities, prepared to wait until such time as the violence in their homelands subsided.[39] Be that as it may, the presence at Delos of so many traders from the Near East tends to support Strabo's assertion that the slave trade lubricated the workings of this emporium. In addition, numerous Roman and Italian families present at Delos exhibited direct links to the Sicilian slave revolts, to Roman landholdings in that province, and/or to slave trading proper (Rauh 1993: 47f.). In many respects, the Sicilian slave revolts and the evidence of economic interests for several Roman and Italian families both at Delos and in Sicily reflect in microcosm the effect that the slave trade was having on Roman society, if not on the entire Mediterranean world.

Equally important, however, is the likelihood that the merchants assembling at Delos from the Near East and from Roman Italy and Sicily, played a role in the development of a Mediterranean luxury trade. Pliny reports (*NH* 13.4), for example, that Delos became a production centre for the perfume trade, a point reinforced by the simultaneous emergence of the Capuan Seplasia, the leading perfume and unguent market in Campania, where many Italian trading firms active at Delos originated (Rauh 1993: 54). Likewise, votive offerings erected at Delos by merchants from distant principalities such as Nabataea (modern Jordan and Saudi Arabia) and Minaea (modern Yemen), point to the likely role of these merchants in the trade of aromatic plants that were the foundation of the commodities. These same men served as go-betweens for related goods such as pepper, precious stones and pearls from India, and exquisite silks from China. In other words, the existence of these dedications not only proves that merchants from such distant regions made the laborious voyage to Delos, but it demonstrates as well that traders at the emporium had the necessary contacts to facilitate exchanges in exotic luxury commodities. Ultimately, these contacts were every bit as siginficant as those of the slave trade. More importantly, the Delian emporium appears to have served as a stepping stone for incipient Roman trade in the Eastern Mediterranean, a duty-free location where traders from the Roman west could bypass the well-established Rhodian-Ptolemaic monopoly of eastern luxury goods.

Overall, the archaeological evidence at Delos indicates that between 150 and 88 BC the island sustained 'boom town' levels of development as a result of these trade links. The island's population attained an estimated 20,000 to 30,000 residents at its peak. Wave upon wave of organised foreign traders relocated to Delos, lured by the island's free-trade status, by its newly expanded harbour, by its convenient location and by the worth of its commerce. Their numbers, indicated not only by the high proportion of foreign youths recorded on ephebic lists such as the one listed above, but also by the emergence of foreign cult centres and votive offerings, eventually dwarfed those of the Athenian cleruchy. Material remains similarly demon-strate the influx of foreigners. Wall paintings, mosaics, sculptural reliefs, statues (including Roman portrait busts and equestrian statues), altar dedica-tions, graffiti, amphorae and ceramic deposits all display decidedly non-Aegean subjects, tastes and nomenclature. The remains of several large headquarters or clubhouses, such as the Establishment of the Poseidoniasts of Berytos and the so-called Agora of the Italians, attest to the wealth and status of these foreign colonies, as well as to their tendency to congregate among themselves. Groups sufficiently large to warrant a collective identity tended to organise themselves religiously as well as ethnically according to the worship of the gods of their homelands. The merchants from Tyre formed themselves into the Herakliastai of Tyre (i.e. the worshippers of Tyrian Melkart) (*ID* 1519), while those from Berytos comprised the Poseidoniastai of Berytos (worshippers of Berytian Baal) (*ID* 1520, 1772–1796). Traders from Italy tended to organise themselves into a number of separate groups, the most celebrated of which were the Hermaistai, the Apolloniastai, the Poseidoniastai and the Compitaliastai, or the worshippers of Roman Mercury and his mother Maia, Roman Apollo, Neptune and the Lares Compitales respectively. The extensively excavated remains at Delos furnish a clear picture, therefore, of evolving patterns in Mediterranean commercial society at the very moment that Mediterranean-wide piracy raised its head. The wealth of this trading community, the abundance of luxury items in its warehouses, and the notoriety of its slave trade inevitably rendered the business community at Delos a likely target for retaliation by elements frustrated by the effects of Roman rule. Delos was home to the elite of the Mediterranean maritime world. Merchants made their fortunes here at other people's expense. The violence directed against the Roman business establishment at Delos in 87 BC offers compelling evidence of the deleterious consequences of slave trade and of Roman domination of the region (Rauh 1993: 68f.)

Apart from the reports of slave uprisings in 132–130 BC, the earliest indications of the emerging danger to the emporium arise with the Roman Law of Piracy of 102–100 BC, records of which have survived at Delphi and Knidos.[40] The Senate expressly prohibited its allies from engaging in any form of communication with the Cilician pirates; moreover, it declared the entire south coast of Asia Minor a newly appointed theatre of Roman military operations. Apparently by 102 BC, the indiscriminate attacks of the Cilician pirates had come to outweigh the benefits of their illegal traffic and provoked the Romans to act against them through a combined programme of diplomatic pressure, legal prohibition and main force. However much the traders at Delos may initially have co-operated with these pirate bands, by the end of the second century BC traders themselves were coming under attack (**20**).[41]

Measures attempted by Roman authorities against the Cilician pirates proved minimally effective, however. The pirates survived a naval assault of M. Antonius 'the Orator' (who apparently got as far as Side in 99 BC), and soon gained newfound support from Rome's greatest adversary in the region, King Mithradates VI Eupator of Pontus. When the Roman conflict with that dynast erupted in 88 BC, the mercantile community at Delos prepared for the worst. An initial assault during the spring of 87 by Athenion's admiral, Apellicon, was successfully rebuffed by a Roman named Orbius, possibly the leader of a makeshift island militia. However, later that year Mithradates' admiral, Archelaus, arrived with a sizable armada and violently destroyed the harbour, looting the Temple of Apollo, killing some 20,000 Romans and Italians on the island and in its immediate vicinity, and enslaving the surviving women and children (Rauh 1993: 68). While not all the residents were eliminated, the damage was extensive. Apart from the plundering of numerous treasures, such as the statues found in the destroyed warehouse in the Piraeus, the troops of Archelaus appear to have focused particular energy on the defacement of conspicuous emblems of the Roman presence on the island. Statues of Roman generals were smashed and knocked over and the symbolic seat of Roman authority on the island, the Agora of the Italians, was fired (Rauh 1993: 69, 289f.). During the course of the Roman counter-offensive, the proconsul and future dictator, L. Cornelius Sulla, directed several of his officers to pass through the island to shore up morale. As soon as Roman rule was restored to Asia, Sulla himself visited the island, leaving behind several memorials (Rauh 1993: 69). In addition, a Delian inscription, *ID* 2612, dated to the years immediately following the Mithradatic assault on the island in 88/87, appears to record a fund-raising effort to restore the Agora of the Italians. Among the subscribers listed on this fragmentary stone (less than half of which survives) are forty-odd Romans and Italians, five Athenians, two Delians and five merchants from Cypriot Salamis, Sidon, Tyre, Chios and Knidos. Quite a few merchants appear to have returned to Delos immediately after its destruction to join the efforts at revival.

20 *Votive Offering (altar) at Delos, dedicated by an Ascalonian merchant, and thanking Zeus Ourios, Palestinian Astarte, and Aphrodite Ourania, for answering his prayers by rescuing him from pirates*

Damage to the *emporium* was severe, however, and ultimately irreversible. The menace of Cilician piracy reared its head even before Sulla's departure and continued unabated in the following decade, culminating in a second, far more destructive assault on Delos in 69 (Rauh 1993: 69). Much of the fire damage visible today in the island's structural remains appears to date from this latter event. Following this attack the *emporium* became so exposed that the Roman legate responsible for the region, C. Valerius Triarius, decided to construct a defensive perimeter around the surviving village. This hastily-built barricade slashed directly across the once thriving business structures and sumptuous residential neighbourhoods of the formerly bustling *emporium* and confirms the extent of the community's decline by 69. At several points along the fringe of the defences – near the lake and beside the stadium – survive traces of graffiti displaying images of warships and equivalent personal testimonials, scratched by the island's defenders. Archaeologists have found a number of coin hoards and, in the *Maison de l'Épée*, a Roman sword placed on the floor of the courtyard in a ritualistic manner. Amid the charred ruins of the *Maisons du Skardhana* and *Fourni*, (**colour plate 20**) they even found the remains of buried and/or executed warriors (Rauh 1993: 71). While there is no denying that Romans continued to reside and even to possess property at Delos, the Lex Gabinia-Calpurnia's reaffirmation of the island's duty-free status in 58 BC proves that the community was wilting. The total absence of collegial documents after 74 BC, the absence of dedications by Near Eastern merchants such as Philostratos of Ascalon, the abandonment of the commercial harbour, the re-use of houses for artisanal purposes, the salvaging of artworks from destroyed residences, and the omnipresent evidence of fire damage point to an *emporium* that had withered under attack and declined. The harbour at Delos was far too exposed to warrant further trans-shipment of expensive eastern cargoes bound for Italy. The destruction of the trading emporium at Delos offered symbolic, if fleeting, cause for optimism, therefore, to the maritime elements opposing Rome.

Rhodes

Unquestionably, the most prominent maritime power of the era was the island republic of Rhodes, a large island (approximately 80km north–south by 40km east–west) situated at the south-east corner of the Aegean. Through a synoicism in 408/7 BC the three ancient communities on this island, Kameiros and Ialysos on the west coast and Lindos on the east, pooled their resources and populations to form the capital city of Rhodes at the island's northernmost point. During the course of the third century BC, this heavily fortified port emerged as one of the leading commercial and cultural centres of the Mediterranean. Rhodian success was partly the result of its unique location at the south-east 'entrance' to the Aegean, making it an important way-station for vessels preparing to confront the northerly gales of the Aegean after coasting along eastern Mediterranean shores. The island's location was also equidistant from a number of important areas of production, including the Black Sea and Egypt, as well as from islands such as Cyprus and Crete, which together with Rhodes formed important landfalls for east–west and north–south traffic across the seas. According to ancient sources, cargo ships sailing before favourable winds from the northern end of the Black Sea (880 nautical miles) could reach the harbours of Rhodes in less than ten days; ships sailing from Byzantium (445nm) in five; while ships sailing from Athens (275nm) required four. From Rhodes these same ships could sail before the winds to Alexandria (325nm) within three or four days.[42] According to Demosthenes (56.3), owing to the reduced occurrence of storms in the eastern Mediterranean, cargo vessels exploiting the diurnal sea breezes of the coast could make the slow return trip from Alexandria to Rhodes even during the winter. Accordingly, Rhodian access to the great Ptolemaic port of Alexandria and its close rapport with the Egyptian dynasty furnished the island republic with its single greatest advantage. As Diodorus Siculus observes (22.81.4), 'the Rhodians derived the majority of their revenues from the merchants sailing to Egypt . . . One could even say that their city was sustained by that kingdom.'

A second advantage to Rhodian naval and maritime prominence was its Peraea, or the authority it exercised over a cluster of neighbouring islands and coastal areas of the opposite Anatolian shore. These included the islands of Karpathos, Chalce, Kasos, Syme, Nisyros, Telos, Megiste and Eulimna, where evidence of Hellenistic ship sheds and slipways of various sizes remains visible. On the opposite mainland Rhodes at its peak in the early second century BC (c. 197–167 BC) also controlled Saros, Loryma, Knidos, Kaunos and Physkos (Marmaris). Archaeological evidence of Rhodian activity is equally visible at identified locations along the Turkish coast including Serce Limani, Bozburun, the Bay of Selimiye and Fethiye. Control of these outlying territories enabled the Rhodians to extend the horizon of their sea power by offering strategically located naval stations for far-reaching operations, supply and repair facilities, and possibilities for emigration and agricultural expansion over time. Accordingly, the Rhodians developed a naval infrastructure whose circumference stretched a good way beyond the headquarters of their fleet. Rhodian control of the adjacent seaboard, its protection of trade routes, and its ability to engage in sudden attacks on hostile craft intruding into these areas furnished the republic with a tactical advantage known to ancient Greeks as *phylake*, that is, the ability to defend and to protect one's own interests as well as the interests of others through the employment of military force. In addition, outlying harbours and anchorages constituted arterial systems of recruitment and logistical support. Subjected regions and allied cities contributed greatly to the recruitment of manpower reserves by providing pools of mercenary forces and rowing labour (Gabrielsen 1997: 41-44).

Rhodes owed a good deal of its success to the adroitness of its inhabitants, as demonstrated already by the decision of the island's three polities to undergo political unification. Isolated far at sea, the inhabitants of Rhodes had for centuries yielded to the military domination of distant maritime empires. In the fifth century BC, the island's communities broke away from the Persian Empire by joining the Delian League commanded by Athens. As this relationship gradually soured, they broke with Athens to form their own federated republic (c.408 BC), thereby enhancing the likelihood of sustained independence. The mettle of this newly formed republic was severely tested by the attempted siege of the Macedonian dynast, Demetrius Poliorketes, in 305 BC. The scale of operations on both sides and most particularly the engineering feats of Rhodian defenders gained the republic worldwide renown. The resilience of the Rhodian population was equally tested by a violent earthquake in 227 BC, destroying most of the city walls and dockyards and causing the collapse of the celebrated bronze statue of Helios, the renowned Rhodian Colossus.[44] Throughout this period Rhodes worked to extend its maritime influence in the eastern Mediterranean and Aegean basins, developing a well deserved reputation for neutrality, for deterrence of piracy, and for quick action in defence of freedom of the seas. In 220 BC Rhodes sent help to the distant city of Sinope on the south shore of the Black Sea, enabling that community to withstand the siege of King Mithradates II of Pontus. Rhodes thereby established itself as a friend to maritime outposts throughout the seas.

When the state of Byzantium attempted in 200 BC to impose tolls on Black Sea commerce passing through the Bosporus, the Rhodian navy lifted the blockade, a gesture that it repeated in 180 BC, when the fleet of King Eumenes II of Pergamum attempted to blockade the Hellespont, and again in 155–153 BC, when the fleet of King Prusias II of Bithynia attempted this again. Rhodes likewise cleared the eastern Mediterranean seas of an assortment of pirates hailing from Etruria, Illyria and Crete. By the beginning of the second century BC, Rhodes assumed command of a naval alliance, known as the Nesiotic League, to protect the island states of the Cyclades. By taking so strong a position throughout the eastern Mediterranean, the Rhodians assumed a central place in the political and economic fabric of the region (Gabrielsen 1997: 45). Its favourable relationship with the grain-exporting Ptolemies of Egypt and its own native production of wine enabled Rhodes to maintain trade relations with numerous maritime states. Evidence of relations exist from Rhode in Spain and Syracuse in Sicily to Tomi and Olbia on the Black Sea, Hierapytna in Crete, the Ptolemaic port cities of Salamis, Kurion and Nea Paphos on Cyprus, and Alexandria in Egypt. These demonstrate not only the magnitude of Rhodian resources but also the island state's confidence in its suppliers (Gabrielsen 1997: 46). Between 220 and 150 BC Rhodian amphorae, presumably used to carry modestly priced Rhodian wine, were the most widely distributed ceramic vessels of the Mediterranean. In fact, the rolled rims, cylindrical necks, pitched, rounded, stamped handles and stump toes of Rhodian wine amphorae serve as the archaeological bellwethers of Hellenistic civilisation at nearly every corner of the sea. More than 100,000 stamped Rhodian amphora handles have been recovered in Alexandria alone, and as we shall see, the data derived from Rhodian stamped handles play an important part in reconstructing the trade patterns of this era.[45] To the extent that specialists associate Rhodian amphora remains with the combined shipments of Egyptian grain and luxury goods from Alexandria, the distribution patterns of these amphora handles offer clear evidence of a Rhodian monopoly of the Ptolemaic grain trade as well. The harbour of this unified polity was a significant centre of trade, as the following description makes clear (**21**).

Situated roughly at the apex of the extreme northern tip of the island on a roughly triangular spit of land, the new capital of Rhodes measured approximately 3km north–south and slightly less east–west (**colour plate 29**). From the region of the eastern harbours the ground rises theatre-like south–west toward a plateau *c.* 90m high, where the acropolis was situated. Unlike most Greek cities, the Rhodians put their defensive energies into the massive circuit walls along the shore, leaving their acropolis unfortified. During the Hellenistic period the capital exhibited five harbours; three of these, the Mandraki, the Grand Harbour and Akandia Bay, were situated on the city's east flank (Gabrielsen 1997: 38). A fourth harbour lay to the south near the district now called Zephyros, while a fifth harbour, today completely silted in, stood slightly west of the city's northern apex. Much like the Piraeus, therefore, the aspect of these harbours gave optimum access to sailing vessels regardless of wind direction, a fact seemingly corroborated by an observation by the second-century AD rhetorician, Aelius Aristides (43.539), that some

21 *View of the Mandraki Harbour of Rhodes.* Matthew Dillon

22 *View of the Crusader Castle in the Mandraki harbour at Rhodes.* Matthew Dillon

of these harbours received those sailing from Ionia (north-west), others those from Caria (north-east), and still others those from Egypt, Cyprus and Phoenicia (east and south) (**22**).

Substantial material remains unearthed by archaeologists in recent times in the Mandraki Harbour reveal elements of what was once a comprehensive and well-maintained naval facility of considerable dimensions and capacity, perhaps double its present size. Among the most conspicuous survivals are the remains of roofed ship sheds complete with slipways to house temporarily inactive warships. Three rows of descending piers have been exposed in a courtyard behind the Rhodian Archaeological Institute. These installations appear to represent the innermost section of a vast dockyard complex. A short distance to the north of this site, excavators exposed four rows of rectangular, Hellenistic-era foundations, constructed with large blocks and following an east/west course. Similar foundations in an area immediately south (near the Cairo Palace Hotel) indicate that a large naval compound extended along the entire shore of the harbour (Gabrielsen 1997: 38).

On the eastern side of the harbour a massive breakwater stands on foundations likewise dating to the period in question. In this vicinity archaeologists discovered rectangular piers sufficiently large to support the roof of a large storehouse. Although excavation work in the other harbours remains unpublished, unearthed remains point to the existence of various dockyard installations there as well, including storehouses for ship's gear, timber, ship-building materials and siege engines (Gabrielsen 1997: 39). Archaeologists have exposed very little, on the other hand, in the way of commercial installations at any of these harbours. One assumes that these were kept physically separated from the naval installations (Gabrielsen 1997: 39).

The founders of the federal harbour reportedly laid out its streets according to a rectangular grid designed by the famed city planner Hippodamos of Miletus (Strabo 14.2.9 (654)). Since the medieval and modern city covers much of the area, excavation has necessarily been sporadic and fortuitous. However, archaeologists working in co-operation with modern developers have exposed at diverse points segments of streets and adjoining buildings that confirm the existence of a basic rectangular grid aligned very nearly north–south by east–west. Exposed remains of underground drains and water-channels likewise conform to this pattern. Some of the streets of the medieval town follow the course of their ancient predecessors (including the famous Street of the Knights) and important stretches of the city's prominent medieval walls likewise conform to the original Hippodamian plan. Although the precise location of the agora cannot be determined, it was probably situated somewhere west of the Great Harbour, where archaeologists have exposed a Roman-era colonnaded street leading to it from the south. The municipal theatre appears to have stood somewhere near the circuit wall on the inland side, and the Colossus, the huge bronze statue of Helios erected to commemorate Rhodes' successful resistance to Demetrius in 305/4 BC, probably stood somewhere in the city centre (Maryon 1956). According to Aristeides (43.6), the town was laid out in a spacious park-like manner. Aerial photography has demonstrated that modern terraces, field boundaries and lanes at considerable distance from the town centre still follow the rectilinear scheme of the ancient grid. Surrounding the whole of this were the city's massive defensive walls, sufficiently strong to thwart the sieges of two kings centuries apart. Very little of the walls has survived, apart from a few sections of the foundation, sufficient to determine its general course. On the east and west sides of the city's triangular topography, the walls essentially followed the coast; along its southern base it exploited the irregular relief of the terrain in a defensible manner. According to Strabo 14.2.5 (653), 'the Rhodians paid great attention to architectural needs, to the manufacture of materials of war, to the store of arms, and to everything else that related to the city's defence.'

The development and maintenance of the city's defences and harbour installations demanded the work of dozens of skilled architects and engineers, schools of whom the Rhodians patiently nurtured, on occasion taking measures to recruit them from without (Diod. Sic. 20.93.5). Rhodian naval facilities remained top secret. Access was prohibited to all but those with the highest clearance. The penalty for spying was death (Strabo 14.2.5 (653)). Consequently, the reputation of Rhodian military and naval engineers became legendary. Ancient sources credit them with inventions such as the fire bearer, used in 190 BC to hurl blazing fireballs onto enemy ships, the *triemiolia*, a sophisticated fighting craft that was part sailing vessel, part naval galley, and a repeater catapult invented by one Dionysos of Alexandria (Gabrielsen 1997: 40).

Due to their successful co-operation with the Romans against Kings Philip V of Macedonia (200–197 BC) and Antiochus III of Syria (192–189), the

Rhodian state obtained its greatest territorial extent during the early second century BC. Roman gifts of territory included the whole of neighbouring Lycia and parts of Caria south of the Maeander River, including the maritime cities of Miletus, Knidos and Halikarnassos.[46] By the outbreak of Rome's war with King Perseus in 172 BC, Rhodes stood equipoised with Pergamum as the leading states of the Aegean, filling the vacuum left by the decline of Ptolemaic naval authority in these waters. As Polybius observed (27.3.7), the Rhodians at this point had assumed the role of protectors not only of their own freedom but that of all other Greeks. Rhodian vessels conveyed grain, wine and luxuries throughout the seas, its vineyards scattered throughout its territories generated significant quantities of wine; its harbour bustled with the commerce of the Hellenistic world.

Although ostensibly a democracy, the Rhodian state was in fact governed by a highly integrated aristocracy from the three constituent urban populations which drew their wealth from combined activity in agricultural production, shipping and the profits of war. More than twenty amphora production centres have been identified in the rural hinterland of the island, several of these closely related to rural warehousing and docking facilities. The same families that produced Rhodian wine and shipped it together with Egyptian grain and luxuries throughout the Mediterranean appear also to have defended their cargoes with privately maintained war galleys. Aristotle (*Pol.* 1304b, 27–31) reports the fourth-century BC occurrence of an oligarchic revolt initiated by disgruntled Rhodian trierarchs who were unable to recover money owed to them by the state. Scholars usually interpret his words to mean that as a general rule, Rhodian trierarchs fitted out and maintained crews and public warships, especially large-decked ships of the line (triremes, quadriremes, quinquiremes), from their own resources and sought reimbursement for their expenses from the state (Gabrielsen 1997: 104). However, the Rhodian aristocracy appears to have relied as well on privately owned warships to fight piracy, to protect coastal areas, and to escort merchantmen. To achieve these goals, the Rhodian aristocracy appears to have maintained a sizeable private navy of multi-purpose warships particularly smaller war galleys such as *lembi*, *myroparones* and *triemioliae*, or oar-driven sailing vessels that could function both as cargo ships and war galleys (Casson 1971: 127f.).

Service appears very much to have been a family affair: epigraphical evidence demonstrates that members of the same families served on the same crews and that entire complements were often recruited locally (Gabrielsen 1997: 104–5). One third-century BC tombstone commemorates three Kamiran brothers, the sons of one Timakrates, who perished in different expeditions against pirates: one as bow officer, one as oarsman, one as troop commander (*SIG* 1225). Direct or indirect involvement in maritime trade appears to have been a prime motive for brothers, fathers and sons to take service on the same ship. The possession of warships as well as of merchant galleys convertible to combat duty presupposes aristocratic control of substantial material and monetary resources, not to mention incentive to exert influence in military and political decisions vital to the economy.

A sophisticated island aristocracy appears to have stood at the core of Rhodian maritime and naval authority. To maintain an emerging empire, the Rhodian aristocracy depended on both locally recruited and foreign manpower. The aristocracy employed well-known mechanisms of *euergetism* to promote and to sustain a large and experienced pool of sailors to man both naval and merchant marines. As the geographer Strabo records (14.2.5 (652-3)): 'the Rhodians are attentive to the common people. Although they do not live under a democracy, they wish, nonetheless, to keep the impoverished multitude in good condition. Accordingly, the common people are provided with food and the wealthy support those in need according to ancestral custom. For they engage in liturgies that furnish provisions to the poor, and in this manner they ensure that the masses are fed and that the city sustains its manpower, particularly insofar as the fleet is concerned.' In addition to controlling a large part of their country's naval infrastructure, the Rhodian aristocracy commanded vital sources of wealth. They supplied the landless masses with food to ensure an adequate pool of fit manpower necessary to row the boats. By recruiting, but firmly controlling maritime manpower, the Rhodians obtained the naval muscle to tap resources further abroad (Gabrielsen 1997: 107).

Rare mention of foreigners has led scholars to presume that the fleet was manned by citizens. Evidence to confirm this is wholly absent, however.[47] By every indication Rhodes obtained a sizable portion of its manpower from native recruits, in part by expanding the Rhodian population base and port facilities into the Peraea. But these numbers can hardly have been adequate to man a navy of more than 100 warships, many of which, particularly large-decked ships such as quadriremes and quinqueremes, required crews of several hundred, not to mention an undeterminable but inevitably sizeable merchant marine. To achieve these ends, the Rhodian aristocracy appears to have cultivated a floating population of foreign maritime labourers. The preserved record of a treaty formed between Rhodes and Cretan Hierapytna during the first Cretan war, for example, stipulates that pirates captured during the joint operations of these two states became the property of the Rhodians along with their ships (Gabrielsen 1997: 110). In short, alongside citizen rowers, the Rhodians employed slaves and maritime foreigners to row their warships. Chained to the oars of Rhodian galleys, even former adversaries, well seasoned maritime labour, were useful to its naval empire. Rhodes chose a dangerous policy, therefore, of recruiting and cultivating a burgeoning maritime population in its harbours, while doing everything possible to insure against the likelihood that this element would ever determine Rhodian destiny.[48]

In the early second century BC this calculation went awry; even the sober aristocracy of Rhodes was unable to contain the anti-Roman passions of the mob now in its midst. Diplomatic failure began, nevertheless, within the ranks of the aristocracy itself. Centuries of eastern Mediterranean political and diplomatic experience had left Rhodian authorities with attitudes incompatible with Roman friendship. Their behaviour toward Hellenistic dynasties during the previous era sufficiently bears this out. Although the Rhodians had by and large adhered to a friendship with the Ptolemies, this never prevented them from cultivating good relations with Ptolemaic rivals in the eastern theatre. Traditional Rhodian policy required the republic to refuse aid to any great power that threatened the republic's own safety and independence (Berthold 1984: 195). To some degree, effective diplomatic relations with conflicting military rivals served to confirm Rhodes' importance in Mediterranean world affairs. Roman authorities, on the other hand, took a dim view of neutral behaviour by any state that directly benefited from Roman friendship. When an emerging anti-Roman faction in Rhodes successfully persuaded the assembly to embrace a friendship with King Perseus of Macedonia, therefore, powerful elements in the Roman Senate grew displeased.[49] In 178 BC the Rhodians undertook the blatant decision to escort Laodice, the Seleucid bride of King Perseus, from Syria to Macedonia.[50] Since Macedonia had no navy and the Seleucids had been prohibited by Rome from sailing beyond eastern Cilicia, Rhodian action in this instance not only won the good feeling of both monarchies, but it served as a pointed reminder of the island republic's independence *vis-à-vis* Rome.

When conflict between Rome and Macedonia erupted in 172 BC, opposition to Rome in the Rhodian assembly was fierce. Pro-Roman authorities in the Rhodian prytanes and council could do little more than maintain an appearance of loyalty, dispatching six warships to the Macedonian theatre in 171. In the meantime the chaos engendered by this war as well as that arising from the simultaneous conflict between Antiochus IV of Syria and the Ptolemies in Egypt in 170/69 hurt Rhodian shipping by provoking severe dislocations in its grain trade. These circumstances actually compelled the Rhodians to obtain Roman permission to purchase grain in Sicily (Berthold 1984: 188). By 169 BC, poor generalship and promagisterial mismanagement had left the Roman offensive mired in the Macedonian highlands. With King Perseus' consent the Rhodians together with King Eumenes II of Pergamum initiated a diplomatic effort to persuade the Romans to accept a negotiated settlement leaving Perseus in his realm. While Eumenes attempted to remain circumspect about his dealings, the Rhodians, perhaps with an inflated sense of self-worth, manoeuvred quite openly. A Rhodian embassy dispatched by the assembly to persuade the Roman Senate to settle for terms arrived in Rome in 168 BC, only to learn on its arrival that the army of the Macedonian king had been crushed by a vigorous, renewed Roman offensive. With hostile senators looking on, the ambassadors did their best to hide the true purpose of their visit. The Roman oligarchy was not so easily fooled.

So careful in their dealings with potential adversaries in the past, the Rhodians had grossly misplayed their hand and now even their friends at Rome were hard pressed to stem the rising rancour against them. Hawkish Roman aristocrats, such as the praetor, M. Iuventius Thalna, spoke openly of war. The ambassador, C. Popillius Laenas, who at Rhodian insistence paused at the island on his way to resolve the Seleucid conflict in Egypt, belligerently addressed the Rhodian assembly to its collective face.[51] Giving vent to the rising anger against the republic, the Roman Senate sent a clear message as well to Rhodian subject states, formally announcing the repudiation of its previous grants of Lycia and Caria and insisting as well that Rhodian garrisons be withdrawn from Kaunos and Stratonicea (Berthold 1984: 202). Anxious to avoid any pretext for war, the Rhodians helplessly stood by and watched the secession of its subject communities. In addition, early in 166 BC the Rhodian people wisely dispatched a reorganised embassy to Rome to secure a treaty of alliance. According to a speech furnished by Polybius (30.31.12) to the ambassador at Rome, the Senate's declaration of the free port at Delos had in one brief year precipitated a dramatic 85 per cent decline in Rhodian harbour duties. The veracity of this assertion has long been doubted, not least of which because the harbour facilities at the Sanctuary of Apollo were hardly sufficient to accommodate a massive rerouting of Rhodian trade at this time. More likely, the threat of conflict with Rome was all it took to frighten foreign shippers and traders away from Rhodian harbours (Berthold 1984: 205, 209). Having been rescued by Roman ambassadors from the clutches of Antiochus IV two years earlier, the Ptolemies were in no position to help. Confident of their place in world affairs only years before, the Rhodians now found themselves completely isolated. Their Roman friend, Cato the Elder, allegedly reasoned with his fellow senators to cease blaming the Rhodians for their arrogance (ORF frg. 169; Berthold 1984: 205). With its empire reduced, its trading partners diverted, and its revenues crushed, Rhodes humbly accepted client status in the new Roman world order and thereby brought an end to both its independent foreign policy and its exaggerated dependence on foreign maritime manpower. The anti-Roman ring leaders of the assembly, Deinon and Polyaratus, were hunted down and apprehended. Thoas, a ship's captain who had served as their courier, travelling frequently between Macedonia and Rhodes with coded messages, was hunted down at Knidos and tortured to reveal what he knew (Polyb. 30.8.5-7).

As will become clear, Rhodian political eclipse did not necessarily correspond with commercial decline. The evidence furnished by Rhodian stamped amphora handles indicates that exports of Rhodian wines continued at the same, if not at an accelerated pace in the following era. Likewise, Rhodian control of the Egyptian grain trade continued unabated. However, the emergence of the thriving emporium at Delos and its newfound maritime contacts of Roman traders in eastern Mediterranean waters, posed a genuine threat to Rhodian maritime prosperity. The Rhodian aristocracy appears to have accepted this as the inevitable consequence of its misadventure during the war with Perseus. Quietly and soberly, Rhodes resigned itself to a secondary role during the last century of the Hellenistic era, humbly acceding to Roman authority in the region and standing loyally by their western allies even its own existence was threatened by a violent siege in 88 BC. Gradually but inexorably, Rhodian influence in the eastern Mediterranean sank into decline, particularly as its remaining trading partners, Ptolemaic Cyprus, Seleucid Syria and Ptolemaic Egypt, succumbed to Roman rule. By the time of the Cilician pirate menace, the maritime elements that had led Rhodes down the inauspicious path against Rome had migrated further east to the mountainous coast of Rough Cilicia and southward to the harbour on the Nile.

Alexandria

Famed for its broad, sweeping, well-sheltered harbours, its rows of richly stocked warehouses, its broad avenues, and its architectural marvels – the Pharos, the Museum, the palaces, the royal mausoleums and the library – Alexandria was the greatest port of the Mediterranean, not to mention a profoundly cosmopolitan city (**23**). Alexander the Great founded the settlement on an oblong stretch of land approximately 6km long by 1km wide, facing the sea to the north and a broad fresh-water lake of Mareotis to the south.[52] Fed by an arm of the Nile, the lake itself furnished a potential water route to the Egyptian interior, once properly harnessed by canal. The advantages of this location to the defence of Egypt were self-evident. On three sides (east, west and south) waterless desert and formidable mountains offered natural protection to the inhabitants of the Nile valley. Forts at Pelusium on the Sinai and at the various cataracts of the Nile effectively secured the approaches from the east and south. The broadest, most exposed front was the coast, and, given the prevailing northerly winds and easterly currents, a naval position on the western end of the Nile Delta offered optimum security. At Alexandria, Alexander the Great converted an otherwise bleak roadstead into a safe, commodious trading centre.

Despite these advantages the approach to the harbour remained treacherous. From Alexandria westward to Cyrene, no major havens existed along this shore. For ships caught in northerly storms the flat featureless terrain and hidden shoals made it implacably hostile (Pryor 1988: 23). As the first-century AD Jewish writer Josephus asserts (*BJ* 4.10.5):

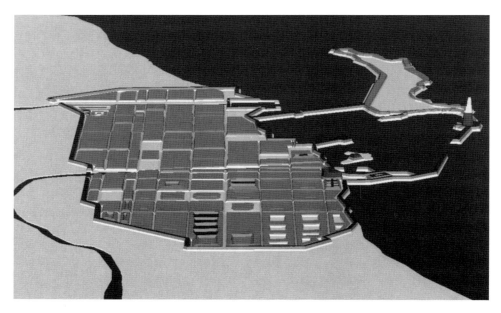

23 *Digital Elevation Model (DEM) view of Alexandria*

Sailors enter the haven of Alexandria only with difficulty, for the passage inward is narrow and full of submerged rocks that oblige incoming vessels to turn against the wind. Its left side is obstructed by man-made structures; on the right lies the Pharos. This island is situated just before the entrance and supports a very great tower that emits the sight of fire to anyone sailing within 300 furlongs (37.5 miles). Distant sighting of the Pharos enables ships to cast anchor a great way off at night and to await dawn before attempting their approach. Along the seaward side of the island the Alexandrians constructed long piers to blunt Mediterranean wave action. The sound of water crashing against these barriers is constant. Thus, navigation into the harbour remains very troublesome, for the approach to the harbour is rendered dangerous both by contrary winds and submerged rocks. However, once a ship passes inside the haven itself, it encounters a capacious shelter approximately 30 furlongs (3.75 miles) in area. Into this harbour comes a wealth of imports, more than adequate to please the native population not to mention a plentiful yield of Egyptian produce destined for export throughout the inhabited earth.

Strabo (17.1.6 (791-2)) likewise comments on the unprecedented massiveness of the harbour's bulwarks, whose design became the model for harbour works, however small in scale, throughout the Mediterranean. Vestiges of these moles survive particularly around the north-western arm of the Pharos Island.[53] The island and its celebrated lighthouse were invariably the first features to arrest the attention of ancient visitors:

> Pharos is an oblong island, very close to the mainland and forms with it a harbour with two mouths. For the shore of the mainland forms a bay. Two promontories project outward into the sea toward Pharos island which sits lengthwise, parallel to the shore. Together these features help to close the bay. Of the extremities of Pharos, the eastern one lies closer to the mainland and to the promontory opposite it and thus makes the harbour narrow at the mouth.

The Alexandrians joined the island to the mainland by means of an extended mole, 1500m long, known as the Heptastadion. This inner construction divided the waterway into two adjoining havens, the Great Harbour to the east and the Eunostos, or 'harbour of fortunate arrival', to the west.[54] Two bridges along the mole, one close to the mainland, the other close by the island, allowed for traffic of smaller vessels between the two harbours as well as for the continuous natural movement of easterly current to minimize siltation in the eastern Great Harbour. The Heptastadion served not only as a roadway to the residential district of the island, but prior to Caesar's conflict in 48/7 BC it also supported an aqueduct. The western harbour was more easily accessible given the prevailing winds and current, but it was also more exposed to their violence. The great eastern harbour was better protected, and owing to the bridge openings remained extremely deep, despite the difficulties posed by its entrance.

Today, the Heptastadion lies buried beneath modern installations and the massive alluvial deposits that now connect the island to the mainland. The former Great Harbour is now too shallow for use by anything larger than small fishing boats, while the former Eunostos has become the dockyard of ocean-going vessels. Nautical exploration has revealed vestiges of breakwaters constructed to insulate the Pharos from wave action, as well as recently discovered fragments of the great lighthouse. However, Alexandria remains by and large an actively inhabited city, minimally exposed to archaeological exploration. Most of the discoveries, as compelling as they are, arise from the sprawling necropoli to the west, south and east of the ancient city (Fraser 1972: 21). Vestiges of the maritime features of greatest importance remain concealed from view, therefore, leaving any attempt at description more dependent than usual on ancient literary sources. Fortunately, quite a few eyewitness reports survive. The historian, Diodorus Siculus, visited the harbour around 60 BC, and describes it in detail. Julius Caesar conducted a winter-long military campaign within the city in 48/7 BC, recorded largely by an anonymous officer under his command in the *Bellum Alexandrinum*. Strabo, the geographer, visited the city between 26 and 20 BC and left a detailed description in his *Geography*. Finally, Josephus, noted above, accompanied the Roman general

Vespasian to his coronation as Roman emperor at Alexandria in 69 AD. The infrastructure of Alexandria so impressed these and other writers that its most important features can be reconstructed with reasonable accuracy.

Surviving topographical features indicate, for example, that the Pharos lighthouse actually stood on a broad rock situated at the entrance of the Great Harbour, directly west of Pharos Island and attached to it by an intervening mole (**24**).[55] The site of the ancient lighthouse currently occupies the fort of Qait Bey, constructed during the fifteenth century by the sultan of that name (Fraser 1972: 18). Owing to the hyperbole of ancient sources, our under-standing of the lighthouse remains hopelessly muddled. The rectilinear shape of the structure appears to have conformed to the available surface terrain of the rock. Its designer, an architect (presumably) named Sosastros of Knidos who left a dedication at its base, erected it in step-like fashion, employed nummulitic limestone obtained from the upper reaches of the Nile. Sculptural decoration as well as other accessory ornamentation was constructed partly of marble and partly of bronze; columns were formed from Aswan granite. At its crest stood an open temple-like structure, a cupola supported by eight columns to form a lantern. Atop this allegedly stood a bronze statue of Zeus Soter, some 7m high. Resinous wood furnished fuel for the signal fire that reportedly was illuminated at great distance by two large convex mirrors. Reports that the lighthouse stood some 600m tall and that the light of its

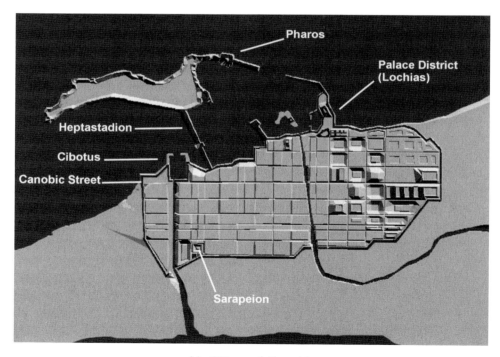

24 *GIS map of Alexandria*

signal fire was visible some 30 miles out at sea are obviously exaggerated.[56] Whatever its actual stature, the lighthouse clearly provided a propitious landmark to Mediterranean merchants and sailors. Sostratos' dedication of the lighthouse to Ptolemy I and his wife Berenice, as the 'Saviour Gods', conveyed a double meaning to maritime workers in this harbour, alluding as much to Castor and Pollux, the 'saviour gods' of all ancient seamen, as it did to these Macedonian dynasts.

Prior to the destruction induced by Caesar's assault on Pharos island in 48/7 BC, the island itself was densely inhabited by fishermen and other maritime elements. According to the writer of the *Bellum Alexandrinum* (17), it was defended not so much by regular circuit walls as by a line of contiguous buildings, some three storeys tall. Passing by the Pharos into the harbour, ancient sailors would have observed a nearly continuous array of docking installations on the east and south. Along the east side of the harbour from the Lochias promontory to the harbour's emporium at the mid-point stood the monumental complex of the Ptolemaic palace establishment (Strabo 17.1.9 (794)). The palace district, encompassing most of what was called Neapolis, stood in the north-east portion of the city between the Canopic Street and the sea. The royal palaces constituted a quarter or even a third of the overall space of the city. All their various elements were interconnected through a maze of passageways, including some leading to a dredged artificial harbour on the Great Harbour's eastern shore. Heavily fortified, this haven was reserved exclusively for royal naval activities. Other passageways connected the palaces to elements such as the celebrated Museum, the *sussytion* or residence hall of the scholars who worked there, the attached library with its holdings of some 700,000 volumes by the time of Caesar, additional monumental edifices such as a pedestrian park (*peripatos*), and most importantly the Sema, or large enclosure that contained the mausoleums of Alexander the Great and the members of the Ptolemaic dynasty. Close by the royal harbour stood a small island known popularly as the Antirrhodos, featuring still another a royal palace and associated harbour. On the mainland behind the Antirrhodos sailors could possibly have discerned the Alexandrian civic theatre. Caesar records (*BC* 3.112) that the theatre was directly attached to the part of the palace where he was holed up in 48 BC and that it offered approaches to the emporium and the naval yards. It was apparently so placed to serve as a make-shift citadel, which is precisely how Caesar put it to use during his siege. According to Strabo (17.1.9 (794)), the theatre faced the sea; from its highest banks of seats, spectators could gaze across the harbour installations.

West of the palace district a projection of land, named after a Temple of Poseidon located there, separated the former district from the emporium (Strabo 17.1.9 (794)). Beyond this to the west the numerous quays and docking facilities of the emporium projected seaward. Strabo (17.1.6 (792)) records that the commercial harbour was divided into several separate installations, presumably by projecting piers and wharves. Much like the other harbours considered above, and probably serving as the model for them all, the wharves and adjoining warehouses (*apostaseis*) of the Alexandrian emporium formed an enclosed district, known as the *exhairesis*, that was separated from the domestic quarters of the city. Similar presumably to the layout at Delos, goods in transit could be loaded and off-loaded here at reduced tariff, so long as they remained inside the emporium. Strabo reports (17.1.6 (792)) that the massive harbour works and the great natural depth of the harbour enabled the largest cargo ships afloat to dock directly alongside the quays by means of *klimakes*, or gang-planks. The remaining area between the emporium and the Heptastadion was reserved for the ship sheds (*neoria*) of the Ptolemaic navy. During the early third century BC, this dynasty launched the greatest navy in the world, more than 400 warships of various size drawn from allied maritime states from throughout the eastern Mediterranean. Catastrophic naval defeats, at Cyprus in 306 BC and at Kos in 256, and the gradual abandonment of overseas territories had by the time of the Cilician pirates reduced the effectiveness of Ptolemaic navy considerably. Nevertheless, as late as 48/7 BC, Caesar reports setting fire to seventy warships in this harbour (*BC* 3.111).

The Eunostos harbour receives less attention from our sources. According to Strabo (17.1.10 (795)), it sheltered an interior artificial harbour called the Cibotus, housing additional military ship sheds. When battling for control of the Heptastadion, Caesar's men were outflanked by small warships apparently issuing from this harbour and passing beneath the bridge close by the mainland (*BAlex.* 19). A navigable canal following basically the same path as the current Mahmoudiya Canal appears to have connected the Cibotus to the Mareotis Lake (Fraser 1972: 26).

The entire extent of the harbour as well as of the city as a whole was defended by circuit walls, traces of which have been identified archaeologically. The disposition of the walls of Alexandria remains nevertheless quite uncertain. The writer of the *Bellum Alexandrinum (2)* informs us that Caesar, trapped in the palace district, confronted an imposing array of defences. 'All the streets and alleys were blocked off by a triple barricade built of rectangular stone blocks and not less than 30 feet high.' This suggests that the defences directly behind the harbour consisted of deliberately arranged curtain walls. Along the southern border of the city, however, perhaps directly facing the Mareotic Lake and the marshes along its margin, the writer reports (*BAlex.* 2) that much like the defences on Pharos island, contiguous tower-like structures, probably the back sides of tenement houses, some reportedly ten storeys tall, constituted the urban defences.

The city itself was a model of urban planning, some 5km east–west by 1–2km north–south. Arranged on a Hippodamian grid, its two chief thoroughfares, the Canopic Street running east–west across the city, and a second, unnamed street running north–south from the harbour to the lake, were more than 10m broad, wide enough to accommodate simultaneous wheeled traffic in both directions. Canals, one emanating from the Cibotus, the other apparently from the palace district, passed through the city connecting the harbours to Lake Mareotis as well as to a tributary of the Nile. The city was divided into five districts named according to the Greek letters Alpha, Beta, Gamma, Delta Epsilon. The Beta district is known to have referred to the neighbourhood of the palace complexes, whereas by the first century BC the Delta district, directly east of the palace district along the shore, was the neighbourhood inhabited by Alexandrian Jews. Along the seaward side of the great Canopic Street, bordering the palace district, stood a number of prominent structures, including the gymnasium, an immense colonnaded complex more than a stadium long, the public courts (*dikasterion*), and the Paneum, an artificial mound dedicated to Pan offering a view across the whole of the city (Fraser 1972: 29). In the south-west quadrant of the city, in the ancient Egyptian neighbourhood of Rhakotis, stood the Sarapeium. Remains of this structure were exposed by excavations conducted in 1944 near 'Pompey's Pillar', a single column standing some 28m tall.[57] Foundation deposits beneath the Sarapeion revealed two sets of ten plaques fashioned from gold, silver, bronze, faience, Nile clay and glass. Inscribed both in Greek and Egyptian hieroglyphic, these indicate that Ptolemy III Euergetes (246-221) constructed the temple in the late third century BC. Archaeologists have also associated the diorite statue of Serapis incarnated as Apis the bull, found at this locale in 1895, and a colossal red granite statue of Isis, found in waters near the Pharos island, with this complex. Along the outskirts at the south-east end of the city stood the stadium, on the south-west fringes the hippodrome (Fraser 1972: 28).

According to Strabo (17.1.7 (793)) the city was supremely livable, boasting a surprisingly mild climate (compared at least to the Nile hinterland) cooled by sea breezes during summer. The city was spaciously arranged with parks, the majority of which were located in and around the palace district. Evidence from papyri indicates that city streets were named according to the divine epithets of various members of the Ptolemaic dynasty (Fraser 1972: 35). Beneath the city was an elaborate system of supply and drainage conduits, connected to the main canals by tunnels, by which fresh water was conducted throughout the city. In 1860 AD the antiquarian Mahmoud El Falaki reported identifying more than 700 such cisterns about the town. Some of these remain in good working order today (Shenouda 1976). According to Caesar's officer (*BAlex.* 3), the cistern facilities of houses belonging to wealthier residents incorporated settling tanks to trap sediment conveyed by the turgid water. The poorer residents, on the other hand, had to content themselves with lesser quality water giving rise, he notes, to frequent pestilence. Beyond the walls of the city especially to the east and west, stood cemeteries of considerable size, testaments to the densely compacted population that inhabited the city during Antiquity. On-going excavations have, in fact, exposed a number of necropolis in all parts of the city, the best known being the catacomb or hypogeum of Kom-El-Shagufa, a short distance south-west of the Serapeion. Carved out of living rock, its three-story marvels include a spiral staircase descending to the triclinium on the first floor and a main burial chamber on the second floor decorated with a mixture of Egyptian, Greek and Roman wall paintings. The extensive remains of these elaborate mansion-like tombs, complete with peristyle courts and side chambers, offer some idea of the likely comforts of Alexandrian palaces and mansions of the past.

The history of the people of this harbour remains inextricably connected to that of its ruling dynasty, the Ptolemies, founded by the follower of Alexander the Great, Ptolemy I Soter (305–283 BC). By the late second century BC, the Ptolemaic empire had fallen on hard times. Formerly the masters of the eastern Mediterranean seaways, naval catastrophes had seriously reduced their ability to remain a world power, just as dynastic disturbances, native rebellions, and the growing instability of the Alexandrian urban populace threatened the dynasty's authority at home. The early Ptolemies had successfully combined naval power, maritime trade, and intensified agricultural production along the Nile to propel themselves to the forefront of Mediterranean hegemonies. At home they had expanded the base of agricultural production along the Nile through colonisation, land reclamation efforts and irrigation projects, particularly in the Fayoum.[58] Equally important were the finished goods of Egyptian artisan shops, both in Alexandria and elsewhere along the Nile. Glass wares, stone wares, metal wares, ceramics, statuary and textiles travelled in all directions from Egypt, particularly the Indian Ocean.[59] Rigorous control of production of all commodities through royal monopolies enabled the Ptolemies to generate significant revenues from their overseas trade.[60] Under meticulous royal scrutiny, the Nile basin yielded sufficient grain harvests to feed the estimated 3.5 million inhabitants of Egypt as well as another 500,000 lives overseas. Alexandrian and Rhodian cargo ships transported Egyptian grain throughout the Mediterranean, from the Greek cities of the Aegean to Roman Italy, Sicily and beyond. In addition, careful development of ports of access to the Red Sea, the most successful route being the overland road from Koptos on the Nile to Myos Hormos and Berenike on the Red Sea, enabled the Ptolemies to acquire a significant hold on the luxury trade to the East. By the mid-second century BC, Ptolemaic navigators learned to exploit the prevailing patterns of monsoonal winds to navigate the Indian Ocean beyond sight of land.[61] The Ptolemies gradually came to dominate Mediterranean trade with central Asia, particularly as the authority of the rival Seleucid dynasty over the overland routes of the Middle East disintegrated.

To protect their trade, the Ptolemies pursued several avenues of defence, including a costly programme of naval construction, expanding alliances with maritime polities throughout the seas, widespread recruitment of manpower for its navy and its merchant marine, and a commitment to the popular notion of freedom of the seas. During the third century BC, the Ptolemies launched the largest fleets of the eastern Mediterranean. By 256 BC Ptolemy II Philadelphos completed a naval build-up sufficiently massive to launch 400 warships, including the design and construction of one or two 'show' vessels of absurdly spectacular dimensions.[62] Many of these were destroyed battling Antigonus Gonatas at Kos in that year, at which point the burden of building and maintaining so vast a naval establishment became prohibitive. From then on the Ptolemaic naval hegemony experienced debilitating inertia, slowly yielding place in the Aegean and the eastern Mediterranean theatres to the emerging might of Rhodes. Unable to safeguard the security of its allies in the Aegean and most particularly along the southern coast of Anatolia, the Ptolemies watched pitifully as these succumbed to the advancing armies of Antigonid Macedonia and Seleucid Syria. Despite their various setbacks, the Ptolemies clung to a handful of Aegean bases until 145 BC, and retained long-standing domains in Cyprus and Cyrenaica until the middle of the first century BC.[63] As noted above, when Caesar landed in Alexandria in 48 BC, more than seventy decked warships, triremes, quadriremes and quinqueremes, were serviceable in its shipyards (BC 3.111).

To build and maintain this naval establishment, the Ptolemies had encouraged maritime settlement and enhanced productivity in numerous underdeveloped areas of the eastern Mediterranean world. Much like their harnessing of the resources of the Nile, the Ptolemies exploited neighbouring regions such as Rough Cilicia, Cyprus, Pamphylia, Lycia and Caria, with an eye toward extracting shipbuilding capacity, forestry resources and maritime supplies (Bagnall 1976: 80f.). The archaeological evidence indicates that Ptolemaic involvement in these regions was extremely one-sided.[64] Alongside shipbuilding and maritime supplies, the Ptolemies levied manpower throughout the region, partly to staff their own fleets, but partly as well to stimulate the development of small local 'auxiliary' navies. Although these squadrons were available for imperial service, they were, nevertheless, equipped, staffed, and maintained by native inhabitants with locally available resources. An unforeseen consequence of Ptolemaic naval hegemony was the militarisation of maritime communities across the region.[65] Formerly allied but increasingly independent naval squadrons from semi-Hellenised communities in Crete, Lycia, Pamphylia, Rough Cilicia and Cyprus would eventually pose a serious threat to maritime security throughout the seas.

Insofar as these developments concerned the evolution of the resident population at Alexandria, the impact of so pronounced and prolonged an effort at naval and maritime supremacy was bound to be significant. According to Strabo (17.1.13 (798)), Alexandria became 'the greatest emporium in the inhabited world. Among the happy advantages of the city, the greatest is the fact that this is the only place in all Egypt that is by nature well situated for maritime commerce. Whether by advantage of its good harbours or its overland commerce, the river easily conveys and brings together everything to this central location.' Given its attractions and its importance, the city became a magnet for immigration. In the second century AD, the rhetorician Dio Chrysostum (32.672) remarked on the ethnically diverse population one encountered in its emporium. Not only were Greeks, Italians, Syrians, Libyans, Cilicians, Arabs and Sub-Saharan Africans present there, but Bactrians, Scythians, Persians and Indians as well. Traders, warriors and sailors from throughout the eastern Mediterranean basin congregated in this emporium, and leading citizens from recently Hellenised states such as Side and Aspendos in Pamphylia, and Kaunos in Caria assumed high-ranking positions within the court. Seeing the imperial advantages of a large resident labouring population in their capital, the Ptolemies maintained a relatively open-door policy. The Alexandrian population vied with that of Rome as the largest in the Mediterranean, possibly 700,000 inhabitants by the age of Caesar.[66] The concentration of so dense and so diverse a population in so small an area generated a highly politicised urban community that gradually came to dominate Ptolemaic affairs.

The reasons for the vigorous political expression of the Alexandrian population were as complex as they were unique to the Ptolemaic experience. The rural character of the Nile population rendered the urban centre of Alexandria the only settlement of its kind throughout the kingdom; its population simply dwarfed those of all other Egyptian communities. In many respects the labouring capacity of the city served as a reflection of the overall health of the Ptolemaic empire at large. For all its worldliness and sophistication, the city of Alexandria was by no means a typical Greek community. It had emerged as rapidly as the Ptolemaic dynasty itself and, accordingly, possessed no traditional home rule, no regular voting assembly, no council, no annually elected magistrates. In essence, the town was governed by royal administrators much like the rest of Egypt and as such the resident population was inherently dependent on the workings and thus closely attuned to the actions and behaviour of the royal court. Alexandria was foremost the residence of Hellenistic kings, queens and courtiers, the headquarters of the imperial army and navy, and the administrative capital of its trade.[67]

Such a relationship might conceivably have functioned somewhat effectively had the Ptolemies managed to sustain some semblance of dynastic stability. This proved impossible, however. To fulfil the ideological aspirations of their subjects, Egyptian as well as Hellenised, the dynasty was required to engage in consanguineous marital relations, brothers marrying sisters, uncles marrying nieces, and nephews marrying aunts.[68] With each rising generation the Ptolemies tended to produce multiple pretenders to the throne, each of whom because of the proximity of blood lines could tender legitimate, dynastic, quasi-divine credentials for the throne. Unlike the destructive tendencies exhibited by Seleucid rivals in neighbouring Syria, the Ptolemies devised a slightly more salutary solution to their conflicts by distributing royal pretenders among three centres of power. In addition to the throne in Alexandria, there was the Cypriot capital in Paphos, and the eastern Libyan headquarters in Cyrene.[69] This separation of warring siblings by maritime space had the advantage of delaying the process of dynastic disintegration. However, the incessant jockeying of rival claimants for control of the main prizes – the capital of Alexandria and its hinterland resources of the Nile – inevitably drew the court and ultimately the urban population itself into these dynastic disputes.

The role of the Alexandrian people in Ptolemaic succession remains poorly understood, nonetheless. Macedonian tradition called for the acclamation of the ascending king by the Macedonian people under arms, that is, by its army (Hammond 1989: 62f.). Conceivably, to build their emporium the Ptolemies had extended the right of franchise to all duly enrolled 'citizens'. In Alexandria this would have included Hellenised military recruits originating from throughout the Aegean and eastern Mediterranean (Fraser 1972: 62f.). For many decades these people maintained a pretence of referring to themselves as 'Macedonians', which was obviously a charade. As time progressed, they abandoned this title in favour of a more workable identity as 'Alexandrians', that is, as a population unique not only to Egypt, but to the world. As the Hellenistic world began to close in around the Ptolemies, this identity took on increasingly local significance.

Given the extreme fluidity of the urban population the precise identity of Alexandrian citizenry might legitimately be called into question. Unlike the exclusive character of civic status experienced elsewhere in the Hellenised world, by the mid-second century BC the Alexandrian body politic probably included any and all 'free' resident males of 'ephebic upbringing' who assumed registered domicile in the community, served in its defence, laboured in its workshops and port facilities, and/or otherwise paid municipal taxes (Fraser 1972: 76f.). The Greek historian Polybius (34.14.6), who visited Alexandria sometime after 145 BC, described the urban population of Alexandria as consisting of three constituent elements. In the south–western neighbourhoods of Rhakotis dwelt masses of native Egyptians, 'quick tempered and uninterested in civic life (*apolitikon*)'.[70] In the Beta district, dominated by the palaces and headquarters of the realm, lived elements of the palace guard and the city's mercenary garrison, 'men at arms grown accustomed to give orders rather than to receive them, the direct result of the ineffectiveness of the kings'. Last came the Alexandrians proper, a 'mixed' population that, however much it professed to be Greek or Macedonian in origin, was largely drawn from an array of communities along the Hellenised borders of the Ptolemaic empire. According to Polybius, this population 'showed similar if lesser tendency to break with the government or to cause disturbances; for even if they were mixed stock they were Greek by origin and remained mindful of the customs common to all Hellenes.' Polybius neglected altogether to mention the thriving Jewish population that by his time had taken up residence in the city's 'Delta' district and had come to play an important part in the military as well as in trade.[71] No evidence exists to demonstrate, however, that any of these elements were expressly excluded from the Alexandrian body politic.

The introduction of the Alexandrian people into the process of dynastic succession appears to have begun in 203 BC when court ministers summoned the urban citizenry to public assembly to support the claims of the infant child of Ptolemy IV Philopator for the throne (Polyb. 15.25.13). Assuming that the process of obtaining acclamation by the Alexandrian 'people' had existed since the time of the first Ptolemy, under normal circumstances this act would probably have amounted to little more than ceremony. In this instance, however, the effort of the courtiers, Agathocles and Sosybius, to replace the deceased king by a child that they could control, an effort they achieved by murdering the queen, Arsinoe, marked an unprecedented departure requiring some legitimate instance of public sanction.[72] The efforts of these courtiers and of all subsequent dynasts to seek popular acclamation by the Alexandrian 'people' arose, therefore, from desperation and political weakness, with the result that each subsequent appeal yielded further and further power to the 'assembly'.

In the course of the following 150 years Alexandrian collective action played a part in the depositions and acclamations of Ptolemaic dynasts on at least eleven separate occasions (170 BC, twice in 164, 131/0, 108/7, three times in 89, 80, twice in 57/6). Usually the violence was incited by the palace guard; however, it typically spread to the streets and on many occasions manifested itself as widespread popular unrest. Two examples, Ptolemy VIII Euergetes II Physcon (145–116 BC) and Ptolemy XI Auletes (80–51), illustrate the gravity of these contests between dynasts and the Alexandrian people, each case revealing a different phase in the progression of popular rule. Ptolemy VII Euergetes II Physcon was generally credited by the sources with having set in motion the 'debasement' of the Alexandrian population through repeated, violent purges of its inhabitants. Already in 164 BC, when he was fifteen years old, powerful courtiers used him as a pawn to expel his brother, King Ptolemy VI Philometor, from the city at the insistence of the mob.[73] On Philometor's death in 145 BC, the peace of the city was immediately disturbed by warring factions supporting Physcon on the one hand, and Philometor's wife, Physcon's sister, Cleopatra II, and her young son by his brother on the other. Returning from his 'exile' in Cyprus to Alexandria, Ptolemy Physcon assumed the title of Euergetes II, married his sister and quickly eliminated the potential rival posed by her son.[74] Plots and conspiracies materialised repeatedly in Alexandria throughout the first decade of Physcon's rule.[75] When the mob set fire to the palace in 131 BC, Physcon retaliated with sudden bursts of violence, repeatedly unleashing the palace guard against the populace and the municipal garrison. According to the third-century AD epitomator Justin (38.8),

Physcon drove many of the leading courtiers and intellectuals into overseas exile: 'The people terrified of these proceedings fled to other countries, and became exiles from their native soil through fear of death.' To replace those departing he encouraged the immigration of new residents, which inevitably altered the composition of the Alexandrian 'citizenry'.[76] Modern authorities question the extent of the urban transformation at this time, but it remains difficult to deny the decided role taken by the Alexandrian population in dynastic successions from here on. Equally questionable is the degree to which this fluid population of mercenaries, traders, maritime labourers, artisans and intellectuals could make any legitimate claim of political enfranchisement as 'citizens'.

Telescoping ahead to the reign of Ptolemy XII Auletes (80–51 BC), one finds the Alexandrian mob so firmly in control that it challenged the authority of the king. A number of developments during the intervening fifty years, including the loss of territories such as Cyrenaica (96 BC) and southern Anatolia (102–67 BC) to Rome, greatly restricted the king's ability to deal with dynastic rivals peacefully. In addition, while dwelling in exile in Lycia, Auletes' uncle, Ptolemy X Alexander (108 to 88 BC), had apparently pursued a poison-pill strategy against his brother and rival, Ptolemy IX Lathyrus (116–108, 88–80 BC), by leaving his realm *ex testamento* to the people of Rome. When he died suddenly at Cyprus in 88 BC, the matter of this inheritance assumed a dangerous and ominous significance in Auletes' dealings with Rome.[77]

The illegitimate son of Ptolemy Lathyrus, Ptolemy XII Auletes ascended to the throne only because the Alexandrian mob had eliminated the last legitimate member of the Ptolemaic line in a fit of violence, dragging him from the palace and murdering him in the gymnasium after he had plotted the assassination of Lathyrus' widow, Queen Cleopatra III (Höbl 2001: 214). Mindful of the will of Ptolemy Alexander and of Auletes' own questionable claim to the throne, the Roman Senate refused to recognise him as king. Citing the existence of the will, magistrates such as Marcus Crassus in 65 BC and P. Servilius Rullus in 64 actually introduced legislation to annex Egypt as Roman territory (Höbl 2001: 224). To retain his throne, Auletes recognised the need for extensive lobbying of powerful Roman senators. With a bribe of 6,000 talents he persuaded the consul of 58 BC, Julius Caesar, to pass legislation recognising him as 'friend and ally of the Roman people'. This removed the potential threat to his hold on power in Alexandria; however, it did little to guarantee the permanence of Ptolemaic authority in Cyprus. The following year the Roman plebeian tribune, Publius Clodius, passed legislation to appropriate that island as Roman territory. Auletes' half-brother, then reigning in Cyprus, promptly committed suicide. With the loss of Cyprus the Alexandrian people, already angered by Ptolemy Auletes' attempt to pay off Caesar through extraordinary tax levies, rose up and expelled him from the city.

Deprived of the former Ptolemaic refuges in Cyprus and Cyrene, Auletes had little choice but to sail to Rome to complain against his people and to seek Roman support for his restoration. Once at the capital he obtained military and financial assurances, respectively, from the powerful general Cnaeus Pompeius Magnus and from C. Rabirius Postumus, one of Rome's leading financiers and publicans. Equally concerned about its future and behaving essentially as an autonomous community, the Alexandrian populace attempted to counter the king's moves at every turn. Dragging Auletes' wife, Cleopatra VI Tryphaina, out of seclusion, they acclaimed her joint sovereign with her daughter, Berenice IV. They then searched furiously for a suitable replacement for Auletes as king. Simultaneously, they dispatched a massive embassy of 100 dignitaries to Rome, determined to match the zeal of Auletes' lobbying effort with the Senate. Auletes dispatched droves of hired assassins to disrupt their mission from the moment they arrived at Puteoli, resulting in rioting and fatalities from that port city all the way to Rome.[78] Word of these outrages elicited protests throughout Rome, but Auletes was able to stifle the Alexandrian mission and eventually secured the necessary support for his restoration. In 55 BC Aulus Gabinius invaded Egypt with Roman forces, defeating the Alexandrian troops arrayed against him and restoring Ptolemy Auletes to his throne.[79] Backed by contingents of Gallic and German mercenaries left behind by Gabinius in Alexandria, Auletes remained at the Egyptian capital until his death in 51 BC.

When Julius Caesar arrived in Alexandria in 48 BC he found the city in its usual volatile state, and for the first time since the days of Ptolemy Physcon, vivid descriptions of the urban population became available (**26**). Caesar came to Alexandria with a small force in hot pursuit of his rival Cn. Pompeus Magnus, having recently driven him from the field at Pharsalus (Caes. *BC* 3.106). He arrived to find Pompey murdered and the young king and queen (Ptolemy XIII and Cleopatra VII) at war. The Alexandrian populace grew immediately alarmed by the sight of his standards in the palace. Caesar and his small army were, nevertheless, indefinitely detained in the city by adverse winds, and as more and more Ptolemaic contingents arrived in the city, they found themselves besieged in the palace by the entire Alexandrian mob (Caes. *BC* 3.106–7).

According to Caesar the Alexandrian population he confronted was determined, unruly, and extremely hostile to Rome. In admittedly contemptuous terms Caesar describes the multitude opposing him as a diverse array of renegades and troublemakers (*BC* 3.110). First he identifies the Gallic and German soldiers, originally recruited during his own campaigns in Gaul and brought to Alexandria by Gabinius in 55 BC, 'men who by now had grown accustomed to the Alexandrian way of life with all its vices and had completely and utterly forgotten the honour and the discipline of the Roman people. These men had all taken Alexandrian wives and many of them now had

25 *Bust of Julius Caesar*

children' (Caes. *BC* 3.106). Next came a motley crew of pirates, bandits, condemned criminals, exiles and runaway slaves. Men, according to Caesar,

> . . . assembled from the remains of the pirates and brigands of Syria, Cilicia, and the neighbouring regions, as well as a multitude of condemned criminals and exiles. Naturally, all our own fugitive slaves find a sure place of refuge at Alexandria, plus guaranteed freedom on condition that they register their names for military service. This way, if any of them is ever seized by his rightful owner; his comrades in arms come to his aid and liberate him, resisting whatever force the slave-owner brings to bear. For since they are all basically refugees from justice, they react to a threat against any one of them as though it were a threat against them all.

As Caesar notes, this nefarious mix had come to play a determining role in the fortunes of the Ptolemaic dynasty and its capital:

These men had grown accustomed to demanding executions of high-ranking ministers of kings, to plundering the property of the rich, to besieging the king's palace with demands for higher pay, to expelling kings, one after another, from the throne and to replacing these peremptorily with substitutes. All of these things they did in accordance with what was by now a venerable tradition of the Alexandrian army... For these men had lived their lives fighting the endless conflicts of the city.

Caesar's description of the turbulent maritime element in control of Alexandria is seconded by several sources. The author of the *Bellum Alexandrinum*, who served with Caesar in Alexandria and was an eyewitness to events, acknowledges the Alexandrians as 'a clever and quick witted people' who were natural 'seafarers trained from childhood by daily practice' (*BAlex.* 12, cf. 16). Otherwise, he views them as 'deceitful, always keeping one aim in view and pretending to another' (*BAlex.* 24). 'If I had to defend the Alexandrians against the charges of deception and opportunism, I could speak for a long time to no purpose; for no sooner does one encounter this population than one recognises its character. No one can doubt that this is a people abundantly skilled at treachery' (*BAlex.* 7). Alluding to Alexandria's ill-famed reputation as a haven for Mediterranean criminals and runaways, the first-century AD Roman satirist, Juvenal (6.83), dismisses the population in a few chosen words: 'that town by the Nile, that Alexandrian cesspool'. The third-century AD historian and Roman senator, Cassius Dio, meanwhile, corroborates the tendency of the Alexandrian people to engage in public protest, to provoke riots, and to display an unappealing zeal for blood (Dio 39.58.1–2, 55 BC).

> For the Alexandrines are always ready to assume a bold front against any authority and to shout aloud brazenly whatever ideas come to their minds. When the time comes for the genuinely terrifying work of war, however, they are utterly useless. This is true despite the fact that during urban uprisings, which with them are very numerous and very serious, they engage in a considerable degree of senseless murder and violence. Setting far less value on life than the challenge of the moment, they pursue destruction in these conflicts as though it were a coveted prize.

Unruly, violent and outspoken, and composed largely of maritime labourers, refugee pirates, runaway slaves and military deserters, the Alexandrian mob appears, nevertheless, highly motivated and resentful of any and all authority. The presence in this city of so many disparate maritime elements at this time charts a century-long migration of Mediterranean maritime elements from Carthage to the shore of Egypt. The Alexandrian 'people' increasingly determined which of the royal claimants reigned in Alexandria and which were shunted off to Cyrene, Cyprus and beyond. Its supporters ridiculed their Ptolemaic rulers through derisive names such as *Physcon* (the Fat), *Lathyrus* (Chickpea), *Auletes* (Flute-player), and *Kybiosaktes* (the Salt–Fish Dealer). As Caesar noted on his arrival in Alexandria (*BC* 3.106), elements within this mob 'republic' demonstrated the capacity to articulate their sentiments in a spontaneous manner, and to formulate collective behaviour, with the actions of one urban element finding resonance in distant neighbourhoods of the city.

> Immediately on landing [Caesar] heard the shouting of soldiers whom the king had left in town on garrison duty and saw them hurrying to meet him because the fasces were being carried in front of him. Hereby the whole multitude asserted that the royal authority was being infringed. Even though this disturbance eventually subsided, frequent outbursts persisted during the following days. Mobs kept materialising throughout the town, and numerous Roman soldiers lost their lives.

The anti-Roman sentiment of the Alexandrian population is equally apparent. As noted above, the site of the Roman fasces in the harbour startled the Ptolemaic garrison and mobilised the population to action. The writer of the *Bellum Alexandrinum* notes that leaders of the action against Caesar harangued their followers with daily anti-Roman rhetoric (*Alex.* 3).

> In their councils and assembly meetings the arguments that their leaders kept driving home were as follows: the Roman people are gradually acquiring the habit of occupying our kingdom. A few years earlier Aulus Gabinius had come to Egypt with an army; Pompeius as well had fled here intending to take refuge. Now Caesar had now come with all his forces, nor had the death of Pompeius in any way dissuaded him from delaying here among them. Unless they successfully expelled him from their kingdom, Egypt would most assuredly become a Roman province.

The absence of home rule did not inhibit this community from seizing the reigns to its own destiny, utilising a spontaneous if anarchic form of street democracy. Everyday citizens shouted out proposals during impromptu public assemblies. Consensus thus achieved quickly assumed the force of 'law'. In defiance of royal authority, the Alexandrians were sufficiently organised to dispatch embassies to foreign powers to articulate the will of the community. Following the example of Athens, they turned for leadership to intellectuals such as Dion of Alexandria, a native philosopher who was murdered while leading the city's embassy to Rome. Despite the seeming lack of military hierarchy, Caesar saw the disparate elements of the Alexandrian community devise and implement effective military strategies and co-ordinate sustained efforts at defence.

The example of the Alexandrian maritime mob demonstrates three conclusions. It confirms the existence of an active Mediterranean maritime labouring culture that enjoyed sustained existence in several strategic ports of the Mediterranean. It also demonstrates the existence of strained relations, if not outright hatred, between unconfined maritime elements of the Mediterranean and the expanding imperium of Rome. Finally, it indicates that this feeling was mutual and that the authorities at Rome engaged in a methodical effort of expelling this unconfined population from west to east, from port after port, across the Mediterranean. In every instance Roman authorities either compelled local authorities (such as Rhodes and Athens) to suppress the influence of the turbulent, independent-minded sailors in their midst, or they removed them altogether with main force. In the latter instances, Roman generals left in their wake plundered, depopulated cities and privately utilised harbours where vibrant, productive communities formerly existed. The features that seemingly most characterised the maritime populations of the ancient Mediterranean, therefore, were their outspoken contempt for authority, their adroitness at collective action, and their virulent aversion to the encroaching influence of Rome.

3

The material remains of Roman maritime commerce

While Ptolemy Physcon was actively suppressing the Alexandrian population in 129 BC, a Roman embassy led by the conqueror of Carthage, P. Cornelius Scipio Aemilianus, visited Alexandria on a fact-finding tour of the east. Ptolemy went to great effort to impress his visitors with the wealth and heritage of his kingdom. Unfortunately, he was dealing with very austere men, even by Roman standards. His extravagant displays of wealth and luxury failed to achieve his intended effect. Woefully miscalculated was his decision to greet his Roman visitors in the Alexandrian harbour dressed in a long transparent silk tunic. With its fabric undoubtedly from China and its cut designed by fashionable Alexandrian tailors, it represented the ultimate in regal *haute couture*. However, its thin, gauzy material reportedly revealed every detail of his obese frame, including his genitalia, leaving Scipio and his Roman associates uncomfortable. They readily indicated as much by walking to the palace at a brisk military pace, with the portly king struggling to stay alongside. Undaunted, Ptolemy went on to celebrate their visit with tremendous pomp, including costly banquets and guided tours of his palace and other royal monuments (Justin 83.8.8–11; Diod. 38.28b.1). Throughout the king's displays of wealth and extravagance his visitors remained unmoved. According to Diodorus Siculus, 'the ambassadors openly quarrelled with the king regarding his itinerary, insisting that the sites he thought marvellous were of no consequence and that they had other things to see.'

Ptolemy's purpose obviously was to emphasise to his Roman visitors not only the abundance of his resources but the importance Egypt played in international trade. Silk from China, food dishes flavoured with spices from southern Arabia, east Africa and India, incense, unguents and perfumes made from aromatic plants from the same regions, precious stones, pearls, ivory, gold and slaves – these were the commodities that his kingdom received from beyond the boundaries of the Mediterranean and, after processing by the artisan houses of Alexandria, redistributed to the markets of the Mediterranean world. However greatly Scipio Aemilianus feigned uninterest, attitudes such as his were fast becoming rare in Roman Italy. Conquest, prosperity and sustained urban growth were heightening demand for luxuries throughout the peninsula. Ptolemy was well aware of the ultimate destinations of the commodities that departed from his harbour in Alexandria. In this age, luxury goods fashioned or trans-shipped through Alexandria invariably landed within the orbit of Rome. Most of Scipio's wealthy contemporaries were willing to pay fortunes to acquire eastern luxury goods and Ptolemaic Egypt was one most logical source.

The pursuit of resources from beyond the eastern rim of the Mediterranean in some way appears to explain the sustained importance of many harbours along this shore. The Ptolemies had worked for centuries to gain access by land and sea to the raw materials that formed the basis of finished luxury goods. At first they dredged and redredged canals across the Suez (Rashke 1978: 649). Eventually, they realised that the prevailing northerly winds and dangerous coral reefs rendered voyages hazardous along the northern stretch of the Red Sea. Accordingly, the Ptolemies moved the hubs of their eastern trade southward, by constructing roads to connect river traffic along the upper Nile with waiting cargo vessels in the southern Red Sea. The most famous of these departed from Koptos, the closest port on the Nile to the Red Sea (Casson 1989: 13), and made its way across the desert wasteland of the eastern mountains to the harbours of Myos Hormos and Berenike. Watched over by military detachments and furnished with way-stations and cisterns for the use of camels and wagons, this route bustled with caravan trains led by *kamelotrophoi* (Rashke 1978: 648). As Ptolemaic authority waned during the period in question, Hellenistic novels and historical sources indicate that armed gangs of bandits congregated in the hills overlooking this road and preyed on this traffic (S. Wolff 1999). That this route remained the main highway east during the Augustan era (27 BC – 14 AD) is indicated by graffiti left by a member of the Roman Peticius family on a large rock at the Wadi Hammamat. His family's stamped Campanian amphorae have been found as far removed as India (Tchernia 1992).

Similarly, along the coasts of Syria and Palestine, harbours such as Laodiceia, Arados, Tyre, Sidon, Ascalon, Azotus, Iamneia and Gaza were linked via caravan routes across the desert lands of Mesopotamia and Arabia to sources of luxury commodities further abroad. The more southerly ports invariably made their exchanges with Nabataean traders who possessed both overland and Red Sea routes to southern Arabia, home to several aromatic plants used in the preparation of foods, unguents, incense and perfumes. The northern ports relied on contacts with caravan centres across the Lebanese Mountains, the most celebrated of which during the Roman era was Palmyra. Long-standing personal experience with the region and its languages enabled Phoenician, Aramaic and Jewish traders to devise suitable routes along the Euphrates, complete with fortress-like way-stations and water reservoirs (Rostovtzeff 1932). Perhaps most importantly, their enormous private wealth, based on extensive landholdings as in the west, enabled desert traders to furnish the equipment and the small private armies essential to the caravans' safe conduct as they made their way across nomad-infested regions, especially the harsh desert hills of western Syria. The presence of so many eastern merchants at Delos, including the Poseidoniastai of Beirut, the Herakliastai of Tyre, the Samaritan colonists from Gerizim, Philostratos of Ascalon and traders from as far abroad as Minaea (Yemen), demonstrate the importance of Middle Eastern connections to the development of Roman trade. Access to eastern trade during the late second century BC would appear to explain the presence of Roman and Italian merchants at a number of eastern ports, not to mention that of eastern merchants at Italian harbours such as Puteoli. It may also explain Rome's curiously friendly relations with powers such as the Hasmonean dynasty of Judaea.

This is not to say that the eastern luxury trade formed the bulk of Mediterranean maritime commerce during the period in question. Obviously, access to finished goods, raw materials, food supplies, and enslaved manpower generated from within the boundaries of the Mediterranean were equally, if not more important to the circulation of Roman cargo vessels at this time. The attraction of the East remained certain, however, and any assessment of the volume of Roman maritime commerce needs to strike a balance between the movement of Mediterranean merchants and their wares macro-regionally as well as regionally. By and large, the presentation of the harbours in the previous chapter indicates that the main lines of Mediterranean traffic trended eastward toward sources of materials that originated beyond the Mediterranean along the broad sweeping arc of the Indian Ocean.

Roman trade with India

The importance of the eastern trade is gradually being confirmed by archaeo-logical work in regions at considerable distance from the Mediterranean. The exploration of archaeological remains of the Roman era in places such as the Arabian peninsula, Somalia, Iran, Pakistan, India and Sri Lanka stands at an early phase, to be sure, and remains sensitive to prevailing conditions of political and social instability. That said, many of the discoveries gained from the limited exploration in central Asia, thus far, offer tremendous insight to the character of ancient inter-regional trade. In Bagram (ancient Kapisa), Afghanistan, for example, French excavators in the late 1930s uncovered a remarkable stock of eastern Mediterranean finished goods, including glass, sculpture, bronze platters and receptacles, steelyard weights and alabaster stone vessels. The presence of a statue of Harpocrates and the alabaster vessels indicates likely Egyptian (Alexandrian) origination for many of these commodities. The glass ware consists of several major Mediterranean types:

millefiori bowls, painted vessels and goblets, cut-glass goblets and diatreta. One of the scenes on the diatreta has been identified as that of the Pharos of Alexandria; others reflect a repertoire fairly typical of Hellenistic glass production in Seleucid Syria, including the battles of Alexander, gladiatorial combats, the duel of Hector and Achilles, and hunting scenes. Also recorded in the remains were lacquers originating from China and ivory plaques, statues and coffers from India. Assigned dates for the Mediterranean finds range broadly from first century BC to the fourth century AD.[1]

As the finds at Bagram demonstrate, the settlement at Kapisa marked a point of convergence for trade routes in central Asia. Chinese silks and lacquers were conveyed south by Indian merchants on tracks leading from far north in the Tarim Basin (Taklan Makan). There, at a number of oasis settlements – Yarkand, Lou-lan, Khotan, Turfan – they procured Chinese goods either from elements of the Hsiung-nu nomads or from merchants representing the Han Dynasty of China, depending on which of the two regional powers happened to dominate the basin at that time (Raschke 1978: 618f.). Chinese sources make clear that the Han Dynasty delivered tens of thousands of rolls of silk and quantities of food annually to the Hsiung-nu as tribute, in an effort to buy peace along their northern frontiers. These efforts at appeasement tended to yield better results than the massive investment made by that dynasty in the Great Wall. The Hsiung-nu utilised military intimidation to develop a highly efficient system of steppe nomadism based on the procurement of provisions and resources from neighbouring populations (Rashke 1978: 612f.). Excess silk and thousands of Chinese prisoners, the proceeds of payoffs and plundering raids, gradually made their way to the trading centres of the Tarim where Indian merchants purchased them in great quantities and removed them southward across the rugged wastelands of Sogdiana and Bactria, across the Oxus River and over the passes of the Hindu Kush mountains to the trading centre of Kapisa and beyond.

Indian works of ivory were conveyed to Kapisa along a southern route that led past Kabul and Jalalabad and descended through various passes to Taxila in the Indus Valley (26). Crossing the Indo-Ganges watershed merchants would arrive at the Sakas/Kushan capital at Mathura, where artisan guilds busily manufactured these items for the kings of the first centuries BC/AD. Driven southward by the expanding hegemony of the Hsiung-nu, the Sakas and the Kushan came to dominate the overland corridors between the Tarim Basin and the Ganges and facilitated commerce by maintaining stability along the length. This is not to say that either the Sakas/Kushan or the federated bands of the Hsiung-nu were inherently traders. Horseback archers garbed in armour, they sustained their warrior elites by extracting essential resources from their subjects. To the extent that taxes levied on merchants engaged in the long-distance trade of the region earned revenue, they showed interest in this trade.

1 (Above) *Watercolour of the Fortress of Qait Bey, on the site of the ancient lighthouse in Alexandria*

2 (Right) *Watercolour of ancient harbours of Carthage. Based on Mohamed Hassine Fantar. Carthage La cite punique.* Paris: CNRS 1995

3 *View of the southern mole of the harbour at Kenchriai*

4 *General view of the harbour remains at Kenchriai*

5 *View of the 'triple gate' of the Acrocorinth*

6 *View of the Hellenistic towers of the Eetionia Gate, with the Kantharos Harbour and hill of Mounychia in the background*

7 *View of Mounychia Harbour, looking east toward Athens*

8 *The so-called Warehouse of the Columns on the western shore of Delos. General view from the east. Island of Rheneia in the distance. Behind the sailboat is the larger of two small islands known as Rhevmataria*

9 *View of the granite columns to the groundfloor interior peristyle of the Warehouse of the Columns. Note the setting holes for retractable table stands*

10 *View of 'Road Five' at Delos*

11 *View of the 'commercial harbour' at Delos showing a line of warehouses south of the Agora of the Competaliastai; the Theater District and Mt Cynthos loom in the distance*

12 *The theatre at Phaselis*

13 *View of insulae at Ostia, Roman Imperial Era*

14 *View of remains of Selcuk fortification walls in Alanya. Lower courses of Hellenistic ashlar masonry are visible*

15 *View of the Antikragos. Remains of Byzantine/Selcuk Turkish castle are visible on the taller promontory; a Late Roman church and necropolis stand on the lower rock to the left. The Pirate's Cove is situated below the lower rock in the foreground*

16 *Ancient Korakesion. View shows the promontory from the north-west with remains of Selcuk Turk fortifications*

17 *View of Hypostyle hall, in the Agora of Theophrastos, at Delos*

18 *View of the South Harbour at Phaselis*

19 *Closer view of the warehouses Alpha, Beta, and Gamma just south of the Agora of the Competaliastai at Delos*

20 (Left) *View of the mosaic floor at the House of Fourni, Delos*

21 (Below) *Will Type 1d amphora in the Alanya Museum*

22 *Remains of pre-Roman fortifications inside the Late Roman walls at Lamos*

23 *Remains of the early Roman city at Antioch. Twin towers mark the entrance to the Roman colonnaded street. The rock in the background is presumably Appian's Kragos*

24 *View of the bath remains (apse with windows) at Asar Tepe*

25 (Above) *The fire jets of the Chimera at Olympos*

26 (Right) *View of the promontory at Iotape from the remains of a Hellenistic Era street*

27 *View of the third-century AD walls of Lamos looking west*

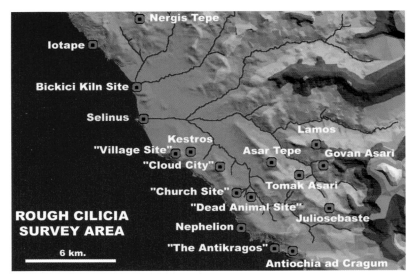

28 *GIS map of the Rough Cilicia Survey Area*

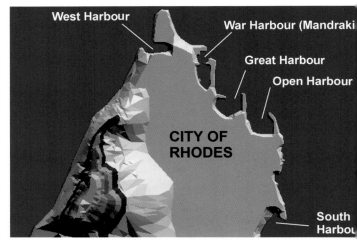

29 *GIS map of Rhodes*

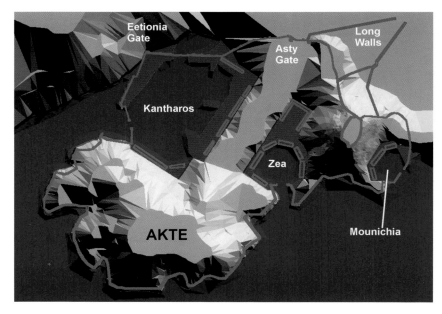

30 *GIS map of the Piraeus*

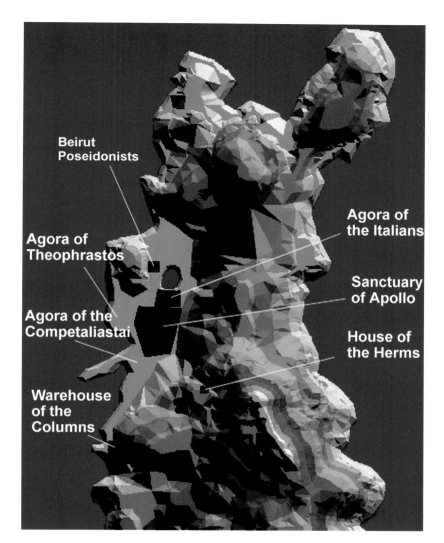

Beirut
Poseidonists

Agora of
Theophrastos

Agora of the
Competaliastai

Warehouse
of the
Columns

Agora of
the Italians

Sanctuary
of Apollo

House of
the Herms

31 *GIS map of Delos*

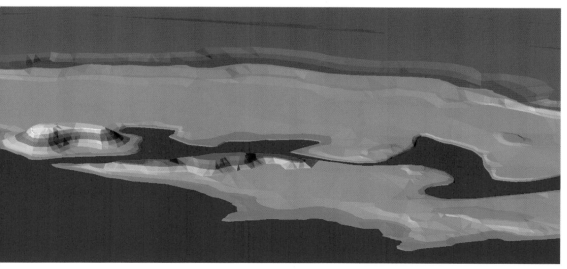

32 *Digital elevation model of the Lechaion harbour of Corinth*

33 *'Pirates' Cove' at Antioch*

26 *Statue of a Kushan King from Mathura*

Other goods from still further east, now lost in the archaeological record (spices, precious stones and silk), arrived at Mathura via roads constructed by the Mauryan dynasty through the ancient capital of Pataliputra, terminating at Tamralipti, the main port in the Ganges Delta. An alternative route went south from the Ganges via Ujjain and the valley of the Narmada River to the Indian west coast, where the major port was Bhrgukaccha (Barygaza, modern Broach) in the Bay of Cambay. According to the first-century AD Periplus writer, the kings who controlled this harbour made careful provision for the protection and piloting of ships in their waters, designating specific ports as emporia.[2] Goods from this port could also be conveyed up the Indus to Taxila and onward to Kapisa. In short, goods from the Far East arrived at Kapisa from several directions. Whether via the Indus, the Ganges or the Tarim Basin, the commodities assembling in Kapisa converged with those arriving from the Mediterranean via the ancient Persian highway across Afghanistan. Alexander the Great had reopened this road network and improved it during his campaigns in the region, and as the finds at Kapisa demonstrate, it continued in use during the period of his successors. Much the same as today, this road veered in a sweeping arc southward to Kandahar then northwards to Herat before crossing into Iran where it linked up with a number of routes leading to ports on the Black Sea and the eastern Mediterranean. This was the overland route exploited by commercial elements throughout the eastern Mediterranean. In many respects it represented a slow, inefficient, extremely dangerous means for the conveyance of materials from one end of the world to the other. Given the inefficiency of overland transport in this era, scholars have long debated the degree to which any significant volume of trade may have passed along these pathways. A far better perspective for the volume of the eastern trade can be gained from the available evidence for the maritime route to the south.

Unquestionably, the most spectacular finds of Roman trade with India arise from the excavations undertaken in 1941–50 and resumed in 1989–92 at Arikamedu near Pondicherry on the south-east Indian coast. Possibly identifiable as the port of Poduke mentioned by the Periplus writer and by the first-century AD geographer Ptolemy, the site revealed a Roman trading settlement of the late Hellenistic and early Roman eras.[3] Large quantities of Roman pottery, beads, intaglios, lamps, glass and coins point to a continuous occupation by merchants of Mediterranean origin as well as to a healthy appetite for Mediterranean finished goods among Tamil inhabitants.

Recent analysis of Mediterranean transport amphorae at Arikamedu by E.L. Will furnishes the most precise information for this trade. All told, her analysis has identified some 400 diagnostic sherds belonging to Mediterranean amphora types. Most of these she identifies as wine jars, more than half of which appear to be Koan, approximately 20 per cent Rhodian, 14 per cent Campanian, 12 per cent Knidian, and 1.5 per cent from Roman Gaul. Chronologically, her analysis shows that the Koan fragments date from as early as the second century BC; the Knidian and Rhodian from the first century BC; and the Campanian amphorae date from the late first century BC and the first century AD. Also included among identified finds were remains of oil jars (Will type 14 and 20), garum containers (Will types 7 and 9), and a fruit jar (Will type 17), all of the early imperial era.[4]

While most of the other data, including Roman coins (gold, silver and bronze) and the inscribed stamps on Arretine fineware, point to the settlement's peak occupation during the Julio-Claudian era (27 BC–68 AD),[5] the amphora data yielded by Will's analysis indicate that the foreign trading presence began much earlier, about the time of the Ptolemaic discovery of the monsoon winds of the Arabian Sea. Moreover, the character of the excavated materials – transport amphorae weighing as much as 50kg when filled and sealed and large quantities of relatively heavy finewares – are the kinds of goods most frequently encountered in Mediterranean shipwrecks (**27**). In Mediterranean contexts these remains are generally acknowledged as evidence of maritime traffic in staple goods, not luxuries. As Will points out, even the wines conveyed to Arikamedu – Koan, Rhodian and Knidian – are more

27 *Koan amphora rim found at Arikamedu.* E. Lyding Will

properly identified as common table wines, the beverages of Roman soldiers, for example, at the legionary camps of Cisalpine Gaul.[6] Their transport containers are found virtually everywhere in the Mediterranean. The possibility exists that these wines were preferred by the inhabitants of Arikamedu, native and foreign alike, because of the use of salt water in their preparation. Acting as a preservative, salt water as an ingredient appears to have lent these wines superior 'shelf life' during the long overseas voyage to India.

The quantities of these transport jars at Arikamedu warrants further consideration. By Mediterranean standards the scale of the excavations at Arikamedu is relatively small. The quantity of Mediterranean amphora finds yielded by these trenches seems significant, therefore. Extrapolating from the available data, the quantity of Mediterranean amphora remains at this site matches those of comparably sized sites in the Mediterranean. In addition, archaeologists found that many of the amphora fragments at Arikamedu were encrusted in hydraulic cement, apparently Italian *pozzolana*, imported by western merchants along with the amphorae to construct commercial facilities at this remote trading outpost (Will 1996: 317). Only a seagoing commerce of significant scale and sustained duration can explain these finds. The presence of such commonplace amphorae at Arikamedu raises important questions, therefore, about the characterisation of Roman trade with India.

The finds at Arikamedu conform to and bring clarity to the archaeological evidence of south India generally (Rashke 1978: 671f.). The barren terrain of the southern end of the peninsula and limited agricultural technology prohibited the development of large agrarian-based polities such as those of the great rivers to the north. Instead, the Tamil rajahs who controlled the southern principalities of Pandyas (Madurai), Ceras (Malabar coast and hinterland) and Colas (Thanjavur and the Kauveri valley) exploited their maritime locations as settings for the development of long-distance trade. When viewed geographically, the southern cape of India forms the tip of two large embayments in the northern Indian Ocean: the Arabian Sea separating India from Africa, Arabia and Iran on the west, and the Bay of Bengal and the Andaman Sea separating the Indian subcontinent from Bangladesh, Burma, Thailand, Indonesia and the Malay peninsula to the east. Both seas are approximately 1,000 nautical miles across and both are dominated by monsoon winds that blow from the south west during summer and the north east during winter.[7] Although coastal traffic had clearly progressed for centuries in both directions, with the discovery of the monsoon winds by Ptolemaic mariners at the end of the second century BC, direct passages from the western shores of the Arabian Sea became possible.[8] Given the navigational logic of ancient mariners, the necessity of making landfall somewhere along the western coast of India became critical to the open-sea route. Forward situated islands such as Charax Spanisou (near the Shatt al Arab) and Socotra (approximately 300km east of the Horn of Africa) and Lakshadweep (the Laccadive Is., 320km west of south-west India) offered advantageous points of departure for ocean crossings similar to those offered by Sicily, Crete and Rhodes in the Mediterranean.[9] As with the Mediterranean islands, commercial traffic tended to cluster at places like Socotra while awaiting favourable winds. Pliny (*NH* 6.84) reports a cautionary tale, for example, of a freedman of an influential first-century AD Roman tax farmer, Annius Plocamus, who while sailing around Arabia was blown off course by a northerly gale. Undeterred, he arrived at Sri Lanka some fifteen days later. This was precisely the sort of sailor's yarn that open-sea runners liked to hear.[10]

Although archaeological information is less forthcoming further east, by this time Indian merchants seeking silk, spices and semi-precious stones had clearly established themselves at trading settlements throughout the Bay of Bengal, and as far removed as the islands of Sumatra, Java and Bali. Learning from their contemporaries in the west, they appear to have exploited prevailing wind patterns to sail westwards across the open sea to the eastern shore of India. At the eastern end of this route, the Andaman and Nicobar islands south of Rangoon offered oceanic launching stations similar to those of Socotra and Charax in the west.[11] The obvious point of intersection for traffic coming from either end of the Indian Ocean was the southern tip of India, precisely the region where the best evidence for Roman trade has emerged. All along the southern coast and even toward the interior where quartz and beryl were available, Roman coins (*denarii* and *aurei*) have been found. In fact, of the 5,400 *denarii* recovered in India by 1978, 99 per cent were found in southern Tamil regions, not to mention 98 per cent of all gold *aurei*.[12]

During the first and second centuries AD, locally inscribed Tamil Sangam literature records frequent interaction between native kings and western merchants, commonly referred to as *Yavana*.[13] One first-century AD king of the Cera tribes along the south-east coast, Nedunjeral Adan, is said to have attacked Yavana ships and to have taken traders hostage in an effort to secure their submission. Sangam literature also attests to the prosperity of Yavana merchants in towns such as Kaveripattinam on the Kauveri Delta and to their settlement in India not only as merchants, but as artisans and mercenary warriors of the kings. The fourth-century AD source for the Peutinger Table even records the existence of a Roman Templum Augusti at Muziris (Rashke 1978: 673). According to the Periplus writer, western merchants trading in south India procured commodities such as pepper, pearls, ivory, silk, spikenard (an aromatic plant), precious stones, malabathrum, tortoise shells and textiles cut to Roman specifications. In exchange for these goods, Yavana merchants brought glass, copper, tin, lead, realgar, orpiment, antimony, wine and currency (Casson 1989: 39f.). The effect of this sustained Roman presence clearly influenced native culture and technologies: red-slipped, rouletted Indian finewares of this period decidedly imitate Mediterranean Eastern Sigillata wares and Indian glasswares copy similar eastern Mediterranean standards (Rashke 1978: 671). In fact, Pliny reports that the Roman Empire endured a significant drainage of its currency in a relentless effort to acquire exotic goods from India (*NH* 6.101; 12.94):

> In no year does India absorb less than fifty million sesterces of our empire's wealth, sending back merchandise to be sold with us at a hundred times its prime cost . . . Moreover, by the lowest reckoning India, China and the Arabian peninsula combined take from our empire 100 million sesterces annually.

Pliny's comments remain highly controversial. The least that can be said is that the currently available data, in the shape of reported finds of Roman coinage in India, fail to bear him out.[14] The amphora data from Arikamedu, on the other hand, would seem to indicate that the true basis of Roman maritime trade with India lay with other commodities. The amphora finds confirm that a good deal of Roman commerce across the Arabian Sea transpired as shipments of heavy bulk commodities such as amphorae laden with wine and oil, ceramic finewares, glasswares, and finished metal wares such as weapons, tools and works of art. The very nature of these commodities suggests that they were conveyed across the seas in large cargo vessels, precisely the type of ships that Strabo reports seeing at the Red Sea port of Myos Hormos, departing for India. Mediterranean merchants regularly shipped these same commodities throughout their home region, making it difficult to classify them as 'luxuries'. In fact, as shall be seen below, discoveries of Mediterranean-produced 'luxury products' such as statuary and marble furnishings are far more commonplace among Mediterranean shipwrecks. This would suggest that the chief markets of Mediterranean luxury goods remained at home.

The evidence acquired thus far from India suggests that Roman merchants sailed to India to exchange basic staple goods with their counterparts from India and beyond (**28**). In exchange they obtained commodities that were unavailable in the west – silk, spices, aromatics and precious stones. As one recent scholar has observed, much like Roman wine and oil, these products were neither rare nor expensive in the regions of their origination (Rashke 1978: 676–7). What affected their prices at the opposite end of the ancient world was the inherent cost of transport and the manifold layers of tariffs they incurred along the way. Widely varying climates of ancient world production areas appear to have rendered one region's staple goods another region's luxuries. Accordingly, the eastern luxury trade of the Roman era needs always to be considered within the context of various socio-economic and political systems in the geographic regions through which it passed (Rashke 1978: 676–7).

Obviously the character of this traffic was far more complex than that achieved by exchanges in currency alone. Questions regarding the volume of this traffic remain more speculative, however. Although archaeological data from the commodities from the eastern ends of this trading network, silk and spices, remain inadequate, the amphora evidence at Arikamedu suggests not

28 *Large cargo vessel under full sail from a sarcophagus in the National Museum at Beirut*

only that Roman maritime trade with India during the first centuries BC and AD consisted of Mediterranean staple commodities but that it circulated at a pace relatively similar to that which transpired within the Mediterranean itself. Roman merchants who established the trading contacts in India utilised those 'finished goods' that the Roman world was most adept at producing. The Auximite kings of east Africa used Roman weapons to assert local supremacy; the Tamil princes of southern India used their geographical position at the centre of ancient oceanic trading routes to raise standards of living of an otherwise unproductive region. Traders from the Far East made the difficult journey to India bearing commodities that, according to available documentation, were readily available in their home regions. No one would argue that commonplace wines from Kos, Rhodes or Knidos bore intrinsic value commensurate with that of spices or silk from the East. Larger quantities of Mediterranean staple goods may have been required to obtain sufficient amounts of the goods in question. This may explain not only the presence of so many Roman amphorae at Arikamedu but the perception as well that the trade with India imposed an unfavourable balance of trade on the West. In addition, repeated references to silk garments in Roman literature and widespread finds of artefacts such as pepper shakers throughout Mediterranean archaeological contexts indicate that, however expensive these luxuries may have been, their prices were not beyond the reach of wealthy elites, not only at Rome, but in relatively peripheral regions of the sea.[15] Assuming that eastern luxury goods were relatively plentiful in the Roman Mediterranean, the volume of traffic across the Indian Ocean must have been significant, albeit unstable. The evidence unearthed at Kapisa and Arikamedu demonstrates, therefore, that merchants from the Roman Mediterranean actively engaged in a wider world economy during the period in question, forming a consistent and sustained pattern of exchanges extending from the eastern Mediterranean along the northern arc of the Indian Ocean. The effects of this trade at emporia such as Alexandria, Rhodes and Delos have already been noted. What remains to be determined is the likely impact macro-regional trade had on regional commerce in the Mediterranean.

The volume of Roman shipping

To gauge the volume of maritime trade in the Mediterranean, the uniqueness of the amphora finds at Arikamedu are matched by more abundant, quantifiable data emerging from archaeological contexts throughout the Mediterranean. Obviously, a question as broad as the relative scale and importance of maritime trade to the Roman economy tends to generate prolonged and detailed discussion. In the pages that follow, it is necessary to restrict the area of focus to available data that best illustrate the character of this trade during the period in question. For example, underwater archaeologists have discovered a diverse array of commodities in ancient shipwrecks capable of demonstrating region-wide participation in maritime trade. The identified remains of shipwrecked ancient cargo vessels themselves and those of maritime transport containers, or amphorae, emerge, therefore, as the principal artefacts of Roman trade during the period in question. Like the cargo vessels that carried them, amphorae were designed almost exclusively for the purposes of commerce by sea.

By way of introduction one might consider the example of the best-known Roman economic writer of the era. The celebrated Roman senator, M. Porcius Cato the Elder (234–149 BC), appears to have been an innovator both with respect to his agricultural practices and his involvement in overseas trade. His surviving treatise, *De Agricultura*, demonstrates the utility of adapting land resources to agricultural production for export purposes. More specifically his writings stress the importance of converting estates to the production of wine and oil; his contemporaries confirm that he had a similar passion for livestock herding (Cic. *De Off.* 2.89). His conservative attitude toward commerce appears symptomatic of a large element of Roman landed propri-etors faced with the decision whether or not to engage in overseas trade in a period fraught with violence. Plutarch (*Cat. Mai.* 21.6) reports that Cato went so far as to invest in speculative trading ventures by purchasing small shares in large mercantile consortia and thereby spreading his risk.

> He used to loan money in the most disreputable of all ways, namely in shipping, and according to the following formula. He required his borrowers to form a large company, and when there were fifty partners and as many ships for his security, he invested in one [2 per cent] share of the company. He even sent his freedman, Quintio, along on all their ventures. In this way his entire security was not imperilled, but only a small part of it, and his profits were large.

Cato's maritime investments are usually taken as an indication of the disincli-nation of Roman aristocrats to engage in maritime trade. Cultural and legal prohibitions actually restricted senatorial participation in this regard.[16] However, the passage also indicates how dangerous maritime ventures appar-ently were. The organisation of large Roman maritime convoys for purposes of security certainly fits with the description of Rhodian trading combines, noted above, as well as with the tendency of Rhodian families to invest in privately owned and manned war galleys as escorts to their cargo ventures. Plutarch's description is not so precise, but the frequent discovery of arms and armour in western Mediterranean shipwrecks demonstrates that large Roman cargo vessels bore their own means of defence on deck. Flotillas of ships as large as the consortium put together by Cato could under normal circumstances probably have sailed at will through hazard-infested waters.[17] It must always be borne in mind that shipwreck data result from cargo ventures that went wrong.

By 1992 some 1,189 ancient shipwrecks had been recorded and published for the Mediterranean region. The vast majority of these have been identified in the western Mediterranean waters of Italy (428, 36 per cent), France (282, 24 per cent), and Spain (134, 11 per cent), some 70 per cent of the total combined. An equally vast majority of recorded shipwrecks date to the Roman era. In fact, Late Hellenistic and Roman Imperial era wrecks represent more than 75 per cent of all recorded wrecks across the Mediterranean prior to AD 1500. By comparison the number of pre-classical and medieval wrecks is extremely small (Parker 1992: 7). This is particularly true in western Mediterranean waters, such as those of southern France, where shipwrecks of the second century BC predominate (Parker 1992: 9). One needs to bear in mind that new shipwrecks are discovered annually, rendering the available published data increasingly obsolete. However, the consistency of the current data is so overwhelming that many years of additional finds will be required before any likely change can be assessed. By and large, shipwrecks dated to the four centuries between 200 BC and AD 200 vastly predominate in the available data of the Mediterranean and suggest in a negative manner that this period marked a peak era with respect to the relative volume of Mediterranean maritime trade.

A second point concerns the size of Mediterranean shipwrecks, and their relative carrying capacity or dead load tonnage.[18] According to Parker (1992: 26), of those wrecks for which tonnage can be determined either from nautical excavation or detailed underwater survey, the commonest class of cargo ships, found in all periods, are also the smallest, namely, those under 75 metric tons or 1,500 amphorae capacity. Next most common are the medium range of wrecks with cargoes weighing 75–200 tons or 2,000–3,000 amphorae capacity. The bulk of this second category falls within the period from the first century BC to the third century AD. The largest class of wrecks exhibiting dead load tonnage in excess of 250 tons or 6,000 amphorae date mostly to the second and first centuries BC with a few additional wrecks recorded during the early Empire (first to second centuries AD). This suggests that small cargo ships supplied the mainstay of Mediterranean trade, but that during the period in question (167–67 BC) larger and larger cargo ships plied the waters of the Mediterranean and probably those of the Indian Ocean as well. As Gianfrotta and Pomey note (1981: 284), prior to the fifteenth century AD, when the Genoese and Venetians regularly constructed ships of 600 tons capacity, Rome generated the largest shipping capacities of the world.

A third point revealed by an analysis of Mediterranean shipwreck data concerns the composition of shipwrecked cargoes (**29**). Drawing on data from 98 well-preserved, thoroughly investigated shipwrecks dated between 400 BC

29 *Merchant galley with amphorae. Mosaic from Tebessa in Algeria*

and AD 400, Parker (1992: 20) determines that 50 or roughly 51 per cent of these shipwrecks carried only one form of cargo. In 45 or 47 per cent of the cargoes sampled, these cargoes consisted solely of amphorae. When data for compound cargoes of two categories of goods, such as amphorae and ceramic fineware, are considered, the number of these cargoes rises to 79 of 98 or 81 per cent of the total sampled. Drawing from a slightly larger sample of 171 identifiable undersea cargoes, 92 or 54 per cent of those cargoes consisted to some degree of amphorae. Not only do these data stress the relative importance of transport amphorae as remains of Mediterranean maritime commerce, but they also suggest, however crudely, that commodities conveyed in amphorae formed the bulk of Roman commerce. Equally importantly, the existence of so many large 'bulk' cargoes of one or two categories of goods indicates that for the period in question prearranged shipment of goods on consignment prevailed over 'cabotage' or small-scale itinerant 'peddling' of merchandise from port to port.

Further information gleaned from shipwreck archaeology indicates that the peak of this consignment traffic occurred during the period in question (167–67 BC). Underwater archaeologists record cargoes of Roman amphorae dated between 300 and 150 BC at a significant number of shipwrecks, more so than those dating from all previous periods combined. Cargoes of Roman amphorae dated to 150–1 BC are recorded on nearly two and a half times as many wrecks as those of the previous interval. In fact, amphora cargoes of the

Late Hellenistic-Roman Republican era form the largest concentrations of all Antiquity. Even the recorded cargoes of early Roman imperial amphorae (first/second centuries AD), great as they are, fail to compare.

Before proceeding with the analysis of ancient Mediterranean shipwreck data, several potentially distorting factors warrant consideration. First, one needs to recognise that numerous shipwrecks in the Mediterranean are known to exist but have yet to be published either by host governments or by sport divers familiar with their whereabouts. In addition, very few recorded ship-wrecks have undergone detailed archaeological inspection. Before Mediterranean host governments acted to outlaw underwater looting, sport divers plundered countless wrecks, thereby obliterating valuable archaeological contexts. Accordingly, as shown above, only a small fraction of the reported 1,189 wrecks are useful for analysis.

Second, the fact that the distribution of more than 70 per cent of recorded shipwrecks emerges from shallow waters off the coasts of Spain, France and Italy, where sport diving by amateurs and diving clubs has thrived for decades, is no coincidence. Deep-water wrecks are obviously more difficult to locate and to explore, and the percentage of ancient Mediterranean shipwrecks awaiting discovery at extreme depths remains indeterminable.[19] Having said that, it stands to reason that the high concentration of Roman Republican shipwrecks found in relatively shallow waters off the coasts of Italy, France and Spain reflects a higher incidence of maritime calamities at that time. This may have resulted from both the greater volume of maritime traffic and a commen-surately higher incidence of navigational failure along areas of relatively treach-erous coasts. As underwater exploration of coastal waters in other areas of the Mediterranean accelerates, the number of recorded shipwrecks continues to rise.[20] However, as the evidence of wrecks such as the *Mahdia* off Tunisia and the *Antikythera* in Greece demonstrates, a significant proportion of unexplored wrecks in regions other than the north–west Mediterranean also date to the period in question, and thus work to corroborate the prevailing pattern of wreck distributions. As Parker notes (1992: 7), the very small number of Late Roman wrecks (third to sixth centuries AD) in the waters of southern France, compared with the vast number of cargoes of the Republican period, cannot be ascribed solely to an accident of statistics. By every indication the Late Hellenistic/Roman Republican era was the greatest era of ancient Mediterranean maritime commerce.

A few additional, potentially delimiting, factors need to be considered. Most of the chronological data for Mediterranean shipwrecks arise precisely from reported amphora finds owing to their durability and to the proficiency of archaeologists at classifying them. Roman imperial evidence for the substi-tution of amphorae by permanently implanted dolia (more difficult to date) or wooden barrels (the remains of which do not survive), if confirmed, would seriously undermine chronological analysis (Tchernia 1986: 285f.). However, in view of mounting evidence for thriving production of amphorae during the Late Roman era, particularly in the eastern Mediterranean, the impact of shipboard use of dolia and barrels appears minimal.[21] Parker (1992: 7), for example, points to the higher incidence of Late Roman shipwrecks in eastern Mediterranean waters as evidence for a revival of trade during the early Byzantine era. This contrasts markedly with the paucity of wrecks in western Mediterranean waters at that time.

One final source of potential distortion to the evidence needs to be considered: namely the possibility that the higher incidence of shipwrecks from the Late Hellenistic/Late Republican era resulted from greater levels of violence perpetrated against maritime shipping.[22] In other words, the volume of maritime commerce during the Roman imperial era may actually have been greater, but the archaeological record in the form of shipwrecks is lower owing to a lower threshold of violence at sea. Arguing against this is the historical record of fairly constant warfare from the early classical period to the foundation of the Roman Empire. Assuming that violence alone explains the incidence of shipwrecks, one would expect to see a higher percentage of wrecks from earlier periods as well. The fact that the quantity of recorded wrecks of the Roman imperial era rank second only to those of late Hellenistic times indicates that maritime calamities resulting from natural risks such as faulty navigation, storms, and contrary winds and currents along treacherous coasts remained the principal causes of shipwrecks throughout Antiquity. The large incidence of imperial wrecks that occurred along the treacherous Strait of Bonifacio in Spain, for example, demonstrates that navigators conveying cargoes of Spanish wine and oil to Rome found this route, however hazardous, the most convenient one (Parker 1992: 9, 19). This suggests that the distribution of Mediterranean shipwrecks has more to do with the general tendencies of ancient navigation than it does with historical levels of maritime violence. Accordingly, distribution records of ancient shipwrecks do indeed appear to furnish a viable indicator of the volume of maritime trade.

A brief description of a few of the more representative shipwrecks dated to the late Hellenistic era will help to clarify the character of maritime trade (**30**). The earliest of the wrecks in question, the *Kyrenia*, was found off the north coast of Cyprus, on a flat sandy bottom 27m in depth, the wreck's cargo forming a tumulus some 10m by 19m. Excavation conducted in 1969–72 by M. Katzev revealed an estimated overall length for the ship of 13.6m, and a beam of 4.4m, suggesting that it displaced 14 tons along with some 20 tons of cargo found in the excavation.[23] From the ship's hold, archaeologists recovered some 343 Rhodian amphorae, as well as 71 others from Samos, Paros, Crete and Palestine. These together with coin finds give the wreck an approximate date of *c*.310-300 BC.[24] Tools, timber and supplies of lead indicate the practical aspects of the ship's business; four sets of dining ware suggest that this was the size of the crew.

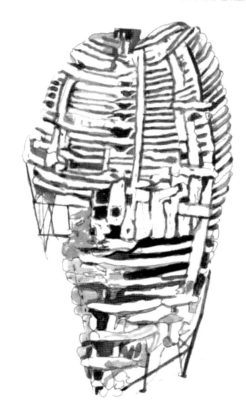

30 *View of the restored wreck of the Kyrenia.* Based on photograph in Gianfrotta and Pomey 1981: 128

The Grand Congloué wrecks were located at the north-east point of the island of that name south of Marseille, at the foot of a cliff some 32–45m in depth.[25] Post-excavation analysis has revealed that the site harbours two super-imposed wrecks, chronologically distinguished by the amphora cargoes they bore. The lower wreck, dated *c.*190–180 BC, contained over 400 Will type 1c (Graeco-Italic) amphorae, some stamped *Ti. Q. Iuventi,* and *c.*7,000 pieces of black-slipped Campanian A fineware, datable to *c.*190 BC; there were also 30 Rhodian amphorae with stamps datable *c.*210-175 BC, and several amphorae from Knidos, Chios and elsewhere (Will 1987: 178). The upper wreck (B) bore a large cargo of *c.* 1,200 Will type 4a (Dressel 1A) amphorae stacked in at least three layers. Most of these jars bear stamps marked *SES* together with production marks indicating that they were shipped by the prominent Etrurian Sestius family, members of which rose to senatorial rank at Rome in the age of Cicero (see below).

Two of the largest wrecks of the era likewise bore cargoes of amphorae. The *Albenga,* found in 1950 in 40–42m of water at a muddy river mouth near the town by that name, underwent excavation from 1957 to the early 1970s.[26] From a tumulus 30m by 10m in area and 2m tall, archaeologists raised more than 1,700 Will type 4b (Dressel 1B) amphorae, mostly bearing wine, along

31 *View of the excavation of the Madrague de Giens.* Based on a photograph in Gianfrotta and Pomey 1981: 56-7

with Campanian A fineware plates and bowls packed between the amphorae in some places. All sources agree that this was a large ship but the estimated size of the cargo varies considerably. Approximately five to six stacked layers of amphorae have been demonstrated, furnishing a potential total between 5,000 and 13,500 in all, along with an estimated dead load tonnage of 500 to 600 tons. Along with finds of oil jars and pottery for shipboard use came the discovery of seven bronze helmets of different types, a clear indication that the crew was prepared for violence.

Arguably the largest wreck from Antiquity is the *Madrague de Giens*, located in 18–21m of water along the north side of the Giens promontory in southern France (near Hyères).[27] Discovered coins and amphora typologies help to assign the wreck a date of 70–50 BC. Excavated in 1971–1983, the Madrague de Giens revealed some 400 tons of cargo, consisting mostly of 6,000–7,000 Will type 4b (Dressel 1b) amphorae, all made in south Latium (**31**). The cargo also included several hundred pieces of black slipped finewares and large quantities of coarse-ware forms apparently packed in boxes stowed on top of the amphorae. Most of this cargo occupied the centre and fore part of the ship; the space in the stern was filled partly with bundles of brushwood and a mass of volcanic sand and partly used for the crew's accommodation. The ship's design incorporated distinctive 'shell first' techniques for fast efficient sailing. The restored dimensions of its hull are 40m long, 9m beam and 4.5m depth inside the hold.

Two additional wrecks have surfaced repeatedly in the historical discussion above with respect to Sulla's siege of Athens. The *Mahdia*, found in 1907 by sponge divers 5km off the coast of Tunisia in 40m of water, contained a large, complex cargo of costly furnishings. Dated by the assorted pottery to *c.*80–70 BC, the wreck contained some 70 Attic marble columns (from 1.85 to 4.4m tall), bases and capitals, full-size and miniature bronze sculptures, marble basins, vases and candelabra and bronze decorative pieces.[28] Most of the bronze work is small but refined, including an archaised herm signed by the celebrated artist Boethus of Chalcedon, and various grotesque statuettes that suggest Alexandrian production. Although most of the goods, including amphorae, bear eastern Mediterranean origins, the cargo also included numerous lead ingots originating from Roman mines in Spain (and stamped accordingly with Latin names). With a keel measuring 26m and a cargo estimated at *c.*350 tons, the wreck's date remains open to an association with the sack of Athens; however, its combined cargo of Spanish lead and Attic elements of entablature continues to generate scholarly disagreement. Most are inclined to identify it with the voracious Roman aristocratic demand for artwork; the presence of the lead ingots indicates, for example, that the ship bore a number of specialised consignments and that it possibly sailed from the Aegean to North Africa to pick up this last waiting portion of the cargo.

Much like the *Mahdia,* the *Antikythera* wreck appears slightly too late for association with the sack of Athens.[29] Found in 1900 in 50–60m of water on the treacherous north-east side of the island of Antikythera, the wreck revealed a stunning array of several dozen statues (now in the National Museum in Athens), numerous amphorae (Rhodian, Koan and Italian forms related to Will type 10), and numerous examples of finely wrought glasswares including mille-fiori bowls. Gold ingots, jewellery and piles of coins were also found. The works of art on board included not only contemporary pieces but also 'old masters' of the fourth to second centuries BC, including the celebrated Ephebe of Antikythera and the bronze portrait head of the 'philosopher' now exhibited in the National Museum in Athens (**32**). An astronomical calculator found on board fixes the date of wreck. Ship's officers used this mechanical device to predict star-alignment in the night sky. Study of its remains shows that it must have been set in 80 BC, the only date that fits both the astronomical situation and also the archaeological date for the site. Resumed excavation in 1976 recovered Pergamene coins dated 88–86 BC, convincing some specialists that the ship was carrying an instalment of the indemnities demanded from the city by Sulla at the end of the Mithradatic War (Parker 1992: 56). Similarly to the *Mahdia,* the *Antikythera* wreck not only demonstrates the volume of trade in costly luxury items across the Mediterranean, but the tendency of this trade to assume a westerly course during the period in question.

Available data from Mediterranean shipwrecks indicate, accordingly, that the period in question represented a high-water mark for ancient maritime commerce. In an impressionistic manner, these records are supported by literary testimony. As the shipwreck data indicate, the greater portion of Mediterranean shipping is presumed to have consisted of relatively small vessels of 300 tons capacity or less. The maritime topography of the Mediterranean all but required this. Harbours with deep draught capacity were few, and possibly restricted to the Piraeus, Rhodes, Alexandria and Syracuse. The

32 *View of bust of the 'philosopher' from the Antikythera Wreck, now in the National Museum in Athens*

majority of Mediterranean maritime settlements were dispersed along shallow protected inlets, alluvial fans, coastal lagoons and narrow coves that could hardly accommodate large, seagoing cargo vessels. Smaller ships, particularly galleys, were preferable for most coastal trade, requiring as it usually did manoeuvring past obstacles without the benefit of sails, or beaching rather than docking along some artificially constructed quay. The sources do indicate, however, that larger cargo vessels, two and three-masted behemoths such as the *Isis* and the *Syracusia*, cruised the 'trunk lines' of the open sea between the major centres (Casson 1971: 184–199). How many of these were under sail at any one time is impossible to say. The smaller carrying capacity of most Mediterranean cargo ships probably means that the number of vessels at sea at any one time was actually quite large. Our best information in this regard arises from military emergencies, as when Hellenistic kings and Roman generals commandeered the available shipping capacity of a given area for a specific war effort. For example, when P. Cornelius Scipio Africanus ordered that merchant vessels sailing along Sicilian coast be seized and brought to Lilybaeum to prepare for his assault on Carthage in 205 BC, his dragnet yielded 400 transports. Similar requisitions by Roman commanders in western Mediterranean waters are recorded in 248 BC (800 cargo vessels bearing grain from Italy to the army in Sicily), 212 BC (130 'laden' cargo vessels seized at Utica), 48 BC (200 cargo ships seized in the same city), and 36 BC (1,000 transports collected from throughout the Roman province of Africa).[30] In eastern Mediterranean waters, kings and generals marshalled similar numbers of cargo vessels during periods of conflict, including 400 transports assembled by King Antiochus III of Syria at the Battle of Raphia in 218 BC; 200 used to convey his army to Greece in 192; 1,600 reportedly assembled by Sulla to convey his army from Greece to Italy in 83; and 100 'extremely large' cargo ships commandeered by P. Cornelius Dolabella in Lycia in 43.[31] Documented numbers of vessels such as these, relatively static over time, present themselves for the eastern and western Mediterranean alike, particularly in the areas such as Sicily and Lycia, where commercial shipping naturally collected. The military character and relative accuracy of these figures notwithstanding, their consistently high counts seem compelling. Despite their annalistic character, these figures, drawn from all points of the Mediterranean, offer potential 'snapshots' of the available numbers of cargo ships, large and small, that plied the Mediterranean sea-lanes at this time. A recent estimate of Mediterranean shipping during the early medieval era posits that something in excess of 5,000 cargo ships sailed the eastern Mediterranean waters during the sixth century AD.[32] The combined shipwreck and literary data for the late Hellenistic/Roman Republican era suggest that a considerably greater number would have been active during the period in question.

Amphora remains

As the preceding discussion of shipwreck data clearly demonstrates, many of the chronological assessments of Roman maritime trade depend on the discovery and proper identification of amphorae found as cargo. Ancient potters designed these ceramic shipping jars to be handled and poured by a single labourer (**33**). For this reason they tend to be fitted with two opposing handles near the top of the jar for handling and a graspable toe or foot at the base for tipping and pouring. Although shapes can vary widely, during the period in question they tended to be closed, cylindrical forms with narrow mouths, elongated necks that broadened slightly to form shoulders, and long tapering bodies that ended in some form of solid, thickened foot or toe. Potters turned the forms segmentally, using relatively coarse, quick-drying clays, then 'soldered' the 'leather-hard' sections together with wet clay, and added final

33 *Hellenistic amphorae of the Athenian Agora. Rhodian, Knidian, Chian and Italian (Will type 10) amphorae recovered from Sullan destruction levels in the Athenian Agora.* Based on Grace 1979: fig. 36

details such as rims, handles and toes before firing. The mouths of amphorae were stoppered in a variety of fashions, most usually with rounded plugs of cork or other wood sealed on top by a layer of pitch or dried clay.[33] During the early Hellenistic period, amphora shapes tended to be stoutly piriform, that is, broad at the shoulder and tapered inward below. However, over the course of the second and first centuries BC the forms of the most widely distributed Graeco-Roman amphorae became taller, narrower and more cylindrical. Italian jars of this period were particularly tall (generally 1m) and heavy with large, collar-like rims, long thick necks and handles, and long thickened toes, frequently fashioned as spikes. This development clearly coincides with the rise in shipwreck data, and hence with the rising volume of Mediterranean maritime trade.

An amphora's upright form and narrow toe rendered it incapable of standing alone; it needed to be leaned against a wall or neighbouring amphora, or set in ring-like stands or tripods specifically designed for this purpose. The weight of a fully laden amphora (as much as 50kg) and its long ungainly form also rendered it an exceedingly difficult container for overland transport. It would have to be positioned upright and balanced carefully on the back of a pack animal or in a wagon to avoid spillage (Koehler 1986). In short, potters designed amphorae for one purpose, to be stacked in the holds of cargo ships. The narrower forms not only enabled better packing in the space provided, but their design also appears to have furnished the vertical resistance necessary to withstand the enormous pressure of the two to five layers of jars stacked above them. More than any other artefact, therefore, amphorae furnish the essential remains of maritime transport. Although primarily used to transport three widely dispensed commodities (wine, olive oil and garum), their functionality, portability and relative ease of production, rendered amphorae useful as shipping containers for a number of products, including fish, fruit, nuts, honey, paint, pine pitch, pine cones and, in some arid regions, potable water.

For the period in question amphorae offer themselves as extremely useful artefacts for purposes of dating. Many other remains of ancient maritime trade, such as woollen goods, textiles and wood products, decompose over time and leave no archaeological record, rendering quantification impossible. Other more durable remains such as metal wares, glass wares and stone elements do survive, but fail as yet to provide adequately precise chronological markers. Although amphorae were produced throughout the Mediterranean and imitations of widely circulating forms were commonplace, the number of amphorae with wide distribution patterns remained relatively limited and uniform, making them uniquely suitable instruments for the analysis of Roman trading patterns over time. Amphora remains are found in virtually every landscape and excavation within relative proximity to navigable waters including inland rivers. Their durability, distinct features, and immense size render even small diagnostic fragments such as rims, handles and toes, relatively easy to recognise. Their recovery from archaeological contexts by the thousands has enabled amphora researchers, particularly over the past 30 years, to identify distinct typologies and morphologies, that is, the chronological progressions to changes and adaptations to specific forms over time. The mere shape of an amphora can reveal a great deal about its origin and period of use. In addition, the presence and/or absence of various amphora types in excavated contexts of several major sites have enabled researchers to assign fairly narrow 'use chronologies' to given forms, generally periods of less than a century. 'Closed contexts' furnished by destruction levels at Carthage and Corinth (146 BC), at Samaria (108 BC), at Athens and the Piraeus (86 BC), and at Delos (87/69 BC) furnish hard dates with which to assess wider patterns of amphora distribution.

The discovery of dozens of amphora kiln sites, often revealed by the presence on the surface of mountains of misfired amphora debris, and the analysis and comparison of amphora fabrics, meanwhile, have enabled specialists to assign numerous widely circulating forms to specific, highly localised regions of production. Literary testimony for agricultural production in these same areas, sometimes combined with analysis of organic residues found inside intact containers, help to identify the likely commodities borne by individual types. The association of individual amphora types with the export production of specific agricultural regions, or even with a specific polity, lends these forms one of their most salient and important characteristics. Market authorities somehow rigorously controlled the design of widely traded amphorae, with respect to both shape and volume. Although literary testimony fails adequately to explain the mechanisms, stamping of amphora handles, rims and shoulders, and graffiti inscribed on amphora necks and shoulders demonstrate that their production and movement was monitored by any number of professionals including the proprietors of pottery firms themselves, associated landholders and merchants, and state officials.

Amphora typologies

It is particularly with respect to the dating and quantifying of stamped amphora remains that the preliminary results of decades of amphora research offer insight to the direction of Roman maritime trade. While allowing for some deviation, a consensus holds that several Greek polities produced a unique style of jar, the shape of which helped to identify the character and origin of its contents. Of the four most widely distributed Greek amphorae during the period in question, three – Rhodian, Knidian, and Koan – were produced by communities at the south-east entrance of the Aegean where maritime shipping so commonly assembled. The fourth, Chian amphorae, represent a sustained history of wine production, documented as early as the sixth century BC. Chian vineyards produced the world's most expensive wine (**34**).

The amphora used to convey Chian wine became an important icon of the island community's productive capacity, so much so that its likeness appears on Chian coins.[34] In the period in question the Chian amphora was tall (*c*.95cm; volume *c*.20 litres) and slender with an extremely long cylindrical neck and similarly long rolled handles turning downward from high on the neck to attach at the shoulder. Toward the base of the neck the form flared outward to

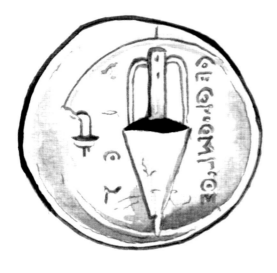

34 *Illustration of Chian silver coin displaying Hellenistic Chian amphora on reverse.* Based on Grace 1979: cover image

an angular shoulder, turning again sharply downward and tapering to a long 'needle-like' toe at the base. The fabric was fine, hard and darkly red. Stamping of Chian jars occurs irregularly, but the form and fabric are so distinctive that Chian remains are relatively easy to distinguish.

As noted earlier, Rhodian amphorae (c.85cm tall; 24 litres volume) were the most widely distributed of the early Hellenistic era, completely dominating the export trade of the Mediterranean and Black Sea basins. With its rolled rim, narrow cylindrical neck, rounded shoulder, inward tapering body, and solid 'peg' toe at the base, its form set a standard for Hellenistic amphorae widely imitated throughout the surrounding region.[35] Its most characteristic trait was its sharply 'pitched' or upturned handles, both of which were stamped during the peak periods of production. The eponymous magistrate who appears to have monitored wine exports from the island, presumably for fiscal purposes, stamped one handle.[36] The magistrate's name is frequently accompanied by emblems, such as the Rhodian rose, or the chariot of Helios. The precise import of the second stamp remains debated. One possibility is that it desig-nated the name of the merchant who ordered production of a batch of amphorae, and thus distinguished his jars from those of other merchants being fired simultaneously.[37] According to this logic the merchant would purchase the amphorae from the production firm and transport them empty to a waiting vineyard. There, he would fill them with the vintage purchased from the proprietor.[38] Owing to such meticulous efforts at supervision, virtually every surviving Rhodian amphora handle from the period in question was stamped. In the case of the stamps bearing magisterial names, this allows for the recon-struction of extended sequences of stamps ranging across five broadly defined periods.[39] These procedures correspond with everything known about Rhodian commerce. As the federated state of Rhodes acquired overseas territory, it extended its production activities to neighbouring islands and the opposite mainland, imposing its standards on the design of Knidian and Koan amphorae in turn. Because of the multiple production areas, the fabric of Rhodian amphorae tends to vary (Hesnard 1986: 72f.). The most commonly encountered fabric is hard, fine buff-red clay, frequently with a cream surface slip. Cut with seawater, as noted above, the wine was common and widely affordable to consumers throughout the seas. In addition, the activity of Rhodian merchants as middlemen to the Ptolemaic grain trade appears to have opened the door for combined shipments of wine and grain. This may explain the form's wide distribution during the first half of the Hellenistic era.[40]

During the period of Rhodian hegemony (197–167 BC), Knidian wine production closely imitated Rhodian standards.[41] Cut with seawater like Rhodian, Knidian wine was relatively inexpensive, and its amphora (c.90cm tall; 39 litres capacity) was closely based on the Rhodian model. The jar's rolled rim and narrow cylindrical neck broadened at the base to form a high rounded shoulder (**35**). The form then tapered inward somewhat gradually to the toe.

Handles were oval and though slightly arched, not as angular as Rhodian. The amphora's most distinctive feature was its toe, pointed with a roll of clay fashioned just above the tip to form a distinctive 'ring-toe'. These toes are easily recognisable when found in isolation. The fabric was fine, somewhat chalky, reddish clay that is buff-coloured at the surface, turning dark red toward the core. Like Rhodian, a cream slip or wash covers the surface. During the period of Rhodian hegemony eponymous magistrates stamped Knidian handles with a regularity imitating that of Rhodes. Knidian nomenclature is not as well recorded, however, and a period of stamps naming *phrourarchoi* has generated considerable disagreement among scholars.[42] Frequently encountered Knidian stamped emblems include the *bucranion*, or facing head of a bull, the *caduceus*, the trident, the ivy leaf, the ship's prow, the anchor, the double axe and the club of Herakles (**36**). Although not as widespread in the wider Mediterranean as Rhodian amphorae, the distribution pattern of Knidian amphorae in the Aegean demonstrates an important trend in Roman maritime trade, as will be seen.

Like Knidian amphorae, Koan amphorae (*c.*80cm tall; 45 litres volume) were strongly influenced by their Rhodian models.[43] Earlier jars exhibit the same rolled rim and narrow cylindrical neck, although not as tall as the Rhodian examples (**37**). An offset ridge tends to separate the neck from the flaring line of the form's broad shoulder. The body remains fairly broad, curving inward towards the base to form a short thickened toe fashioned with a small projecting basal knob to absorb shock. The fabric is relatively coarse and ranges from tan to red to brown, frequently displaying a pale green surface wash that presumably results from 'seawater slipping'.[44] The unique Koan handles, small, closely set, double-rolls of clay sharply pitched in imitation of the Rhodian handle, are the most salient features of all Koan amphorae. By the end of the second century BC the body was made slimmer and more streamlined, but the double-rolled handles continue to identify Koan remains in archaeological contexts. Koan jars were irregularly stamped, possibly one jar per batch has been suggested, and some of the later stamps appear in Latin, indicating gradual acquisition of the island's wine production by Italians, as will be seen (**38**).[45] As noted above, Koan wine was highly prized by Tamil kings in India. In his agricultural treatise, Cato indicates widespread popularity in Italy as well, so much so that he furnishes a recipe for doctoring the taste of homegrown Italian wine to imitate that of Koan. Italians were not alone in this regard. By the middle of the first century BC production of 'Koan style' amphorae became widespread throughout the Mediterranean, from the coasts of Spain and Campania to those of southern Anatolia. The presumption of specialists is that the rolled rims, narrow necks and double-rolled handles of these forms were meant to signify that, wherever produced, the wine's bouquet resembled that of Koan.[46]

35 (Left) *Early second-century BC Knidian amphora in the Alanya Museum*

36 (Above) *A Knidian amphora stamp with bucranion at Delos*

37 *Koan amphoras of the Mithradatic era at the Delos Museum*

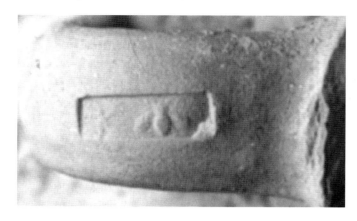

38 *View of Koan amphora handle (probably third century BC) stamped with a 'bee'. From Kinet Hüyük*

Italian amphora production

Roman amphora specialists have for a long time worked with classifications of Roman amphorae according to broadly defined 'families' of forms. This has led to considerable confusion. In the course of nearly sixty years of field research, E. Lyding Will has furnished more precise analysis, based on fabrics, forms, stamps and contexts.[47] The earliest 'Roman' forms consist of Will types 1a–d, known more generally as Graeco-Italic amphorae (early third century to mid-second century BC). Will type 1a, an early Graeco-Italic wine jar with wide distribution, was manufactured in various places throughout Greek-speaking regions of the Mediterranean, most significantly in Sicily.[48] Will type 1a amphorae exhibit a narrow mouth and low flaring rim, a short neck extending to broad shoulders, and a disproportionately wide body. Its short toe is cylindrical and hollow; its short handles S-shaped and oval in section. Its fabric consists generally of fine buff clay.[49] Will views type 1b as a transitional form and type 1c as a relatively rare form, even though hundreds of type 1c amphorae were discovered in the lower wreck at Grand Congloué.[50] On the other hand, Will type 1d (*c*.250–150 BC) occurs very widely throughout the Mediterranean, with particularly large concentrations found at the Italian harbour of Cosa. Closely resembling Will type 1a, type 1d is larger, with a longer neck and handles (**colour plate 21**). Its toe is solid and the clay at Cosa tends to be coarse, sandy, pinkish yellow-buff clay. The appearance of stamps and graffiti marked [. . .] *ES* and *M. SE.* on these forms indicates that production at Cosa was initiated by the wealthy and prominent Etrurian family of the Sestii, mentioned above. The production of this wine amphora coincides with the development of the port at Cosa, including a winery and commercial fishery (**39**).[51]

During the late second century the Sestii and other western producers adapted the form of this small amphora to meet the growing demand for exports from Italy. The new form, known generally as the Dressel 1 after the

German epigraphist who first catalogued their presence at Rome, became the bellwether of Roman commercial activity throughout the Mediterranean. The point of intersection between the new form and the previous Graeco–Italic jar appears, once again, to lie at Cosa. On the basis of the abundance of Sestius stamps and the common pinkish buff fabric, Will has successfully demonstrated a progression from Will type 1d to Will type 4a, a form of Dressel 1 produced in massive quantities at Cosa. Will's type 4a (late second to mid-first century BC) are remarkably uniform in dimension, suggesting closely co-ordinated production on a mass scale. The Sestii most probably achieved this through the employment of large numbers of slave potters at workshops in the harbour, as indicated by the wide array of production marks that appear in Sestian stamps. Will type 4a amphorae are very tall (generally over 1m; 22 litres capacity) and

39 *Will type 11, type 10a, and type 4a amphorae at Delos Museum*

slender (average diameters 28–30cm), with long necks in relative proportion to their bodies. The thick collared rims of type 4a slope or flare out into a pendant fold, constituting one of the type's main characteristics. Mouth diameters average 14–16 cm. Both the cork and the *pozzolana* stopper in type 4a are regularly set well down into the neck (Hesnard and Gianfrotta 1989) (**40**). The form's neck narrows towards the bottom into a sloping shoulder that merges with the body at a distinctly angular join. The body then tapers gradually to the toe, which is somewhat short and squat, but solid (average diameter 5–6cm). Equally long close-set handles flank the form's long neck. The fabric is characteristically coarse, pinkish buff, with a lighter surface slip; the Sestius stamp is usually impressed on the rim.[52]

That the Etrurian port of Cosa was the primary production centre of Will type 4a amphorae seems certain: 70 per cent of the amphora remains at the port excavations at Cosa consist of Will type 4 amphorae, and some 86 per cent of the stamped remains are Sestian.[53] In addition, as noted above, marine archaeologists discovered some 1,200–1,500 of these amphorae (Will type 4a) in the upper wreck of the Grand Congloué, most, if not all, stamped with Sestian production marks (Will 1987a: 174). In 44 BC, Cicero mentions that his political ally, the senator, L. Sestius, possessed *navigia luculenta*, splendid ships, that he could lend to the effort mobilising against Mark Antony. As Will and others have noted, the upper Grand Congloué wreck was quite possibly one such example.[54] To judge from the wide distribution of Sestius stamps at sites in western Mediterranean area, especially France, Sestian wine production dominated the western Mediterranean markets until the mid-first century BC.[55] A slightly later version of this form, Will type 4b (Dressel's form 1b, *c.*75–25 BC), were likewise produced at Cosa, though its primary production areas appear to have been southern Latium and Campania.[56] The Sestii also produced a third form, Will type 5 (often called Dressel 1c), apparently to carry garum from the Cosa fishery (**41**).[57]

The production of several additional Italian amphora forms is more complicated and awaits further discussion by Will. One very complicated 'family' of amphorae, produced along the northern Adriatic coast of Italy and Istria, Will has now classified into a range of separate forms (Will types 3, 6–10, 13–14).[58] Commonly known as 'Lamboglia 2' after the Italian archaeologist who first attempted to classify them, Will has identified one particular form, Will type 10, as an olive oil jar, based, among other things, on the presence of a graffito (*OLEA*) found on the neck of one of these forms at Delos.[59] From the thick collared rim down to the shoulder these forms display a development similar to the Will type 4s: slightly shorter (*c.*90cm tall; 31 litres capacity), their necks tend to be wider, flaring outward to an offset join at the shoulder. From here the form displays a sagging bag-shaped body, tapering sharply inward at the base to form a long spiked toe. The handles are long, thick and round. Those at Delos, where archaeologists continue to excavate significant quantities, tend

40 (Above) *Stamped stopper to a Will type 10 Italian amphora at Delos*

41 (Right) *Will type 5 Italian amphora at Delos*

to exhibit a gritty pinkish-buff fabric with a slightly green 'seawater slip' on the surface and are frequently stamped on the rim. Less frequently encountered in the western Mediterranean, the form was clearly exported eastwards where it shows up in significant quantities in the Aegean and beyond. Will's type 11 amphorae represent a similarly complicated group, commonly referred to as 'Brundisian Ovoid'. Kilns for Will type 11a (first century BC) have been identified near Brindisi, convincing Will and others that the form transported the celebrated olive oil of Venafrum, mentioned by Varro for both its high quality and massive production.[60] Although the collared rim bears resemblance to those of the other Italian forms (the one in the photograph slopes inward from the top, with a groove near the base; the diameter of the mouth is 16cm), the body is nearly spherical, and the thick, rolled handles are short and bowed (**39**). The fabric is orange buff with a cream 'seawater slip' on the surface. These too occur in large quantities at Delos and are frequently stamped on the rim (**39**).

Together with the eight classifications of widely circulating amphorae noted above, the distribution of one last form requires comment, this one from Carthage (**42**). Despite the fact that the Roman destruction in 146 BC interrupted its production, discoveries of the Mana C form (named by the scholar who classified it) at Athens, Delos, Ephesos, Bodrum and at several ports in

42 *Mana C amphoras in the Delos Museum*

Israel, including Ascalon and Joppe, demonstrate that its distribution continued in the following period.[61] 'Torpedo-shaped' and generally 1m tall (*c.*35 litres capacity) the form exhibits a broad, platter-like rim (frequently moulded) and funnel-shaped neck that narrows to rounded shoulders. Its long cylindrical body ends in a long, thick spiked toe. Lug handles characteristic of Phoenician forms from earliest times are set just below the shoulder. The fabric tends toward a reddish buff while the surface generally exhibits a thick layer of greenish-white 'seawater slip'. Although distribution totals and analysis of their stamps remain preliminary, it is clear that the contents of this form, Carthaginian wine, oil or garum, was enjoying widespread popularity throughout the Mediterranean before as well as after the sack of Carthage.

Distribution patterns of stamped amphorae

Forms, volumes, archaeological contexts and inscribed stamps of widely circulating transport containers offer a crucial insight, therefore, into the history of Roman trade in this period.[62] As the literary testimony indicates, some sort of transition clearly occurred during the decades between the war with Perseus and the defeat of the Cilician Pirates (167–67 BC). Evidence of amphora distributions indicate that Rhodes lost its dominant maritime commercial position in several long-standing markets – the Western Mediterranean, the Adriatic, and parts of the Aegean, and to a good degree expanding exports from Roman Italy account for this loss. Recent analysis of the remains of stamped amphora handles appears to furnish reliable quantifiable data capable of putting developments in perspective. Despite a number of limitations with this form of evidence, the consistency of the patterns of distribution of stamped amphora handles at key centres such as Athens, Delos and Alexandria in the late second century BC remains striking. The ratios of Rhodian, Knidian and Italian stamped handles at these places has remained relatively fixed over time, notwithstanding the continuing discovery of whole amphorae and stamped handles. This suggests that the ratios reflect reasonably reliable records of the patterns of distribution of commercial transport jars to permit their use in historical analysis.

Amphora remains of the third and early second century indicate that Rhodian wine exports dominated all three markets of Athens, Delos and Alexandria. In the decades following the foundation of the free port at Delos, however, conditions in Athens, Delos and elsewhere underwent a dramatic change, with expanding distributions of Knidian wine jars supplanting the formerly dominant Rhodian ones. For example, of 40,000 stamped handles collected in the Athenian Agora by 1979, 65 per cent originate from Knidos, displacing Rhodian stamped handles by a 3 to 1 ratio (Grace 1979: 12).[63] At Delos, where most of the contexts date to the late second and early first centuries BC, specialists report that from a total number of 7,079 stamped handles examined by 1965, 61 per cent are Knidian, 22 per cent Rhodian and 9 per cent Italian. As excavations continue at the Athenian Agora and at Delos, the relative distribution of these types of stamped amphora handles appears to hold steady. Knidian wines appear to have gained supremacy in these markets by the end of the second or early first centuries BC, and similar patterns of surging Knidian imports are demonstrable elsewhere, such as Tenos and Argos. Rhodian and Italian handles finish a distant second and third respectively. When compared in this manner, Rhodian handles might appear to be more numerous than Italian, but one must allow for the likelihood that a very large percentage of Italian handles and rims (perhaps 90 per cent) are unstamped (Will 1987a: 183). Accordingly, the quantity of Italian wine jars may actually have surpassed that of Rhodian jars at Delos.

A similar pattern appears to emerge for the distribution of Chian and Koan amphorae at Delos (Grace and Savvatianou-Petropoulakou, 1970: 281). The count of stamped amphora handles of these jars – each less than 2 per cent of the total pattern in 1970 – is small in comparison to Knidian, Rhodian or Italian, but the infrequent and indeterminate manner by which Chian and Koan amphorae were stamped undoubtedly distorts their patterns of distribution. Some specialists argue that the quantities of these jars were probably much greater than the count of their stamped handles indicate. Insofar as Koan amphorae are concerned, however, the emerging quantities of Koan remains at Indian Arikamedu suggest that a large percentage of Koan wine travelled out of the region altogether.

The ratios of distributions of stamped amphora handles at Alexandria, in the Graeco-Roman Museum and in the Lucas Benaki collection, demonstrate an opposite tendency, namely, an increasing Rhodian monopoly of the Egyptian wine trade toward the end of the second century. In 1965 Virginia Grace reported identifying 80,000 Rhodian handles, 6,860 Knidian, and 980 Italian. By 1979 she had studied 90,000 stamped handles, identifying 85 per cent as Rhodian (Grace 1979: 12). In a later, chronologically-oriented analysis of approximately 17,435 specimens in the Benaki collection, Grace was able to demonstrate that the Rhodians exported 68 per cent of these jars (11,885) between the years 146 and 88 BC. She also noted that dated Knidian handles, and hence exports of Knidian wine to Alexandria, fall off sharply after 166 BC (Grace 1979: 26). In short, the distribution pattern of Rhodian stamped handles at Alexandria statistically overwhelms those of the Knidian and Roman distributions. Unlike developments in the Aegean, Rhodian wine exports to Egypt appear to have risen dramatically in the period after 166.[64]

A regional count of stamped amphora handles in Cyprus supports evidence for a sustained flow of Rhodian wine at that Ptolemaic outpost as well. Specialists believe that Rhodian exports to Cyprus during the second century actually drove locally produced Cypriot amphorae into extinction and helped to establish a Rhodian commercial monopoly. Most of these exports occurred, however, during the first half of the second century, before 166 BC. The quantities of Rhodian handles in Alexandria remain staggering, all the same, and raise significant implications for an expanding Rhodian monopoly of the Egyptian grain trade. Recent, more precise analysis of Rhodian amphora stamps in Egypt indicates that the period between 140 and 120 BC possibly represents the peak of the Rhodian amphora trade.[65]

Rather than experiencing commercial decline after the emergence of the Delian free port, Rhodian wine producers appear to have concentrated their wine exports at eastern Mediterranean markets like Alexandria, apparently at the expense of other long-established markets in the Aegean and elsewhere. Apart from Athens and Delos, Rhodian wine exports to the western Mediterranean, Adriatic and Black Sea regions decline dramatically in the late second century. This information needs to be coupled with the overwhelming archaeological evidence for a massive penetration of Italian wines in Gaul and Spain, where archaeologists have unearthed millions of Will type 4 and 5 amphorae of the late second and early first centuries BC, and the Adriatic, where Will type 10 and related amphorae are the forms most commonly discovered. Even though the precise volume of Rhodian wine exports to Adriatic and western Mediterranean markets before 166 BC remains difficult to establish, by the end of the second century Italian wine and oil producers appear to have secured a virtual monopoly in these regions.

The position of Italian wines in the Aegean and eastern Mediterranean remains more difficult to evaluate. Large quantities of Will type 10 and related amphorae have emerged at Athens and at Delos, yet, as the distribution ratios demonstrate (9 per cent of the total stamped handles at Delos), their numbers do not compare with those of imported Knidian wine jars. The high ratio of Rhodian to Italian stamped handles in Alexandria likewise tends to confirm the low yield of Italian amphorae in the eastern Mediterranean. Despite what was undoubtedly a fairly significant commercial presence in Alexandria, Italian wine merchants do not appear to have penetrated this market extensively. This would suggest that the movement of Roman exports into the eastern Mediterranean waters was limited and confined largely to the Aegean areas where Roman settlements and provincial administration aided in their circulation.[66] This restriction of Roman trade evidence to the Aegean seems telling not only with respect to the large Roman presence in Alexandria, but also with respect to literary reports, noted above, of Roman collusion in a slave trade with the eastern Mediterranean pirates of Cilicia. This trade reportedly continued from 138 BC until at least 102–100 BC when Roman authorities began waging war against the pirates. Assuming that exchanges at Delos involved amphorae laden with Italian agricultural exports, one specialist hypothesised that much like in France, remains of Italian amphorae should be detectable at settlements of the Cilician pirates.[67]

Since 1996 a regional survey directed by the author has explored the vicinity of one supposed pirate base, the promontory of Antiochia on the Kragos Mountain, presumably the same Kragos that is mentioned by Appian

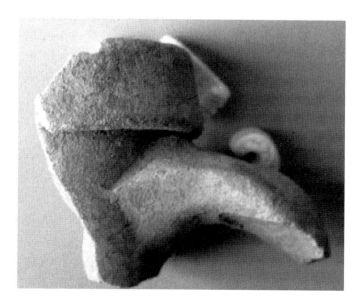

43 *Remains of a Will type 5 amphora found at Kinet Hüyük*

as the stoutly fortified citadel of the pirates. Preliminary indications, such as the presence of a Will type 1 (**colour plate 21**) and a Will type 10 amphora (found in neighbouring waters) in the Alanya Archaeological Museum, the misidentified publication of a stamped neck of an Italian amphora at the excavations at Tarsus in Cilicia Pedia, and confirmed finds at Issos and Israel, led the author to believe that surface remains of Italian amphorae would be detectable in the survey area (**43**).[68] Provisionally, the author can report that seven seasons of pedestrian survey in the wider vicinity of Antiochia on the Kragos, some 120 square kilometres of surface exploration, have yielded practically no evidence of Republican-era transport amphorae from Italy.[69] As will become apparent below, what little surface information has emerged for 'piracy' in the region of the Kragos is complicated and subject to varying interpretations. With respect to Italian amphorae of the period, though, the evidence seems to indicate that their trail grows colder the further one advances eastward from the Aegean.

Assuming that the ratios of amphora distributions confirmed by exploration and analysis at Athens, Delos and Alexandria are accurate and provide tentative proof of the reliability of other published ratios throughout the Mediterranean, these ratios reveal several patterns of distribution. For some reason Rhodian wine exports to traditional markets in the western Mediterranean, the Adriatic, the Aegean and the Black Sea declined in the latter half of the second century, although the extent of a decline in Rhodian amphora production remains debatable. Overall production and exportation of Rhodian wine may actually have accelerated in this period through a methodical effort at monopolising Rhodian control over a restricted range of the eastern Mediterranean markets such as Cyprus and Egypt. In the western Mediterranean, meanwhile, Italian wines became dominant in Italy, Sicily, Gaul, Spain and the Adriatic and point, as Will suggests (1989: 298), to a deliberate programme of Italian economic expansion. Following the destruction of Carthage, Italian amphora remains in the Aegean region likewise become significant; however, their concentrations decline the further eastward one advances beyond the south-east corner of the Aegean.

By far the most significant development in amphora distribution patterns of the Aegean during the period in question arises with Knidian amphorae and their dominance of amphora remains in Athens and Delos. As noted earlier, specialists have suggested that the inhabitants of Knidos and Kos adapted the volume and shape of their amphorae at this time to Athenian standards precisely to exploit the demand for wine at the burgeoning emporium at Delos. If true, this would demonstrate a categorical shift in Knidian and Koan wine production away from their former Rhodian influence to that of Athenian-run, Roman-dominated Delos. Such a development can only have worked to the disadvantage of Rhodian wine traders – at Delos, at Athens and throughout the Aegean, most particularly in the Roman province of Asia.

The shift in amphora distribution patterns in the Aegean, particularly the replacement of Rhodian amphorae by rising quantities of amphorae originating from Knidos, Kos, Chios and Italy at Delos and Athens, appears to mark the epicentre of the changing fortunes of Mediterranean trade in this era. Italian amphorae became dominant in the west; Rhodian amphorae remained dominant in the east. Here at the point of convergence, the amphorae of a number of less conspicuous maritime powers appear to have surged. A cursory examination of the historical background of these three states indicates that they had entered into a relationship of economic co-operation with Rome. Chios, for example, enjoyed status as a *civitas libera*, that is, a free and independent city, prior to the Mithradatic War. Despite solid evidence of a Roman commercial presence and property interest on the island, the city was presumably immune from Roman tribute. Since its harbour lay situated within the confines of the Roman province of Asia, commerce passing through it probably remained subject to Roman *portoria* or customs dues. This alone could explain the prominence of the Roman community on the island, with its host of tax collectors (*publicani*), subcontractors (*mancipes*), and associated *negotiatores* and *mercatores*, and its service as a *conventus civium Romanorum*. By 88 BC, Appian (*Mith.* 47) reports that Italian entrepreneurs had acquired direct possession of the city's most prized agricultural estates. In other words, Italian entrepreneurs probably seized control of these particular vineyards, precisely at the moment that Pliny assigns the initial importation of this luxury wine to Italy (*NH* 18.45).

Prior to the Mithradatic War, Kos and Knidos, on the other hand, appear to have stood outside the limits of the province of Asia and were not in the least subject to its Roman governor. Kos enjoyed status as a *civitas libera*, and Knidos perhaps even greater status as a *civitas libera et foederata* (a free and allied city with treaty relations with Rome). While Roman officials possibly subjected their inhabitants to other exactions – military requisitions and levies, hospitality toward visiting Roman dignitaries – these cities presumably were exempt from Roman tithe collection. Having said that, the similarities in the patterns of amphora distribution and in commercial and social tendencies among the Chians, Koans and Knidians appear remarkable, particularly when combined with the political evidence for a neighbouring maritime city, the independent and autonomous state of nearby Kaunos. Although we know nothing about the likely export trade of Kaunos in this era, its example supports the emerging pattern of commercial co-operation between the independent maritime cities of south-western Asia Minor and Rome. Rome specifically recognised the freedom and autonomy of Kaunos when it seceded from the Rhodian alliance in 167 BC, and the city remained outside the Roman province of Asia, free and independent down to the Mithradatic War. By 88 BC, large numbers of Romans and Italians had taken up residence there, undoubtedly taking advantage of its attractive harbour-lagoon. The Kaunians nonetheless massacred these Romans and

Italians during the Mithradatic invasion of that year. The *civitas libera* of Kos likewise hosted Roman residents in 88. Augustan-age evidence to suggest that the Koans enhanced the status of these *Romaioi*, as opposed to other resident alien *paroikoi,* by furnishing them with the privileged right of property ownership: *egktesis ges kai oikias.* Much like the *Romaioi* at Chios, therefore, the Roman residents of Kos very conceivably owned wine-producing estates on the island. As noted above, the inhabitants of Kos modified the standards of their wine jars and their coinage at this time, presumably to conform to the Athenian standards in use at the *emporium* at Delos. In addition, archaeologists at Kos have found Koan amphorae stamped in Latin.

The inhabitants of the *civitas libera et foederata* of Knidos, meanwhile, appear to have received their initial treaty from Rome toward the end of the second century BC. Like the Koans, the Knidians modified the standard of their amphorae to conform to those in use at Delos.[70] In addition, the prominent display of the inscribed stele bearing the Roman 'Law of Piracy' (101–100 BC) in the 'Trireme Harbour' of Knidos demonstrates that a large concentration of Roman and Italian merchants conducted business and sought assurances of public safety in that harbour, and hence worked, if not resided, at Knidos.

Independent or otherwise, the status of Chios, Kos, Knidos and Kaunos does not appear to have precluded close economic and commercial co-operation with the merchants and traders of Roman republican Italy. This co-operation included daily traffic of Roman and Italian traders in each of their harbours, the residence of Roman and Italian merchants in three and possibly all four cities, the opportunity for Romans and Italians to enjoy property rights and to engage in the production of the very wine in question in at least two of these locales, and the adaptation of 'municipal' wine jars to conform with the standards of the burgeoning (Roman) emporium at Delos in three. All four of these states held strategic positions in the eastern Mediterranean – Chios a crucial stepping stone to the coastal cities of the Roman province of Asia, Kos, Knidos and Kaunos at the eastern entrance to the Aegean where owing to the character of the winds, maritime traffic invariably tended to collect. For Roman traders seeking routes to eastern luxuries these maritime cities offered substantial advantages.

The behaviour of Kos, Knidos and Kaunos becomes all the more remarkable when contrasted with that of their neighbours and rivals, the Rhodians, in the same period. Unlike Chios, Kos, Knidos or Kaunos, the *civitas libera et foederata* of Rhodes, having received a treaty from Rome in 165 or 164 BC, adhered to its own traditional standards of amphorae and coinage, apparently undeterred by administrative developments at Delos. Unlike their neighbours, the Rhodians appear to have admitted very few Roman and Italian merchants into their community, or at least there is very little evidence for this. In contrast to the growing appeal of Knidian, Koan and Chian wines, the consumption of Rhodian wine declined in the Aegean as Roman influence expanded. When one pauses to consider that the Rhodians had only recently dominated the foreign and commercial affairs of Kos, Knidos and Kaunos in much the same manner as the Romans were doing now, the inference seems obvious. The inhabitants of these free and independent cities had in some unknown fashion fallen under the sway of Roman 'commercial hegemony'.

Differences in attitude and behaviour between Rhodes and its former allies, Kos, Knidos and Kaunos, continued into the Mithradatic War. Unlike those cities the Rhodians adhered faithfully to their Roman alliance, readily receiving the fleeing army of C. Cassius, the governor of Asia, along with droves of Roman refugees, and valiantly resisting the siege of Mithradates' admiral, Archelaus. This contrasts remarkably with the actions of its neighbouring states. Though the Koans were able through extravagant bribes to spare the lives of the Roman refugees holed up in their Temple of Aesculapius, they greeted the Mithradatic forces of Archelaus gladly. Mithradatic elements likewise controlled Knidos when L. Licinius Lucullus arrived in the region in 85 and 'persuaded' its inhabitants to revolt (along with those of Kos). The Kaunians, as noted above, actively participated in the Pontic king's massacres of Romans and Italians. As closely aligned commercially with the Romans as these three 'independent' cities had been in the preceding years, their loyalty to Rome during the war seemed grievously wanting. One might even suggest that the more tightly integrated the inhabitants of these Greek cities became with the Roman trading elements, the more palpable was their display of animosity during the Mithradatic conflict.

Assuming that Kos, Knidos and Kaunos were autonomous, independent, and immune allied states prior to the war, three plausible explanations come to mind for their close commercial co-operation with Rome at the end of the second century. One, the location of these cities in the same corner of the Mediterranean as Rhodes, combined with the presence of Roman wine producers and merchants in their harbours and their total exclusion from the harbour of Rhodes suggests that these cities co-operated closely with Roman and Italian trading firms active in the East, even as the Rhodians did not. The location of all these harbours at the area where westward coastal traffic confronted the northerly winds of the Aegean cannot be overlooked. As noted earlier, before the prevailing winds the outbound voyage to Alexandria was relatively manageable by a number of routes; however, the return trip invariably entailed a labourious crawl along the coasts of Palestine, Syria and southern Anatolia. Close commercial and economic co-operation between Kos, Knidos, Kaunos and Rome may reflect little more than the value of these places as layover points for the Roman and Italian merchants struggling to make the return leg to Delos from the East. These harbours provided Roman traders with three friendly points of shelter – apart from Rhodes – in the face of adverse winds.

A second possibility concerns the tendency of commercial relations to anticipate legal and diplomatic ones by several years. The amphora evidence quite possibly documents the earliest patterns of Roman trade in eastern Mediterranean waters and does so at a time when Rome possessed no territorial rights beyond the Aegean. Roman and Italian traders who sailed into these waters probably found the legal forms of status available to them in regional harbours – status in various degrees as resident aliens – unacceptable, and shopped around for concessions. In lieu of support from any official Roman presence, they probably relied on informal arrangements with the inhabitants of allied cities, or at least with the inhabitants of those cities willing to welcome them into their harbours. Benefits and concessions earned in this fashion would not necessarily surface in the legal or diplomatic historical record. The eagerness of cities such as Chios, Kos, Knidos and Kaunos to compete openly with the Rhodians for market shares in the Aegean maritime trade may alone account for their extraordinary openness towards Roman merchants at this time.

A third explanation for close co-operation with Rome assumes the likelihood that merchants in these cities served as middlemen to the Roman slave commerce and eastern luxury trade at Delos. Although Strabo (14.5.2 (669)) insists that these slave sales occurred in the Delian harbour, his testimony lacks confirmation in the Delian remains where no explicit reference to a slave trader, a slave market, or a Cilician 'trader' has survived. According to Strabo, the Pamphylian port of Side served as an intermediary harbour in this trade. Merchants reportedly purchased prisoners from Cilician pirates at the municipal dockyards, most likely for intended resale to the Romans at Delos and beyond. Cicero provides similar testimony for the Lycian states of Phaselis and Korykos and for Pamphylian Attaleia.[71] Perhaps the harbours of Kos, Knidos and Kaunos functioned similarly. Pirates or pirate-aligned middlemen from states such as Side, Attaleia and Phaselis possibly transported prisoners to these harbours for resale to the Roman and Italian traders and property holders recorded there. While there is no proof, the role of these maritime cities as 'stepping stones' in a slave and luxury trade that extended from Cilicia to Delos would attractively explain not only the significant presence and distinct status of the Romans and Italians working in these harbours but the expanding importation of Knidian and Koan amphorae at Delos. Local merchants would naturally have added wine and other locally produced goods to the cargoes being loaded in these harbours. Given the westward trending direction of this coasting traffic, the emergence of significant concentrations of Knidian and Koan amphorae in the central Aegean becomes logical.

Regardless of the precise reasons for the close commercial co-operation between the independent cities of Chios, Kos, Knidos, Kaunos and Rome, the evidence for this co-operation underscores the importance of eastern Aegean harbours to developing patterns of trade. The evidence thus assembled not only addresses the volume of Mediterranean trade but its direction, and that direction was consistently one of eastwardly expanding commerce by Rome.

Not only does it conform to the shipwreck data furnished earlier, but it demonstrates as well how the Romans managed by the late second century to assemble a trading network that extended from Spain and Gaul in the west to eastern Aegean states such as Chios, Knidos, Kaunos and Kos, and by association with Koan amphorae conceivably all the way to Arikamedu in India.

The shifting distribution patterns of Roman and Rhodian amphorae throughout the Mediterranean, with Roman wares driving Rhodian out of the western Mediterranean and moving into the Aegean, indicates as well that this expansion came at the expense of the island republic. Accordingly, the decision of cities such as Kos, Knidos and Kaunos to co-operate with Rome in and of itself implies a tacit divergence on their part from long-standing ties with Rhodes. Romans were visible in these harbours, they were invisible at Rhodes; Roman influence in the Aegean was expanding, Rhodian influence waning. The implications for commercial hegemony raised by the evidence at Chios, Kos, Knidos and Kaunos point to the existence of closed trading networks that in some manner excluded Rhodes. The behaviour of the inhabitants of Kos, Knidos and Kaunos during the Mithradatic War seems equally informative. Evidently one of the dangers independent states confronted after entering into commercial co-operation with Rome was the tendency of Roman traders never to leave, once installed in eastern harbours. Their financial prowess, their commercial contacts, and their political influence enabled these Romans and Italians to intensify their presence in nearly every instance, ultimately enabling them to acquire possession of the most productive agricultural estates of the host cities. Antipathy to this Roman presence during the Mithradatic War, if not outright hatred, appears to have been a quite natural consequence. The inhabitants of the Rhodian republic seemed well aware of this. They were apparently willing to accept the full consequences of exclusion from Roman imperial markets as the inevitable price for their commercial and political independence.

Conclusion

Shipwreck and amphora data extending from the coast of west Spain to the east coast of India tend to confirm the pattern of historical movement described in the previous chapter. Roman amphorae and cargo vessels drove formerly dominant Hellenistic mercantile elements out of the western Mediterranean in the same manner that Roman legions eliminated maritime populations in Carthage, Corinth and the Piraeus. Distribution patterns of internationally traded amphorae indicate that once the Roman senate had humbled Rhodes, Roman merchants pushed ever further eastward towards Alexandria, the main emporium for goods arriving from the Indian Ocean. The history of the Roman conquest of the Mediterranean world was to no small degree a history of Roman domination of foreign trade.

4

Roman trading society
merchants, sailors, and the maritime mob

The years marking the transition from the Hellenistic to the Early Roman era were characterised by urban development, rising material prosperity, nagging social tensions and highly destructive conflicts. From end to end the Mediterranean bustled with agricultural, artisan and maritime activity. Cities large and small formed the nodes to a maritime transportation network conveying the grain of Egypt, the metals of Spain, the garum and fish of North Africa, the wines of the Aegean, the statuary of Asia, and the dyed textiles of Syria and Phoenicia to the emerging core society of Rome. The reactionary, ever-wary foreign policy of the Roman senate during the course of the second century BC kept not only the capital city of Rome but also the entire Mediterranean empire in a decidedly unfinished state. Forced movement of hundreds of thousands of slave prisoners from the region's periphery to its centre had destabilised urban societies and settled agricultural communities everywhere. Repeated urban disturbances flared up throughout the seas. Piracy raged throughout the eastern Mediterranean waters, along with conflicts provoked by King Jugurtha of Numidia in North Africa and King Mithradates VI of Pontus in central Anatolia. Ethnic hostilities in Seleucid Syria and Judaea, rebellions throughout Spain, the Aegean and the Balkans, and eventually open civil war in the Italian heartland all testify to seething animosities that inaugurated the 'new world order' of Rome. In the midst of this confusing, highly unstable situation, Mediterranean merchants and sailors busily assembled the trade routes that enabled the basin's economy to expand.

Roman merchants

Ancient merchants lived within the margins of Mediterranean urban society (**44**). Cicero (*Verr.* 2.5.167) publicly describes the bulk of the Roman traders as 'obscure men of limited means', a highly revealing expression. A century later Tacitus (*Annales* 4.13.2) could refer to the lifestyle of a descendant of the

44 *First-century BC Roman fresco showing Roman merchant galley under sail approaching the coast.* Based on a painting from a villa near Sirmione

illustrious Sempronius family, reduced to the status of a common merchant after falling out of favour at the imperial court, as wholly inappropriate to that man's station in life. These observations serve as indicators to the social disparity that existed between aristocrats and traders. Rarely did actual members of the urban elites exhibit themselves in the trading emporia, onboard cargo ships or at distant centres of the luxury trade. Epigraphical records at Delos and in Italy demonstrate that traders bearing Greek names conducted the bulk of the trade for the land-dwelling aristocracies of the Italian peninsula and that a high proportion of these traders hailed from slave origins (Rauh 1993: 30f.).

Roman senators and the members of town councils throughout the Mediterranean could afford to hold themselves aloof from trade. Most of their wealth lay in land, and as landholders employing an array of working elements to conduct their farm work, they produced sufficient resources to furnish their everyday needs without undue dependence. However, in order to obtain the luxury goods that our sources indicate they desired, they needed to liquidate some portion of their accumulated assets by participating in the wider commercial economy. Converting their best lands into efficiently run estates to produce export quantities of agricultural produce, such as wine and olive oil, marked one avenue widely employed at this time. However, once accumulated the money raised by this and other means, including profits from warfare, could itself reap greater return when invested as liquid capital. As Plutarch (*Cat. Mai.* 21.6) relates about the second-century BC Roman senator Cato the Elder, 'he used to loan money in the most disreputable of all ways, namely, in shipping.' As noted earlier, Cicero's friend and senatorial ally, L. Sestius of Etruria, is known to have possessed a commercialised estate at Cosa, seagoing cargo vessels and personal interests in southern Gaul. Thousands of amphorae stamped with the Sestian logo have been recovered not only at their kiln centre at Cosa, but in shipwrecks and at excavations throughout France.[1] In short, at this level of society private affairs were so extensive, and assets so manifold and dispersed, that their proprietors arguably directed whole portions of the commerce of the empire.

To accumulate greater wealth, Roman senators put their money in the hands of equestrian capitalists, non-senatorial members of elite aristocratic families who specialised in managing the business of the empire. This last-mentioned group was of course highly diverse: some such as Cicero's friend Atticus maintained the pretence of being too 'well bred' to engage in the 'sordidness' of commerce, an affectation that stands in direct contrast with the unabashed commercialism of the era. Nevertheless, people such as Atticus possessed considerable accumulated assets, investments and property throughout the Mediterranean. Atticus' agents, usually freedmen or Italian businessmen of lesser means, could cash letters of credit for Cicero in the province of Asia, monitor Atticus' loans in Athens, and manage his valuable herds in Epirus. What little 'commerce' Atticus did engage in might be said to have been conducted 'informally' and exclusively among friends – albeit among friends situated in high places (Rauh 1986). Despite the presumption that people at the highest levels of society attended solely to private affairs, such affairs invariably entailed overseas trade.

Others at the top, with fewer pretensions than Atticus, took active roles in the business of the empire, as publicans or investors in public contracts. Poised at the top of the business world, these people were powerful, aggressive and influential. Cicero would not dream of calling their work sordid, however inclined he may have been to disparage that of their employees labouring in the company offices throughout the provinces. Given the degree to which publican financial interests were bound up in the affairs of state, these people took an avid, even aggressive interest in the political conflicts of the late Republic and behaved in an extroverted manner quite at odds with the retiring demeanour of Atticus. According to Cicero, C. Rabirius Postumus, the agent of Pompey who assumed control of the finances of Egypt in 58 BC, 'was very active in the public arena, conducting a great deal of business, for he possessed considerable shares in the publican companies'. Postumus also lent money throughout the Mediterranean, employed a freedman agent at Ephesus and

Naxos, engaged in overseas commerce with his own cargo fleet (importing paper, linen, and glass from Egypt), and produced wine and oil for export on his own profitable landed estates.[2] The careers of these men were in many ways as public as those of Roman senators, therefore. When their interests were at stake, Roman publicans could be counted on to browbeat Roman senators by shoving their way through the voting assemblies in the forum.

Beneath these elements the ranks of the business world subdivided into layers of various professionals. *Negotiatores* were merchants who engaged in overseas *negotia*, an ambiguous term that usually entailed money-lending along with several other activities integral to foreign trade. These professionals conducted private business and grew prosperous, laying the foundation of status promotion for future generations of their families. Enjoying similar status were the managers of publican companies and financial agents of the Roman aristocracy. Active at local levels as the agents directly responsible for overseeing the collection of Roman tithes and tariffs, these people had to navigate their way past bad harvests, defaulting provincial landholders, impoverished councils and communities, merchants cunningly evading import and export duties, the greedy concerns of stockholders back in Rome and, not least, the meddling and often directly competing interests of corrupt Roman officials. Beneath publicans stood private businessmen of lesser means, *mercatores*, or common traders who engaged in some limited facet of overseas trade. *Mercatores*, declared Cicero (*Verr.* 2.5.167), were 'poor men of humble birth sailing across the seas to shores where they were unknown, arriving among strangers and without benefit of acquaintances to vouch for them'. Their decision to go to sea was determined most likely by unexplained circumstances that jeopardised their families' inherited estates, since few men of any means voluntarily went to sea to conduct trade. As Plautus has the son of the wealthy merchant explain in the *Mercator* (78), 'When grandfather died, father sold the farm and with the money bought a cargo ship of 15 tons burden and sailed about selling cargoes of merchandise everywhere, until at length he acquired the wealth he now possesses.'

A decision to sell one's farm cannot have come easily. The anxiety induced by a trading career generated nerve-fraying potential. When the son of Plautus' merchant came of seagoing age, his father 'built me a Corcyrean galley ship, bought merchandise, loaded the now completed vessel with cargo, and lastly counted me out 6,000 drachmas with his own hand. A slave who has been my guardian since I was a boy was assigned to monitor my efforts. Having undertaken these preparations, we weighed anchor. We arrived at Rhodes, where I sold my whole cargo quite to my satisfaction. In fact, I made a big profit over and above the price my father set for the merchandise and thereby obtained pocket money for myself.' Accumulated profits such as these ultimately enabled merchants to retire from the sailing business altogether and to remain on dry land, in many instances by speculating financially in the ventures of others as a resident alien, or metic, at some foreign port. As a former merchant residing in the Piraeus during the fourth century BC explains ([Dem.] *against Apaturius* 4-5), 'I, men of the jury, have by now for a long time been engaged in foreign trade, and up to a certain time risked my own life at sea. About seven years ago I gave up voyaging and, having accumulated a modest capital, I try to put it to work by making loans on overseas ventures. As I have visited many places and spend my time in your exchange, I know and am known to most of the seafarers among you.'

The actual shippers and traders tended, by and large, to be men of servile origin, acquired through the Roman law of slavery by families intent on maintaining their control over distant commercial operations. These people will have originated primarily from eastern Mediterranean regions, Greeks from Asia Minor, Phoenicians and Jews from Syria and Palestine, Egyptians from Alexandria. Emerging as they did from regions long inured to trade with the East, these traders enjoyed the advantages of good business sense, proficiency in the required languages, and personal knowledge of regions far removed from trading horizons of native-born Romans and Italians. They were naturally skilled in the logic of identifying useful trading goods, negotiating advantageous contracts, handling accounts, making profits and enduring risks.

The fact that their home regions were fast sinking into political disarray furnished additional incentive for eastern Mediterranean merchants to engage in business for Roman creditors. At the close of the Hellenistic era, the Seleucid dynasty in Syria imploded into a century-long ordeal of dynastic disputes and civil wars, leaving the region seethed with ethnic animosities. The Ptolemies in Egypt – long weakened by their border wars and court intrigues – regularly battled urban Alexandrian uprisings and native agricultural mutinies in the hinterland. To maintain what little they could of their former share of the eastern luxury trade, the Ptolemies had succumbed to the confidence rackets of Cilician pirates cruising the seas, as well as to armed robber bands that controlled the overland highway between the Nile and the Red Sea. Given the prevailing chaotic conditions, some eastern merchants sought access to Roman trading communities as the surest means to negotiate their escape from the approaching chaos, with the prospect eventually of transferring their assets westwards.

Although a maritime career could rebuild a noble's fallen fortunes or enrich that of an ambitious freedman, it did not come without risk. Unlike landholding elements, ancient merchants wilfully exposed themselves to an inescapable variety of dangers. Hard-won knowledge of the sea could enable maritime voyagers to avoid submerged rocks and shoals, or failure to make landfall through erroneous navigation, but it could do little to divert violent storms, contrary winds that drive vessels off course, sudden raids by pirates, or worse, confiscation by warring states at sea. Adrift at sea with expensive, heavily mortgaged cargoes stored in the hold, the Roman merchant had no acropolis for refuge when confronted by armed hosts with hostile intent. Even assuming that one were fortunate enough to escape the perils of jettisoning cargoes during storms at sea, of running aground on jagged rocks, or encountering armed ambuscades by pirates lurking amid the islands and craggy heights that bordered the main sea-lanes, endless rounds of swindling and bureaucratic difficulties awaited merchants in every crowded port.

In the cramped, dingy harbour towns of the Mediterranean seaboard, a foreign merchant entered a culture of outlandish lies and masculine bravado (**45**). The bravado came naturally from the various risks of travel by sea and the courage this travel required. The lying arose from endless rounds of negotiation. Merchants had to play their hands like gamblers, since the nature of the business required that each and every participant secure profit while enduring numerous financial nicks and cuts from the fees of tax collectors, moneylenders, market officials, warehousers, shop dealers and innkeepers. On every quay merchants confronted harbour dues, import and export fees, display fees, weights and standards fees, sales taxes, storage fees and the daily cost of lodgings. The universality of lies and deception in the marketplace inherently kept merchants alert and dealings sharp. A foreign merchant had little choice but to make friends quickly with local business authorities (usually with

45 *Sailors unloading a cargo of amphorae. Relief found at Portus and now in the Torlonia Museum in Rome*

substantial financial priming) in order to staunch the financial bleeding. This same foreign merchant would just as quickly double-cross his friends, creditors and sureties if profit warranted, by promising tithes to Mercury and Hercules, the gods most inclined to overlook the perjuries of businessmen. Fraudulent dealings often gave way to lawsuits, and, given the international composition of the maritime population, these marketplace contests often assumed overtones of ethnic hostility, particularly when merchants from the 'Roman West' locked horns with those from the 'Greek East'.

Since the highest profits accrued from commerce conducted in war zones, the most dogged of merchants followed closely in the wake of armies, offering stores and supplies at inflated prices while purchasing prisoners and captured booty for a discount at military auctions. The tendency of our sources to recount the bizarre deaths of merchants who strayed too close to the front – besieged by Gauls outside the Roman camp at Aquileia, squashed by elephants near the battlefields of Numidia, ambushed by Celtiberians in the remote Spanish highlands – provide some insight to the risks their activities entailed.[3] The maritime world was both coarse and violent; it was definitely no place for the weak. Merchants strolled about the wharves in broad-brimmed hats, loud-coloured cloaks, and patches over one eye. As Plautus bellows, 'That's the maritime mode – look smart, look trim.'[4] Roman traders assessed the risks of a maritime venture and gambled with both their lives and their livelihoods. They stored accumulated resources in warehouses throughout the Mediterranean and gradually but perceptibly constructed the lines of trading empires. The endgame of any merchant slave working for Roman creditors was freedom, profit and fame (**46**).

The remains of merchant-like bravado are frequently plain to view. For example, a Roman trader at Delos, C. Ofellius M. Ferus, erected a giant statue of himself in a prominent place within the ground-floor portico of the so-called Agora of the Italians – with statue, niche and portico all having been bought and paid for by Ofellius himself. The statue's nude form of a robust athletic youth reveals the mindset of this wealthy merchant. Bearing a lance in its right hand, a sword in its left, it deliberately imitates the stance of a celebrated and often imitated study of Alexander the Great (Queyrel 1991). In other words, C. Ofellius, the Roman merchant, commissioned the celebrated Athenian sculptors, Timarchides and Polycles, to create his likeness in the mould of the greatest of all world rulers. He might as well as have proclaimed that he was buying and selling the world that Alexander had previously conquered.

At the level of a common trader one arrives at the great social divide between impoverished landholding elements and servile elements rising from below. While many freeborn merchants were forced to sell their estates and risk their worth on cargo ventures, the successful freedmen began with nothing, yet, managed through hard work, ability and luck to accumulate sufficient

46 *The statue of C. Ofellius M.F Ferus from the Agora of the Italians at Delos. In Delos Museum.*

47 *The house of the Herms at Delos* – The Maison de l'Hermès at Delos, *excavated in 1949-1950; view from the north*

assets to purchase their freedom and to obtain financial security. In a speech fragment Cicero (*Orator* 232), for example, claims to have known of slave traders, merchants and 'Syrian and Egyptian eunuchs' who were wealthier than any member of the patrician Cornelian, Claudian, or Fabian families at Rome. At Delos, large, magnificently furnished mansions, such as the House of the Herm (**47** & **48**), with its elaborate terrace design, its double-storey Doric marble peristyle, its statue group by Praxiteles, its niches, its eight marble herms, its assortment of additional statues and statuettes, its multiple stairways, and its external liturgical paintings were inhabited by wealthy slaves, perhaps the very slave traders in question (Rauh 1993: 219f.). Another merchant recorded at Delos, C. Heius T. f. Libo, was probably identical to the provincial landowner by the same name who resided at Messana in Sicily. His elegant mansion exhibited gold embroidered tapestries from Pergamum and statuary by Praxiteles, Myron and Polyclitus – pieces so prized that people throughout Sicily and Italy flocked to see them (Rauh 1993: 56). Despite its satirical bravado and grotesque exaggeration, Petronius' description of Trimalchio's rags-to-riches story in the *Satyricon* (76) captures the essence of the entrepreneurial spirit rapidly pervading Rome (**48**).

48 *View of the interior groundfloor peristyle court of the House of the Herms at Delos*

My master left me coheir with the emperor, and I thus acquired his patrimony and my freedman's toga. But easy wealth never satisfies anyone. I yearned to try my hand at business. To cut to the chase, I had five ships built and stocked them with wine – worth its weight in gold at the time. Then I shipped them off to Rome. I might just as well have told them to go drown themselves since that's precisely what they did. Yes sir, all five of the vessels shipwrecked. No joke. In one day old Neptune swallowed down 300,000 sesterces. Was I licked? Hell no! The loss just whetted my appetite for more. So I built some more ships, bigger and better and a good deal luckier. No one could argue that I didn't have the guts. Like they say, big ships make a man feel big about himself. I purchased a cargo of wine, bacon, beans, perfume and slaves. In the end my wife Fortunata had to bail me out, selling all her gold and the very clothes off her back just to put 100 gold coins in the palm of my hand. Those coins proved to be my winning ticket. What the gods want done gets done in a hurry: on that one voyage alone I cleared 100,000. Right away I repurchased my master's property. I built a house; I went into slave trading and cattle-buying. Everything I touched turned to profit. Soon I had acquired the worth of all the people in my home town combined, so I cashed in my chips. I retired from trade and turned to money lending through my freedmen.

Men such as these generally pass into view when conducting business with their Roman superiors – facilitating some transaction for Atticus and Cicero, arranging purchases and maritime shipments of statues and slaves, or appealing to some Roman governor for assistance. These were the people with the most at stake in local harbours and who did their best to assemble the requirements of a marketplace wherever they conducted business. The overseas population of Roman business people (including freedmen and slaves) appears to have been prodigious – 20,000 scattered throughout the Aegean, 80,000 to 100,000 in the province of Asia by 88 BC (Rauh 1993: 27).

Much like the inhabitants of the House of the Herm at Delos, Trimalchio and his wealthy freedmen dinner guests represented the *nouveau riche* of Mediterranean maritime society. Although their slave origins prohibited them ever from obtaining aristocratic social status, their entrepreneurial skills left them garishly wealthy and free to flaunt their superiority before the impoverished orders below. These were the 'big shots' of the everyday maritime world, the kind of men ordinary traders, shippers, sailors and slaves looked up to and aspired to become. People like Trimalchio faced the dangers, borrowed the money, and established the trading contacts with distant producers, proprietors and luxury traders from remote ends of the ancient world. When smart and lucky they took their profits. The religious dedication that stood above the door to Trimalchio's fictional mansion (*Satyricon* 60) unabashedly proclaimed the merchant's patron saints: 'Wages, Good Fortune and Profit'.

In the mind's eye of the wider Mediterranean public these merchants fared rather poorly. Almost universally the sources decry their behaviour as rapacious, corrupt, ruthless and sometimes downright murderous. When they were not busy corrupting Roman officials, 'railroading' innocent provincials through promagisterial tribunals, or fleecing elderly matrons of their ancestral estates, Roman *equites, publicani* and *negotiatores* can be seen charging outrageous rates of interest, subjecting defaulting provincial borrowers and taxpayers to heinous forms of torture, and seizing their family members as slaves.[5] A closer inspection reveals, however, that 'Roman' traders generally toiled with the everyday tasks of conducting business in a high-risk environment. The nature of their work required them to construct cosmopolitan communities remarkably open to Hellenistic Greek ideas, customs and people. The degree to which Mediterranean outsiders sought access to Roman business communities suggests that they appreciated this 'openness' and exploited it. Successful outsiders such as the fictional Trimalchio, for example, acquired Latin verbal, written, and commercial skills, and by working toward manumission (and personal prosperity), assimilated themselves into the mainstream of 'lower-class' republican society. As the houses and statuary of the emporium at Delos demonstrate, Romans there were receptive to the advantages of Hellenistic Greek household science, architectural design and sculptural trends. Although the material remains of this island confirm the prevailing mindset of its *nouveau riche* community, merchant appreciation for sophisticated trends in Hellenistic art, for example, seemingly contradicts various descriptions of these professionals as rustic, uneducated boors. By accepting the character of the Roman business community as it was, warts and all, one is able to recognise its place at the vanguard of Mediterranean cultural development.

As closely as they lived and worked, the members of the Roman merchant class, nevertheless, stood a considerable distance from the labouring classes beneath. As explained below, the greatest difference between merchants and ordinary seamen was the degree of risk they incurred. The very notion of risk possessed different shades of meaning at different ends of the social spectrum. Those at the top – aristocrats, *equites*, publicans and moneylenders – saw risk purely in terms of the capital they invested in mercantile ventures, either as bottomry loans, purchases of cargoes, construction of ships, hiring of crews or consignment of agricultural surpluses. More often than not, these entrepreneurs opted to remain safely within the confines of their agricultural estates and urban townhouses. The common seaman, on the other hand, could be dispatched into harm's way under any circumstances. In a word, Roman merchants essentially controlled the course of maritime life for all who laboured beneath them; a common sailor could only pursue the fate his wages assigned.

Mediterranean sailors

Far less is known about the experiences of common seamen during Antiquity than about those of their merchant superiors. Seamen emerged from a lower stratum of society that generally leaves little record of itself, forcing one to compensate for this ethnographic meagreness by reconstructing the phases of their work lives. To an overwhelming degree the lives of ancient sailors were moulded by their workplace, the seagoing merchant vessel. One must necessarily begin with descriptions of these formidable machines.[6]

The ancient cargo ship was a highly complex machine, the most technologically advanced workplace of its era. Its full mastery required of its workers knowledge and experience with a wide array of tools and equipment. The great majority of ancient Mediterranean seagoing ships were built shell-first by the so-called mortise-and-tenon or draw-tongue joint technique. The best-preserved example is unquestionably the Kyrenia wreck noted above, dated c.310-300 BC.[7] The ship's 13.6 m. hull was constructed of Aleppo pine, with tenons of Turkey oak and a pulley-block of mulberry; it was sheathed below the waterline in lead and carried a single sail. Its hand-made construction serves as an impressive example of craftsmanship. Its keel, stemposts, sternposts and strakes were carved with the adze to a complex shape and fitted painstakingly together with thousands of joints. The shipwrights constructed each join by drilling and chiselling out two mortises on each end of two adjoining strakes, placing them together over a false tenon and locking the whole joint with two holes bored through the strakes and the tenon, made fast by driving in small treenails. The interior framing was then attached to the hull segment by segment, with the shipwright relying on the emergent hull shape, rather than lofted lines, to cut most of the frames. This type of construction produced a strong, firm hull, but was expensive in terms of both skilled labour and high-quality timber. It was also more appropriate to smaller vessels, since shipwrights would have found the job of lifting inboard and trimming the frames of large ships such as that of the Madague de Giens gruelling work.[8] In the period in question hulls were strengthened in a number of ways. Archaeologists have identified lead sheathing, such as that employed with the Kyrenia, on fifty-seven shipwrecks whose dates indicate that this was very common during the period in question. However, other designs of the period employed double layers of bottom planking, sometimes lined with thick fabric in between. Most wrecks reveal extensive use of caulking both inside and out with pitch, resins, paint and vegetable pastes to reduce leakage and to discourage marine fouling.[9]

An Egyptian papyrus of a ship's lease from the third century AD details the sorts of equipment required by any sizable merchant vessel: 'mast, yard, linen sail, ropes, jars, rings, blocks, two steering oars with tiller bars and brackets, four oars, five boat poles tipped with iron, companionway ladder, landing plank, winch, two iron anchors with iron stocks, one one-armed anchor, ropes of palm fibre, tow rope, mooring lines, three grain chutes, one measure, one balance yard, Cilician cloth, one cup-shaped two-oared skiff fitted with all appropriate gear, and an iron spike'.[10] A merchant ship was too big and unmanageable a machine to be run by novices; it took tremendous skill, experience and co-ordinated effort by a crew of four to six men to make it sail.[11] To operate such a large vessel an experienced sailor was trained in the exercise of fixing a vessel's machinery and of applying it to the purposes of navigation. This training included knowledge of riggings and sails, how to steer the ship, how to splice lines, and how to read the winds, the weather, the skies and the moods of his superiors.

Going to sea required an organisation of labour sufficient to enable a sailing vessel to exploit the advantages of wind, water and currents. The ancient sailor laboured on what was in essence a frail wooden vessel surrounded by omnipotent forces of nature, often imparting a special urgency to his co-operative effort. The physical demands of his work required extraordinary strength, stamina, dexterity and agility; its dangers required courage and a constant renewal of initiative and daring. The character of seafaring work and its lonely setting – isolated as it was from mainland populations – contributed to the formation of a strong labouring identity among sailors (Rediker 1987: 83). As we shall see, it created a separate maritime culture for an ethnically diverse underclass of wage labourers.

To direct the ship and its crew, Roman merchants and their investors selected a small cadre of officers who most generally rose from the ranks of ordinary seamen – the *navicularius* (ship's owner), the *magister* (ship's captain), *gubernator* (second officer), *proreus* (first mate), the *toicharchos* (second mate) and the *faber navalis* (ship's carpenter). Beneath these served the *nautae* or ordinary seamen (Casson, 1971: 300f.). The *navicularius* was most often an entrepreneur who specialized in the management of one or more merchant vessels. The *navicularius* was the one who organised the arrangement of cargoes of various merchants on board, determined their intended destinations and, most particularly, secured the necessary financing to fund a merchant run. As Petronius (101) remarks about the ship's captain Lichas, 'Lichas of Tarentum is an extremely respectable man. He not only runs this ship, he owns it. Moreover, he's a large landowner and the head of a trading house. At the present moment he's shipping a cargo on consignment.' Given the weight of his responsibilities and financial and contractual obligations they required, a *navicularius* was generally a freedman or freeborn. The degree to which *navicularii* actually travelled with their vessel(s) remains uncertain, since their work largely required their presence on shore. Once at sea, the *navicularius* assigned all aspects of sailing process, particularly on large vessels, to the direction of the ship's *magister* or captain.

The *magister* was generally responsible for fitting out the vessel, including the hiring of a sailing master and presumably the rest of the crew, for maintaining the ship in good repair, and for all administrative matters, particularly arrangements concerning cargo and passengers. Naturally, he also exercised considerable authority over the crew and directed much of the ship's activities once underway, including handling the tiller. The skill required to pivot the ship's huge steering oars with its fragile steering bar earned the respect of land-dwelling passengers such as St Augustine (*Enarratio in Psalmum* 31.4), who marvels at the dexterity of the helmsman in high seas, 'manipulating the steering arm, keeping the bow to the waves, and preventing the ship from broaching to'. Barring mutinies or panic-induced crises, the captain's authority on board was absolute; together with the *navicularius* and *proreus* he formed the ship's tribunal with the authority to judge any crimes committed on board (**49**).

When out at sea the *gubernator*, or sailing master, enjoyed fairly wide authority in all matters relating to the ship's handling, barking commands for the direction of the ship's sail and its course. Ancient merchantmen of all sizes were basically square-rigged vessels employing one broad square sail set amid ship. Some of the largest seagoing vessels employed two- and three-masted square rigs, and fore and mizzen sails were also added, though their function remained secondary (Casson 1971: 239f.). The mainsail was the ship's primary means of propulsion and in most representations of ancient freighters it dwarfed the rest of the canvas. The *gubernator*'s basic chores – steering, rigging, and sails – were crucial, therefore, to the rate of the ship's progress, which in

49 *Scene from a relief showing sprit-rigged cargo ship entering the harbour in a strong gale. From the sarcophagus in Ny-Carlsberg Glyptothek, Copenhagen*

turned depended directly on the work performed on this equipment. The *gubernator*'s skilful performance ultimately determined the speed and hence the profitability of a given voyage.

The *proreus* was the *magister*'s second in command for the direction of the ship and would assume command in the event that anything untoward occurred to the *magister* himself. The *proreus* stood on the foredeck to study the depth of the sea, using a sounding lead to detect the closely rising sea bottom (Oleson 2000). Sounding leads are fairly commonly discovered in ancient shipwrecks, varying in weight between 3 and 13kg (*c.*20cm tall by 16cm wide at the base). Somewhat bell-shaped, they were hollowed out underneath in various manners to receive fat or grease with which to collect samples of sediment from the sea floor. The character of the sediment, sandy, muddy, if any, would indicate to the *proreus* the quality and proximity of the seabed. This form of underwater 'divination' obviously required many long years of experience. Otherwise, he attended to the ship's maintenance and saw to it that hull and gear remained in good working condition. The administrative side of things was in the hands of the *toicharchos*, who combined the functions of a purser and supercargo, taking care of both passengers and cargo. Among the likely duties of this officer were the settling of passengers' and merchants' nerves during rough sailing and in the worst likely circumstances, determining which cargoes would be jettisoned during storms.

50 *Ship's faber completing a boat, late second or early third century AD. Relief from the tombstone of P. Longidienus, Archaeological Museum, Ravenna*

The *faber* or ship's carpenter was another extremely important officer in a world of hulking wooden vessels (**51**). His responsibilities were to maintain the soundness of the ship, repairing masts, yards, boats and machinery, checking the hull, applying pitch to the seams of planks, and wooden plugs to leaks to keep the vessel tight. Tools, sometimes an impressive basketful, have been recovered from at least forty-nine ancient shipwrecks, carefully maintained for odd jobs and repairs on board.[12] Evidence of repairs, such as the replacement of two strakes on the Madrague de Giens wreck, is visible on many shipwrecks, indicating that ships' carpenters worked to maintain the seaworthiness of merchant vessels for as long as possible (Parker 1992: 27). Thirty-two ancient wrecks have produced the remains of ship's pumps, most significantly the wreck of the Dramont D, where four bronze piston-driven machines were discovered.[13] Sometimes the vertical wooden trunk and continuous disk-chain that raised water to the deck level survives, but quite often, as with the Grand Congloué, the Albenga, and the Madrague de Giens, archaeologists have found the lead collector and twin pipes that evacuated the bilge-water overboard, lying on top of the cargo (**51**). The carpenter's search for a leak often required that he wade through stagnant bilge water with potentially overpowering vapours. Bilge water was so great a problem on ancient merchantmen that the *faber* frequently detailed a seaman, generally the least able member of the crew, to keep a constant eye on it. A seaman thus sentenced endured an arduous voyage of baling and manning the pump. As Plautus opines (*Menaechmi* 401), 'What ship are you talking about? A wooden one that's been scraped, caulked, and repaired time and again. It has more pine plugs patching its planks than a furrier's shop has pegs for display.' Since a tight ship demanded little pumping, sailors revered the skilful carpenter who could keep this dreaded back-breaking work to a minimum. Large cargo vessels required additional subordinates including a cargo clerk, quartermasters and ships' guards. In addition, pilots to navigate vessels through particularly treacherous waters were essential labourers to be hired from approaching localities.

In the reverse logic that so typified ancient commercial thinking, the positions aboard ship most directly associated with contracts and the handling of money such as the *magister* and *toicharchos*, would normally be entrusted by the ship's owners and investors to slaves, thus guaranteeing the firmest possible control over their activities. But the rest of these offices, whose skills ultimately demanded years of training at sea, would be entrusted to experienced sailors risen from former crews. Captains and mates needed to possess first-hand knowledge in navigation, particularly in an era when navigational aids were rudimentary. Good handbooks were available, supplying brief notes on distances, landmarks, harbours, anchorages, and so on, but there is no evidence for use of charts.[14] This placed a premium on the kind of experience that could only be acquired from years of sailing along designated maritime routes. The knowledge of seafaring was contained largely within a broad system of apprenticeship.

51 *Illustration of bronze spigot to the pumping mechanism found aboard the Nemi wreck.* Source: Gianfrotta and Pomey 1981: 290

For the common seaman, work at sea formed a ceaseless existence of physical toil, intense discipline, and risk of bodily harm. The bulk of the seafaring labour process was quite simply the movement of cargo – loading, sailing and unloading the merchant vessel – under frequently challenging conditions at sea. As such, it demanded a co-operative labour process on the part of its workers. Sailors were required to perform a unified set of tasks involving sophisticated machinery within a highly enclosed setting, all of this occurring under intense supervision (Rediker 1987: 83).

First the ship had to be loaded. The arrangement of cargo was important, for its stowage had to take into account the weight, form and type of every commodity as well as the overall balance of the ship. The heaviest goods had to be placed nearest the keel on the very bottom and at the centre of gravity of the ship; other items were stowed according to their packaging. All goods had to be secured to prevent shifting in rolling seas. Sacks carrying 10,000 almonds were packed into the Kyrenia hold alongside 400 amphorae and a heavy load of something perishable such as bales of fabric located in the forepart of the ship (Parker 1992: 231). Other wrecks such as the Grand Congloué and the Madrague de Giens display rows of amphorae carefully packed with brushwood and stacked three and four layers deep.[15] Ballast was often added because a ship required a proper amount of tonnage on board to sit properly, neither too light nor too heavy in the water. More than forty ancient shipwrecks have produced such ballast, often boulders, pebbles, beach rock, clay or sand. Heavy goods such as lead ingots would naturally be loaded carefully at the bottom of the hold to help trim the ship. At the Kyrenia a collection of twenty-nine millstones were laid along one side of the ship's centre-line to compensate for the asymmetry of the hull.[16] The leakiness of a given ship likewise determined the manner in which goods would be stowed, since some forms of cargo had to be housed bilge-free to avoid water damage. For the crewmen the tasks of loading and stowing cargo entailed lifting, hoisting, heaving, stowing and pumping, all supervised by the *magister* and the *proreus*. Deeper-keeled ships needed harbours with quays, but they were better suited to fast open sea passages (Parker 1992: 25). In large harbours with deep moorings and stone quays, such as Alexandria or the Piraeus, winches and wheel-driven cranes may have eased the physical burden somewhat off the backs of common sailors, but in most places the shallowness of the waters necessitated that larger ships moor at a good distance from the shore, making the process of loading cargo from lighters and smaller boats all the more toilsome and hazardous. Rabbinical sources report that large ships in Palestine would anchor off shore where the depth of the water was about ten hand-breadths (*c.*1m). As a rule the ship was brought so close in that its keel very nearly touched bottom. The *proreus* stood at the prow of the ship sounding the depth of the water with a pole, taking care lest the ship run aground on a rock or sandbank. When the ship reached the minimum depth, the anchors were let go and the unloading or the loading began. The stevedores entered the water and waded to the ship carrying merchandise to or from the shore on their heads and shoulders.[17] Another way of unloading and loading was to set up a chain of men stretching from the shore to the ship. The man standing on the ship would hand the load to the man standing in the water next to the ship or fling it to him if the distance was great. If several ships were anchored near one another, the merchandise would sometimes be flung from one ship to the next. Even more strenuous, sailors and stevedores would jump from one ship to the next (Patai 1998: 62). However complicated, the job of loading was difficult and physically draining (**52**).

Once the cargo had been loaded and secured, the emphasis of work shifted from handling the goods to handling the ship. One of the widest misconceptions of ancient maritime activity is that very little rowing occurred in connection with merchantmen. This distinction applied only to the largest of cargo vessels, and even these regularly demanded the oarsmanship of crewmen in 'tugboats' and lighters to make clear of ports and narrow waters before setting sail in the open sea (**53**). The vast majority of small- and medium-sized vessels that plied the rocky, uneven coasts of the Mediterranean relied on a combination of both means of propulsion, sail and oar, like the broad-beamed Corcyrean galley employed by Plautus' merchant son, noted above. Merchant galleys employed rowers not only to supplement wind propulsion in the absence of prevailing winds, but also to steady the movement of the ship when excessive wind prevailed. During the equally common 'stills' of the Mediterranean summer, the progress even of larger sailing craft would inevitably require the strained efforts of seamen exerting themselves from the deck with poles and oars. Rowing was equally essential to smaller oared craft,

52 *Sailor transferring an amphora between ships. From a mosaic at Ostia.* Gianfrotta and Pomey 1981: 47

53 *A harbour tugboat. Third-century AD relief from a tomb in the Isola Sacra between Ostia and Portus*

such as the lifeboats and skiffs that sat on the decks of large ships to cope with the necessities of rescue, and the loading and offloading of cargoes in shallow waters. As a result, galley rowing was almost as fundamental to the merchant vessel as it was to the warship, and a considerable portion of the maritime working population undoubtedly drifted from one occupation to the other depending on circumstances, wages and demand. To the shout of the mate or the beat of the drum, ancient seamen would churn their oars in unison. The poet Statius comments on their inevitable fatigue (*Thebais* 6.799–801), 'when after long wandering over the sea the signal is given from the poop to cease rowing and rest their arms for a while . . . then, following a brief moment of repose, a second cry recalls them to the oars.' (**54**).

Ideally, on reaching deep water the ship and its crew could rely on the propulsion of a favourable breeze. To capture its force required skill, discipline and the co-ordinated efforts of several hands. On any sailing ship raising a heavy sail was back-breaking work. A mast and sail was fitted with a half a dozen or so different ropes each of which held a specific function. Larger sailing ships had to have considerably heavier gear, and most large vessels were equipped with winches and capstans forward to handle the operation (Gianfrotta and Pomey 1981: 289f.). The square-rigged mainsail was sewn with numerous 'brail' lines enabling the sail to be raised, lowered, and tilted at angles to capture the force of the wind. Archaeologists recovered some 176

54 *Relief showing a Roman merchant galley. From Avezzano, now in the Torlonia Museum in Rome*

lead brail rings and several wooden toggles at the wreck of Kyrenia, for example.[18] Virgil (*Aeneid* 3.267–8) describes the effect of the *gubernator* giving the order 'to shake loose the brails and slack them off, as the south wind filled the sails'. This manoeuvre required that the crew, several of whom would be hanging aloft from the yard arms, unfurl the stiff canvas by whipping the brails briskly to get them to run through the blocks and 'fairlead' pulleys. Once the canvas began to flow the seamen would adjust the brails to the proper amount (**55**).

To maximise sail efficiency the yard arms themselves could be raised and lowered by various ropes and pulleys. They could also be tilted at angles verti-cally and swivelled side to side. Given the inherent limitations of square–rig sails in the face of adverse winds, bracing the yard round until it ran from bow to quarter and adjusting its slant toward the wind provided the only effective means to keep the sheet forward of the mast, thus enabling the ship to 'tack' or be driven in opposite directions by the same wind. The crew accomplished this, as Lucan notes (*Pharsalia* 8.193–9), by 'slacking off the lines toward the prow and taking in those toward the stern. The sea sensed the movement and changed its sound, as the prow cut a new course through the water.' Each shift in this manoeuvre required, as Virgil notes (*Aen.* 5.830–2), that the crew guide the lines to 'unfurl the sails, now to port and now to starboard', and that 'they together in unison brace the lofty yards about, then brace them round again

55   *Sailing vessel entering port. Shows sailors climbing the ropes and perched on the yardarms while furling the sails. From the tombstone of Naevoleia Tyche, a shipper of Pompeii*

on new course'. In smaller craft or during strong gales on large merchantmen, the ship, according to poet Achilles Tatius (3.1.3–6), would, 'heel over, lying one side in the water amidships and going high in the air on the other side. Since the ship is all aslant, we all change our position to the high side of the vessel.' Aristotle (*Mech.* 851b) observes similarly that, much like modern day yachtsmen, ancient sailors 'join in the fight against the wind by leaning their bodies in the direction opposite to it'. With each adjustment of the rudder, yard, and sail, the ship would careen from one side to the other, as Tatius notes, 'a third time, a fourth time, many times, we go through the same procedure keeping up with the gyrations of the ship' (**56**).

56 *Cargo vessel under full sail. Third century AD relief found at Portus, now in the Torlonia Museum in Rome*

When the wind blew too forcefully for normal sailing, the crew could swing the yard arms lower on the mast to lower its centre of gravity; in lighter winds it would be raised higher for better speed. Storms, particularly the sudden and violently unpredictable Etesian gales of the Aegean summer, posed a more serious challenge to labouring seamen. As Petronius ominously describes (114), 'the sea suddenly grew rough and great thunderheads towered up on every quarter, utterly blacking out the light of day. Shaking with terror the sailors scrambled to their posts and hastily furled the sails against the gathering storm. But the raging winds cracked down on the ship from every side at once, battering us so wildly that the pilot completely lost his sense of direction. At one moment we seemed to be driving straight for Sicily; at the next we were caught by the North wind, that squalling tyrant of the Italian coast, and pitched about completely at its mercy. But even more ominous than the winds was the sudden darkness, blackness so intense that the pilot, standing on the stern, could no longer see the prow.' Storm gusts inevitably demanded sailors' skill at adjusting the sail, as Achilles Tatius makes clear (3.1.1–2), 'a wind arose from low over the water and struck the ship head on. The captain ordered the yard braced around, and the sailors quickly complied, furling the canvas aloft toward the yardarm by main force on one side because the wind blew too strongly for them to haul the lines against it. As for the yardarm on the other side, they kept just as much of the original spread of the sail as would take the wind at the proper angle to bring the yard around.'

Often the very force of the winds could render impossible the crew's efforts to manipulate the billowing mainsail and the wind-induced rigidity of the yard arms. In these instances the mainsail could, if possible, be lowered and replaced by a smaller sheet referred to by sailors as the *nothos* or 'bastard sail'. In the remarkably detailed account of his stormed-plagued trip from Alexandria to Ptolemais in Libya, the fourth-century AD bishop Synesius (*Epistle* 4) describes how the fifteen-man crew of the ship on which he and some fifty other passengers had taken passage was driven out to sea by strong southerly gales. At nightfall an opposing storm 'commenced to blow from the north, the violent wind soon raising the seas into mountain-sized waves. When this gust suddenly fell on us, it drove our sail back inside-out against the mast, and nearly capsized the ship by its stern.' With the force of the wind intensifying and huge waves menacing the vessel, the panicking passengers frantically joined the crew's efforts to shorten the sails, but they 'were thwarted by the ropes, which were jammed in their sea-swollen blocks.' At dawn the winds abated sufficiently to enable them finally 'to work the rigging and handle the sail'. However, when they called for the *nothos* to replace the mainsail the ship's embarrassed captain informed them that he had left it at port, 'in the hands of a pawnbroker'. Fortunately, they were able to take in the mainsail like 'the swelling folds of a garment. In four hours' time we who had imagined ourselves clasped by the jaws of death were able to disembark in a remote desert place.'

Another tactic with storms at sea was to deploy anchors to create sufficient 'drag' to steady the movement of the ship and thereby to resist the violent force of the winds. During another celebrated storm-swept voyage, that of St Paul from Caesarea to Rome (*Acts* 27), the crew 'put out a sea-anchor and let her drift'. As conditions deteriorated further, 'the sailors tried to abandon ship. They had already lowered the ship's boat, pretending they were going to lay out more anchors from the bow, when Paul said to the soldiers of his guard, "unless these men stay on board you cannot and will not reach safety." At that the soldiers cut the ropes of the boat and let it drop away.' Even the smallest sailing craft were likely to carry several anchors, while the larger ships obviously deployed more, invariably raised and lowered by crewmen plying thick cables through capstans.

The dangers posed by life-threatening storms could ultimately require that the ship's crew jettison cargo, particularly if the ship had taken on too much water or if the rolling seas caused the weight of the cargo to shift and the ship's keel to lie at some perilously exposed angle. As Plautus wryly observes (*Rudens* 371), 'Old Neptune is an unforgiving market inspector: all trashy goods must go overboard.' The already difficult job of unloading stowed cargo on a pitching deck in a howling wind was inevitably rendered all the more difficult by the violent resistance of merchants whose wares were being discarded. The reassurances of legal redress provided by the universally recognised Rhodian Sea Law, which equally distributed losses incurred during jettisoning among all surviving cargoes and their proprietors, was small compensation to a businessman whose hard-acquired, extensively mortgaged commodities were being cast over the side. In life-threatening gales the captain might finally order the crew to cut away the cable and cast off the halyard in order, as the poet Lucilius notes (*ROL* 3.193), 'to save mast, sail and all the other tackle'. 'Next day,' the writer accompanying St Paul observes (*Acts* 27), 'as we were experiencing very heavy weather, the crew began to lighten the ship; and on the third day they jettisoned the ship's gear with their own hands. For days on end there was no sign of either sun or stars, the storm was raging unabated, and our last hopes of coming through alive began to fade.' During Synesius' anguishing voyage, the yard arms ultimately cracked and fell to the deck, 'very nearly killing us all.' 'Yet,' Synesius reflects (*Epist.* 4), 'it seems this very accident, by failing to destroy us, became the means to our salvation. For we should never have been able to resist the force of the wind, as the sail had once again proven intractable and had defied all our efforts to take it in.'

In the worst of scenarios the ship would go down leaving all hands to the mercy of the deep. The first-century AD Jewish writer, Josephus, recounts his own near-death experience in stark terms (*Vita Josephi* 15): 'I reached Rome after enduring great danger at sea. For our ship was wrecked in the middle of the Adriatic and we, some 600 in all, had to swim all night. About daylight, through God's good providence, a ship of Cyrene appeared and I and certain others, about 80, outstripped the others and were taken on board.' As the fourth-century AD sophist Libanius coldly observes (*Progymnasmata* 8.349–51 F.), 'whenever sailors, having weighed anchor, leave the harbour, they sail side by side with death, knowing that their only salvation rests in the wood on which they labour . . . for when the sea begins to boil with the force of the winds, its towering waves and frightening foam become the verisimilitude of disaster.' At all times, and most particularly during storms, the execution of the merchant ship's manoeuvres demanded the skilful, co-ordinated efforts of numerous seamen straining under the watchful shout of the *gubernator*. Nimble sailors are described by Lucan (*Phars.* 2.697–8), 'swinging themselves aloft by the ropes and with remarkable ease running the length of the yard while holding on to the lifts high above the deck'. The ancient sailor was an athletic, skilful tradesman to the ancient world's largest, most graceful, yet, most unsettling machine.

On arrival at port, the process of setting sail was reversed: the sail was furled by men going aloft to secure the canvas with gaskets, all lines were snugged down, anchors dropped and equipment neatly stowed. Once the ship was in port attention turned back to the cargo. Breaking bulk, or discharging the first part of the cargo, began with the same equipment and labour used in loading. Cargo was lifted, hoisted, or heaved from the hold and transferred with the help of other workers into smaller craft or directly onto quays. At smaller ports the seamen generally had to row the cargo ashore or wade with it in their arms (**57**). At this point, safe on shore and with the work momentarily completed, the sailors of the crew might be allowed a brief respite in the inns and taverns that lined the harbour. More often than not, however, they were ordered to begin stowing new cargoes as the ship's hold was reorganised for an ensuing destination.

The confrontation between man and nature, the seaman's perpetual evervigilant struggle to survive in the face of the nearly omnipotent forces of the deep, was central to seafaring work. The crew's chances of survival improved

57 *Sailors hauling a block of marble to Rome. Detail from statue base of the Tiber in the Louvre Museum.*
Souce: Gianfrotta and Pomey 1981: 212

markedly as the ship's company became an effective, efficient collectivity, bound together in skill, purpose, courage and community (Rediker 1987: 154). In all activities the authority of the *magister*, the *gubernator*, and the *proreus* was absolute, and they directed the efforts of the crew through the narrowly composed language of sharply assertive commands. The language of work was thus central both to the socialisation process and to the nature of social life at sea. Passengers could observe the shout of the *gubernator's* commands, 'Slack off the brails!', 'Contract the sails!', 'Mind the helm!', 'Turn the sheet left!', 'Turn it right!' Any newcomer who failed to learn the language of the ship would inevitably obstruct the rhythm of a crew's combined efforts. Caesar (*BC* 1.56) learned this painful lesson during the siege of Massilia in 49 BC, when the sailors and pilots of his warships, 'having suddenly been recruited from merchant ships', had difficulty manoeuvring their vessels because 'they were not yet familiar with the names of various tackles in the warships'.

Under such close scrutiny seamen worked the sails in a whir of activity: hauling in lines and turning the capstan on deck, swinging from lines in the air, and shaking them while suspended from the yard arm. Their days were long and their fatigue overwhelming. These factors heightened the risk of bodily harm, particularly injuries that resulted from the daily employment of equipment capable of breaking men's bones, dislodging eyes and cracking skulls. With a contempt all too readily expressed by land dwellers for the ancient seaman, Synesius (*Epist.* 4) sneers at the crewmen of his vessel, and the manner in which they 'accosted their comrades not so much by their real names, as by the distinguishing marks of their misfortunes, calling out 'Hey, Cripple!', 'Yo, Ruptured!', 'Look about, Squint!'.' 'Each one had his distinguishing mark,' he continues, 'and to us this sort of thing was no small source of amusement. However, the moment we were in danger it was no longer a laughing matter, for we began to lament our fate, entrusted as it was to the hands of men with defects such as these.'

Another risk of bodily injury arose from the extensive use of corporal punishment by captains and mates when asserting their authority at sea, particularly violence towards slaves. 'Where's the man who dared cut his hair on board my ship in the dead of night?' Petronius (105) has Lichas the ship's captain bellow, when it was learned that the *Satyricon's* heroes had violated this ancient seaman's superstition. 'Bring the culprits here this instant. By the gods, I want to know who's going to lose his head in order to get this ship purified again!' 'In order to appease the patron goddess of the ship,' Encolpius, the novel's hero explains, 'it was decided that each of us would be given forty strokes with the lash. The order was executed immediately. Sailors armed with knotted ropes threw themselves on us, determined to placate their goddess with our blood.' Despite Petronius' lighthearted treatment of this activity, corporal punishment formed an overpowering reality to a seaman's everyday existence.

The ship's officers exercised their authority over sailors in additionally demeaning ways: they apportioned the sailors' meal and drink rations while on ship, the duration of their free time both ashore and on board, the degree of danger in tasks assigned on deck, and the extent and thoroughness of medical treatment in the event of injury or illness. Remains of personal effects on ancient shipwrecks indicate that, though minimal, supplies were probably adequate for the crew. Aboard the Kyrenia plates, bowls, saucers, cups and wooden spoons were found in sets of four, suggesting that this was the number of the crew.[19] Clusters of roof tiles and kitchen equipment at numerous wrecks indicate the presence of small covered cooking hearths. Individual amphorae, clearly not part of the cargoes, serviced the crew's needs for wine, oil, garum, supplies and water (Parker 1992: 29). In exchange for their work efforts, both slave and freeborn sailors received wages, and even military rowers, who are presumed to have enjoyed far higher status than common merchant seamen, were notoriously underpaid. Conditions for the destitute sailors of common merchant vessels were significantly worse: the sources describe them labouring naked aboard ship, and going about barefoot, dressed in a mere tunic, when ashore (Casson 1971: 320f.). In essence, working at sea meant virtual impoverishment and incarceration. Compounding the seaman's misery was the fact that work at sea represented a form of cultural isolation, exposing the seaman to the deprivation of many common benefits of mainland social relations. Ancient maritime existence restricted the movement of seamen to a liminal world of pitching wooden decks at sea and the squalid unkempt bars and taverns of Mediterranean harbours on land.

Ancient sailors were the cast-offs of Mediterranean society, freeborn as often as they were slave. Generally speaking, ancient sailors arose from the displacement of rural subsistence labourers by a number of forces, for example, the relentless violence and warfare of the era, particularly throughout the eastern regions. Short of actual warfare, landholding elites throughout the Mediterranean flagrantly expelled neighbouring small farmers from their lands. In conditions such as these many subsistence landowning families found it difficult to retain their place on the land and thus compelled male children in their early teens to seek alternative means of livelihood. In addition, native elites, such as the elder hierarchies in Rough Cilicia, sent their youth to sea to expand control over neighbouring waters.[20] While more fortunate workers found employment as agricultural day labourers, artisans and dockyard stevedores, the truly destitute, used-up and socially discarded elements were pushed out onto the sea.

As the trade routes of the Hellenistic East and Roman West expanded and merged during this era, the Mediterranean maritime population absorbed an increasing array of antisocial labouring elements, compelled to sell their mind and muscle for money. Synesius (*Epist.* 4) complained that the crew of his passenger ship consisted of Jews, 'a graceless race and fully convinced of the piety of sending to Hades as many Greeks as possible', and 'farm boys who up to last year had never gripped an oar'. Slaves and expelled farm boys manned the sails of most Mediterranean merchantmen. Alongside these laboured, branded and whip-scarred criminals incapable of finding honest work elsewhere, and, therefore, like the others, ejected onto the sea. Sources such as Plautus repeatedly allude to the inhabitation of maritime bars and taverns by elements such as runaway slaves and criminals. As Plautus has a pimp's slave in a maritime brothel complain (*Poenulus* 831f.):

> How men are debauched in these resorts! May the gods help us! Every kind of person can be seen there, the same as if you visited the Underworld. Equites and hoplites, freedmen and slaves, in fact, slaves of every description – robbers and runaways, convicts, chain-ganged and debtor slaves! No matter who, no matter what, everyone is welcome so long as he can pay.

The universal designation for the runaway slave was the branded forehead, a visually commonplace marking in the maritime world.[21] Branded faces, foul odours, bad language, physical infirmities, and leather-hardened skin all physically separated maritime workers from their land-dwelling contemporaries. Ancient seamen displayed a dialect and manner peculiar to themselves, making them objects of suspicion and contempt. Synesius (*Epist.* 4) cannot resist the urge to sneer at the reviled Jewish captain and crew of his merchant vessel. Like the New Testament writer of the *Acts of St Paul*, he portrays the sailors of his storm-tossed ship as cowards, eager to escape an endangered vessel in lifeboats while abandoning the ship's passengers to their doom. Cicero similarly warns his freedman Tiro, about to embark on his return to Italy from Greece, to beware reckless sailors (*Fam.* 16.9): 'Do not to be too hasty in taking ship. Sailors out to make money are apt to hurry things.' These expressions inevitably reflect more about the underlying bias of land-dwelling elements than they do about uprooted socially displaced sailors. The very fact that so many thousands of merchant vessels successfully plied the Mediterranean Sea, annually delivering luxury and staple goods intact and in good working order throughout its confines, suggests that the vast majority of merchant crews performed their arduous tasks effectively and without complaint.

The maritime mob

The abuses inherent in a labour system dependent on meagre wages and slavery drove ancient seamen away from official society as they had known it and towards fundamentally different ways of life on the margins of the sea. To a far greater extent than most of his contemporaries, the seaman confronted his labour as something external, something alien, his incarceration on a merchant vessel resulted in a radical loss of social ties, liberty and personal autonomy, and an intensification of emotional strain. In addition to working as one of the first collective labourers, the ancient sailor was also one of the first alienated workers (Rediker 1987: 200). Within harbours throughout the Mediterranean maritime labourers formed separate communities whose social agendas stood at odds with those of land-dwelling contemporaries. Although the fear of proletariats made many skilled and landed workers regard their seafaring neighbours at a distance, seaman through their mobility helped to link various social and geographical particles of ancient underclass culture. Through their constant movement, they transcended localism and served as the bearers of culture and information among far-flung groups and places. The mobile seaman was both a carrier of information and ideas between different groups of labouring people and someone who by way of new experiences was sometimes able to generate new ideas and practices (Rediker 1987: 294). As such, ancient seamen contributed to the processes of cultural standardisation and communication among working class elements throughout the ancient Mediterranean world.

Among the experiences and characteristics that earned a seaman authority and esteem were an understanding of the techniques and technicalities of the work place, knowledge of the trade routes and the sea's winding geography, a command of maritime vocabulary, having survived a shipwreck or two, a good singing voice or a nimble dancing step, physical strength and courage, good humour, and among the men at the bottom of the labouring hierarchy, scars on one's back from the whips of social superiors – the telltale symbols of defiance and endurance (Rediker 1987: 211). Their informal, collectively-defined system of hierarchy was based on the social and cultural relations of the workplace. It arose from the daily experience of labour and had little or nothing to do with profits, productivity, or the social ordering of land-based society.

To distinguish themselves, seamen resorted to a number of behavioural traits guaranteed to set them apart from land-dwelling society, including hard language, defiance of physical abuse, and a willingness to engage in violent demonstrations against the prevailing Mediterranean social orders. Ancient seamen had tongues as nimble as they were razor sharp. They spoke in immediate, direct, clear, expressive and forceful ways even if it got them in trouble, as it sometimes did. To ameliorate the harshness of their work environment, seamen performed their labour with volleys of oaths, sometimes addressing their officers with abusive and reviling language. The very tools of their labour, such as the *nothos* or bastard sail, came to acquire a sailor's precise epithet. Abusive language, accordingly, provided texture to their work environment and enabled ancient seamen to obtain social leverage vis-à-vis their superiors on deck, not to mention against contemptuous land dwellers. Under the relative anonymity of darkness or mass assemblies a sailor's abuse was likely to grow loudest, as Horace makes clear in his description of a voyage he made along the Italian coast (*Satires* 1.5): 'From here we went to Forum Appia, a place crammed with sailors and rascally innkeepers . . . presently night began to spread her shadows over the earth and to scatter the stars across the heavens. A Babel of voices arose, slaves abusing sailors and sailors abusing slaves.' Non-deferential, sometimes defiant speech expressed one of the ways in which maritime culture was linked to the process of counter cultural identification.

As a functioning tool a sailor's voice was every bit as important as his hands, essential to his labour and equally important to his creation of a palatable social environment. Most particularly the sailor enjoyed a fondness for music and song. Continuing his lament about his ferry outing, Horace moans about his difficulty sleeping (*Sat.* 1.5), 'while a sailor and a passenger, soused with flat wine, rivalled one another in singing to their absent mistresses.' Plutarch (*Pompey* 24.3–4) observes how the pirates of Cilicia, predominantly renegade sailors as we shall see, brought Roman supremacy into contempt by 'their flute-playing, their stringed instruments, and their drunken revels along every coast'. Cultural forms such as the work song and the specialised language of the sea assumed integrative roles, helping to forge occupational identity and solidarity.

Ultimately, the willingness of a sailor to engage in free expression was determined by his ability to endure pain, particularly the pain inflicted by maritime authorities such as ship's captains, slave masters or the whip-bearing peace officers who patrolled Mediterranean harbours. The ability not only to endure but even to laugh in the face of pain earned sailors, convicts and runaway slaves high standing in maritime society. Effective banter laced with allusions to physical abuse encouraged solidarity among those most experienced in the same. As Plautus demonstrates in the greetings of two street-smart slaves, the language of corporal punishment could serve simultaneously as insults and as badges of honour (*Asinaria* 297f.):

> – There you are, you whip softener!
> – What do you want, jailbird?
> – Why, you're one to talk, you fetter farmer!
> – Say it ain't so, you rod tickler!
> – How much do you think you weigh, stripped naked?
> – Damned if I know.
> – I knew you wouldn't know; but by the gods, I know for I've weighed you. Stripped and tied you weigh twenty minas, when hanging by your heels.
> – What's your proof of that?
> – I'll show you my proof and my means of calculation. When a solid twenty minas is fastened to your feet, and your handcuffed hands are firmly lashed to a beam, you weigh precisely the weight of a good-for-nothing scoundrel!
> – Oh, go to hell!
> – Precisely where you yourself are destined in slavery's will!
> – Let's cut this war of words. What business do you want of me?

The threat of physical abuse gave stinging clarity to the void that separated maritime culture from the dominant social orders. To retaliate against the deprivation of freedom and autonomy and to assert some place in society, the ancient sailor forged his own community based on physical appearance and behaviour deliberately set at odds with those of landed ascendancy. Collective labour at sea passed easily into collective self-defence as seamen sought to protect themselves from harsh conditions, excessive work and oppressive authority. Solidarity within maritime society frequently expressed itself through the exhibition of defiantly retaliatory tendencies – deception, theft and civil disobedience. The maritime inhabitants of Alexandria, sneers one of Caesar's officers (*BAlex*. 24), 'were a deceitful people, always keeping one aim in view and pretending to another'. The shrewdest elements within this society knew from experience how to assess the cost/benefit ratio of physical abuse.

Gruff talk and the ability to endure physical violence insulated the seaman against the indifference and visible contempt of mainland society. Another particular aid in the sailor's flight from poor treatment, physical abuse, or imprisonment was the mobility inherent to his trade. Seamen were in many ways nomads, voyaging without firm geographical boundaries or stable residence, and their mobility insured a rapid diffusion of their culture (Rediker 1987: 158). Movement in the form of desertion was, therefore, a crucial resource to the sailor's quest for autonomy. As a form of struggle and a means of survival, desertion was widespread among maritime workers. For slaves, desertion offered the added advantage of starting life freshly anonymous in harbours at a considerable distance from where they last saw their masters.

As noted above, numerous sources allude to the existence in harbour taverns of runaway slaves alongside criminals and maritime labourers. Once a runaway slave had escaped into the subterranean world of maritime taverns, it was nearly impossible for his slave owner to find him, particularly in ports such as Alexandria or Puteoli, where sailors could count on the support of maritime sympathizers. As Caesar complains (*BC* 3.110), 'all runaway slaves of ours had a guaranteed refuge and a guaranteed way of life at Alexandria, provided they enrolled and became soldiers. If any of them was arrested by his master, he was snatched away by agreement among the soldiers, who protected their companions against violence as though they were themselves in danger, because they were tarred with the same brush.' To Roman eyes,[22] the ruling classes of Alexandria, Corinth or Carthage engaged in 'class treason' by allowing their populations to evolve into 'maritime republics'. As Caesar explains, the openness and accessibility of maritime cities rendered them vulnerable to political seizure by the *ochlos nautikos* or 'maritime mob', a mixed collection of free and unfree, rootless, destitute, mobile labourers. The Alexandrian mob, for example, 'was led by a small faction of buccaneers . . . that habitually demanded that friends of the king be put to death. They plundered the property of the rich, they laid siege to the king's residence to win higher pay, and they removed some and appointed others to the throne.' (Caes. *BC* 3.109-110) Plutarch observes a similar pattern with Themistocles' fifth-century BC development of the Piraeus (*Them.* 19): 'Themistocles strengthened the position of the common people at the expense of that of the aristocracy, and filled men with boldness, since power now settled into the hands of sailors, boatswains, and helmsmen.'

Despite their opprobrious tone even, Caesar and Plutarch would acknowledge, however, the importance of the maritime population to the well-being of the Mediterranean world system, its economy, its administration, and its permanence. Armies as well as cargoes inevitably needed to travel by sea; strong navies guaranteed the safety of each. The careers and livelihoods of numerous professionals – including diplomats, military officers, merchants, soldiers and citizen sailors – depended heavily on maritime transport and its labourers. As a result, exposure to maritime culture was for many property-holding, land-dwelling elements unavoidable, particularly the subterranean world of the maritime tavern, through which all voyagers inevitably passed. Ancient Mediterranean taverns formed highly egalitarian settings characterised not only by the attractions of their cultural life but by the mobility and impermanence of their transient populations. Roman aristocrats found it exceedingly difficult to restrain the effects of these establishments on their peers. As Juvenal makes clear about the first-century AD Roman consul Lateranus, respectable land dwellers succumbed time and again to the egalitarian fervour of the taverns (*Satires* 8.171-178):

> If, Caesar, you wish to find Lateranus, that muleskinner you've now made consul, then send someone off to the harbour town of Ostia. Send someone off, I say, but be sure to have them hunt for your legate throughout the waterfront taverns. There they will find him, stretched out drunk amid gangsters of every description, sailors, thieves and runaway slaves, murderers, coffin makers, and Syrian priests flat on their arses but still banging away with their cymbals. Everyone's freed in these establishments – free and easy. They hoist their cups in unison, not to mention their wenches, and table hop with egalitarian fervour.

For the ancient seaman, the maritime tavern was a home away from the sea. Maritime establishments offered safe havens from the monotonous life of toil in the open waters; they likewise functioned as the nodes of social intercourse for a complex array of social elements. In Mediterranean taverns and brothels, for example, the ancient seamen was able to fraternise with hired female companions who generally shared eastern Mediterranean origins like themselves, not to mention important cultural affinities such as language and religion (**58**).[23]

Through their ability to entice aristocratic and freeborn citizens into their otherwise predominantly working-class followings, these same women

58 *Bust of drunken elderly prostitute.* Capitoline Museum, Rome

constructed potentially important lines of communication vertically through the social orders. Some courtesans, such as the dazzling Praecia who compelled Roman senators to bow to her will in 74 BC, exploited their influence in the taverns to challenge and to destabilise the hierarchy itself. Plutarch acknowledged the significance of women such as Praecia (*Lucullus* 6.3): 'In other respects she was nothing more than a courtesan, but she used her associates and companions to further the political ambitions of her friends, and so added to her other charms the reputation of being a true comrade, and one who could bring things to pass. She thus acquired the greatest possible influence.'

Ancient maritime taverns and brothels thus furnished important flashpoints for the relay of information from one working-class element to another. When the force of some outrage prompted labourers to take to the streets in protest, ancient seamen were ready to join in rowdy and rebellious demonstrations, as the riots that repeatedly erupted in Alexandria make clear. Caesar's own arrival in 48 BC, for example, incited violent protests throughout the city (*BC* 3.106): 'for a period of days the crowd continued to assemble and provoke frequent disturbances.' Seafarers joined in these tumults because they were footloose in the port towns between voyages, and hence available. In addition, the ancient seaman carried ashore a source of an oppositional culture (Rediker 1987: 250). Due to their work experience, sense of collectivism, experience from co-ordinated work effort, and ability to withstand the dangers of the sea, harsh physical conditions and physical abuse, seamen brought to the ports a militant attitude toward arbitrary and excessive authority. They tended to empathise with the grievances of others, to co-operate for the sake of self-defence, and to use purposeful violence and direct action to accomplish collectively defined goals.

Seamen were instrumental, therefore, to the formation and extension of ancient working class culture. They influenced both the form and the content of underclass protests by their militant presence in maritime crowds. They manifested and contributed to the anti-authoritarian and egalitarian traditions within early labouring culture. The ancient seamen, who, as Horace notes (*Sat.* 1.1.29), 'so boldly sailed throughout the seas', used their strategic position within the social divisions of labour to mediate exchanges of experience and information between working-class populations in distant maritime communities. Their movement helped to define and to extend the community and culture of working people throughout the Roman world.

5

Cilician piracy and Mediterranean maritime discontent

Native attitudes in the Bay of Pamphylia[1]

In 334/3 BC, Alexander the Great conducted his field army through a dreary winter campaign along the south-western coast of Anatolia, trudging as far as the plain of Pamphylia before heading inland to seize an important crossroads on the Anatolian plateau. This rugged march along the narrow mountainous coast of Lycia and the rolling plain of Pamphylia was necessary to deny this region and its strategic harbours as a staging ground to a Persian counter-offensive. As he approached the inhabitants of the Pamphylian urban centres, attitudes began to harden. Apparently surmising that Alexander, short of money and supplies and equally pressed for time, could ill afford to linger in their vicinity, and guessing as well that the absence of his siege train (dispatched earlier into the Anatolian highland by the alternative route) severely limited his options, the inhabitants pulled their populations and movable assets within their walls and attempted to wait him out. Few of the cities showed a willing-ness to receive Macedonian garrisons. Instead, they coldly, almost disdainfully, offered gestures of submission and modest financial and material contributions. Aspendos exhibited perhaps the most flagrant instance of disregard, at first offering 50 talents and a large number of horses, then reneging on their offer (Arrian *Anabasis* 1.26-27). Recognising that his resolve was being tested, Alexander wheeled his forces into position to assault the city with or without siege weaponry. The townspeople soon relented; however, the weakness of the king's position was revealed. Alexander needed repeatedly to deploy his army outside the gates of Pamphylian cities. One should add that occasionally, particularly at Sillyon and Termessos where strong defences thwarted any genuine assaults, even these displays of force proved futile (Arr. 1.26-28). At face value this test of nerve appears more peevish than genuine. With the exceptions of Sillyon and Termessos the inhabitants of the plain of Pamphylia knew that they were no match for the battle-hardened army of Alexander. Realising that Alexander's true objectives lay elsewhere, the inhabitants were simply stalling for time. As often as Alexander showed his determination, resistance usually ceased. Despite Alexander's rapid success along the Aegean seaboard, his experience in Pamphylia indicated that he was uninitiated in the hegemonic dealings of the eastern Mediterranean. As he and others learned, the rules were different along the seaboard of the Bay of Pamphylia; a region that nurtured piracy. Why native elites in certain peripheral regions of the Mediterranean encouraged the development of piracy remains a topic worthy of elaboration.

Alexander's experience with the urban populations of Pamphylia illuminates the perspective of the inhabitants of this region towards outsiders. For centuries Pamphylian communities had yielded to the imperial aspirations of several 'off-shore' empires – to the Lydians and the Persians during the sixth century BC, to the Athenian commanders of the Delian League during the fifth century, and to the Persians again shortly thereafter. In the centuries following Alexander's passage through Pamphylia, regional dominance rotated among the Ptolemies, the Seleucids, the Attalids, and after 101 BC, the promagistrates of the Roman Republic. Isolated by the enveloping, dramatically vertical barrier of the Tauros Mountains, Pamphylia, with its well-watered plains and accessible harbours, presented itself, for better or for worse, as a convenient way-station for the naval advances of Aegean and Eastern Mediterranean empires as well as for the general movement of Mediterranean maritime trade.

While settlements along the Bay of Pamphylia furnished useful stepping-stones to prizes and profits further abroad, they were rarely in themselves the objectives of military campaigns. The merchant shipping that passed through these waters was likewise generally destined for more famous commercial centres abroad. Ancient merchantmen hugged the coast of the bay more often than not to evade the prevailing northerly winds of the open Mediterranean during summer, preferring instead the gentler shore breezes generated by temperature changes between the sea and neighbouring mountains. Likewise, military leaders such as Alexander, Kimon, Antiochus III or Cn. Manlius Vulso, conducted themselves largely as passers-by. Even Mopsos, the mythological Trojan hero credited with founding the cities along this coast, rather than linger, continued eastward to greater renown in eastern Cilicia and Syria. Despite its well-watered plains, its rich agricultural yields, the abundant timber supplies in neighbouring mountains, and its breathtaking natural splendour, travellers found the shores of the Bay of Pamphylia unwelcoming. The climate along the coast was and remains insufferably hot and humid during summer, despite the general aridness of the landscape. Numerous marshes and coastal lagoons rendered the region pestilential, so much so that the wealthy land-holders of Antiquity much like the emerging Turkish middle class of today retreated to highland 'yaylas' of Termessos and Laertes during the torrid summer months. The inhabitants, meanwhile, were, if not overtly hostile to foreigners, then certainly calculating in their treatment, largely because they shared few genuine cultural affinities with peoples beyond their horizons. As its handful of Greek dialectic inscriptions demonstrates, Pamphylia exhibited an ethnically diverse culture incorporating Anatolian, Hellenic, and Phoenician attributes to form a hybrid mix (Rauh *et al.* 2000: 152). Since few visitors ever came to Pamphylia to stay, the natives appear generally to have reacted to their arrival through a xenophobic combination of hostility and opportunism. Modern Turkish tourists from regions of Istanbul or Ankara will tell you privately that things have changed little in the resorts of Antalya and Alanya after two thousand years.

This behavioural tendency of the Pamphylians bears significance on the emergence of piracy in these waters during the late Hellenistic era, specifically the so-called phenomenon of Cilician piracy (*c*.139–67 BC). Nearly all the cities and fortresses specifically associated with Cilician piracy by textual sources – from West to East, Olympos (**59**), Korykos, Phaselis, Attaleia, Side, Korakesion (Coracesium) and the 'Kragos Mountain' were in fact situated on and looked out across the arching waters of the Bay of Pamphylia. In Pamphylia proper, Side and Attaleia openly consorted with pirates. By this time the most prominent commercial centre of the bay, Side allowed the pirates free and unrestricted access to its harbour, permitting them to sell captive victims 'at public auctions on the municipal wharves while plainly admitting

59 *View of the site of Olympos in Lycia*

their freeborn origins'.[2] With its well-situated harbour, its fortifications, its coinage and its reputation as a regional 'outlaw state', the settlement at Side appears to have acted as a 'fence' for plundering pirates, eventually provoking a response by more respectable powers.[3] For example, what little is known about the military operations of M. Antonius 'the Orator', the first Roman general commissioned by the Republic to suppress Cilician piracy in 102 BC, indicates that he viewed the seizure of Side as the primary objective to his campaign.[4] Pirate troubles did not cease here, however. Q. Oppius, the Roman proconsul of 'Cilicia' in 88 BC, was apparently on the verge of a punitive expedition against Pamphylia as well, when his plans were interrupted by defeat and capture by King Mithradates VI.[5] During the confusion of the Mithradatic war, Pamphylian cities continued to elicit punitive expeditions from Rome. Cn. Cornelius Dolabella, the Roman governor of Cilicia in 80–79 BC, dealt severely with the inhabitants Aspendos and Perge for unspecified misbehaviour.[6] In 77–76 BC, the Roman commander, P. Servilius Vatia Isauricus, reasserted Roman authority in Pamphylia while en route between his more celebrated campaigns in eastern Lycia and the mountain highlands of Isauria. More specifically, he suppressed the inhabitants of Attaleia and deprived them of their lands after they had apparently gone so far as to forge treaty relations with the pirates.[7] In other words, despite clear evidence that Pamphylia had existed under Roman hegemonic control since 101 BC, a sufficient number of reports suggest that the cities of this region remained recalcitrant and suspiciously outlaw.

The name 'Cilician' may, accordingly, be misleading for this piracy, given that its points of origin were scattered across the Bay of Pamphylia. Other pirate settlements, Olympos (**60**) and Phaselis (**colour plate 16** & **18**), stood technically in Hellenistic Lycia and had both existed as members of the Lycian League since at least the early second century BC. Sometime before 77 BC, the pirate chief Zenicetes incorporated both cities into a small piratical empire. He menaced shipping throughout the Bay of Pamphylia (and the wider Mediterranean) from his fortress beneath the eternal flames of the Chimaera, where he and his pirates conducted mysterious rites in honour of the god Mithras (**61** & **colour plate 25**).[8] Recent Turkish survey work has revealed preliminarily the existence of a Hellenistic-era fortress (Goktas Kalesi) on a narrow peak above the flaming vents of the 'Chimaera' as well as the remains of a stone-cut shrine near the harbour that appears to have functioned as a Mithraeum (Atvur 1999: 27–8). The willingness of the inhabitants of Phaselis, like Side a crucial Mediterranean way-station, to collaborate with this pirate chief demonstrates – along with several previous instances of antisocial behaviour – their lack of regard for maritime peace and security.[9] To some degree, the topographical barriers posed by the jutting ridges of the Tauros Mountains formed psychological barriers as well. The behaviour of the inhabitants of Phaselis and Olympos stood in sharp contrast to the good reputation

60 *View of the acropolis at Olympos*

enjoyed by fellow Lycian communities further west.[10] According to Strabo (14.3.2 (664)), the latter populations 'conducted themselves in a civilised and decent manner even as the Pamphylians seized control of the seas as far as Italy'.

Similarly, along the vaguely defined eastern boundaries of the Bay of Pamphyli,a pirate enclaves presided. Historical sources seem to agree that Korakesion/Coracesium (**colour plate 16**) (modern Alanya) served as the chief naval base and headquarters of this pirate menace and that it was here that the Seleucid pretender Diodotus Tryphon first installed the naval squadrons that converted to piracy after his demise in 139 BC.[11] It was here as well that Pompey the Great defeated the last resisting pirate elements in a naval battle before this promontory, compelling the survivors to surrender by threat of siege, thus bringing the Cilician pirate episode to a close in 67 BC. Presumably, this was where the pirates amassed their large quantities of weapons, timber, metals, sailcloth and rope, as well as where they maintained the enslaved labourers who constructed their warships and necessary material (App. *Mith.* 92, 96). Surviving courses of ashlar masonry beneath superimposed Seljuk mortared work in the Alanya castle's fortification walls offer substantial indication of the strength this position enjoyed at the time of the Cilician pirates. Approximately 60km further east at a point where the Tauros Mountains rejoin the sea, the urban site of Antiochia ad Cragum stands on a sheer promontory

61 *View of the area of the fire jets of the chimera at Olympos. The open area at left mid-ground is the chimera zone*

300m in altitude (**62** & **colour plate 23**). A Roman client king named Antiochus IV of Commagene founded this provincial capital during the reign of the Emperor Claudius, presumably at the location where the Cilician pirates had previously constructed their impregnable fortress known as the 'Kragos'.[12] According to Appian (*Mith.* 96), this pirate base consisted of two citadels, the Kragos itself and the Antikragos projecting out in front. Although Appian is the only source to mention this bastion in connection with piracy, he clearly states that Pompey assaulted it in 67 BC on his arrival 'in Cilicia'. While the surviving remains date to the Roman and Byzantine eras, the site's topography certainly matches the description of Appian. Standing remains of a bath and palaestra, a colonnaded street, a basilica, churches and tombs are visible at the 'Upper City' beneath the jumbled ruins of an acropolis; a heavily fortified

(Byzantine) bastion survives on the lower promontory down below (**colour plate 15**). The lower citadel is in turn flanked by a middle crest of rock sheltering two hidden sea coves, one of these open to the sea, the other accessible via a broad, deeply-eroded passage through the rock (**colour plate 33**).[13]

Going by the literary testimony alone, therefore, the Bay of Pamphylia appears to have bristled from end to end with fortresses and pirate harbours at the time of the Cilician uprising. Viewed from the north, the 'pirate bases' at Korakesion and the Kragos Mountain to the east, and Phaselis, Korykos and Olympos to the west, would appear to have formed projecting arms to an urban hegemony centred in Pamphylia. This bay, with its pincer-like arms, was most probably the origin of the sustained pirate menace of 'Cilicia'. As the '*lex de provinciis praetoriis*' and related sources demonstrate, in *c.*102–99 BC, the Romans ultimately declared these 'Cilician' waters a '*provincia*', or 'sphere of operations', and thereafter assigned the eradication of the pirate menace to a series of Roman pro-magistrates. Given the fact that many of the pirate atrocities occurring at this particular moment were located in eastern Lycia (Olympos and Phaselis), the Romans obviously conceived of this 'sphere of operations' in a broad sense. Its specific 'maritime' orientation was probably restricted to the confines of this bay and to whatever populations within its waters openly participated with, supported or surreptitiously harboured pirates.

Genuine understanding of this pirate phenomenon calls for a sensitive appreciation of regional developments in the eastern quadrant of the Mediterranean world: for example, the unique social and cultural system that prevailed in this region, as well as for the peculiar conditions of maritime society that tend to generate piracy in any historical period. While the role of maritime society as a breeding ground for piracy will be considered below, the promotion of piracy by native elements in the Bay of Pamphylia demands immediate attention, particularly with respect to the pirate bases in western Rough Cilicia. Several scholars have demonstrated that the peoples dwelling along the mountainous coasts at the eastern end of the bay remained at odds with offshore cultures throughout Antiquity. No imperial power successfully dominated the tribal elements of the Cilician Mountains, no matter how much the Assyrians, the Persians, the Seleucids or the Romans claimed to have done so.[14] Textual remains indicate that societies along the eastern shores of the bay remained more isolated than those further west. In sharp contrast to the evidence for assimilation of Greek culture in Lycia and Pamphylia, for example, only four Hellenistic-era inscriptions survive in the western Rough Cilicia, indicating more gradual acceptance of Greek forms of communication.[15] In their nomenclature and material remains, meanwhile, the inhabitants of western Rough Cilicia preserved the purest vestiges of traditional Luwian culture to survive in Anatolia.[16] In the mountains behind Korakesion and the Kragos, several Luwian peoples known collectively as the Isaurians (the Lalasseis, the Cietae, the Cennatae and the Homonadenses), posed a continual

62 *View of the precipice of the Kragos from the Antikragos*

menace to coastal settlements through the early Roman era.[17] Ruled by 'tyrannoi', the inhabitants of Rough Cilicia viewed banditry as a badge of honour, a code that regarded collaboration with any outside power as a sign of lost face and illegitimacy. Inaccessible, hostile and outcast, the Isaurian tyrants loomed over and peered down on the Mediterranean *oikumene* of Flat Cilicia (Cilicia Pedia), plundering its coastal cities and farmlands but otherwise remaining aloof from its social and economic order.

Accordingly, the degree to which any of these elements involved themselves in the affairs of the Cilician pirate bases on the western coast becomes difficult to assess. The consistent degree to which the ancient sources refer to the pirates as *Kilikes*, and to their chieftains as 'tyrants', seems to imply that the pirate commanders drew on the mountain peoples of the Taurus hinterland for manpower, or that the mountain chieftains themselves somehow dominated the pirate bands.[18] In this regard one can point to analogous relationships between coastal pirates and mountain bandits in regions such as Illyria, Aetolia and Crete. The emergence of Cretan piracy in the Hellenistic era has been convincingly portrayed, for example, as a downward and outward progression of bandit populations from secure mountain fastnesses to neighbouring coastal harbours, and then to piracy (Brulé 1978: 117–184). Some scholars argue for a general fluidity between mountain bandits and pirate elements throughout the Mediterranean. This theory finds resonance in the testimony provided by Appian (*Mith.* 96, 117), for example, who insists that the 'Mountain Cilicians', hence the Isaurians, supported the pirates against Pompey. He and other sources refer repeatedly to the leaders of the Cilician pirates as '*tyrannoi*', and he adds that Pompey led many such tyrants in his triumph in 62 BC. The likelihood of co-operation between the pirate bands that infested the Bay of Pamphylia and the xenophobic natives of its hinterland needs to be recognised, consequently, as must the realisation that the native inhabitants of Rough Cilicia are far more likely to have left their imprint on regional archaeological remains than any temporary settlements of pirates.

The questions raised by the behavioural pattern of Luwian natives in western Rough Cilicia, the character of their archaeological remains and their likely involvement in 'Cilician piracy' bear directly on the efforts of the Rough Cilicia Archaeological Survey Team to recover and to identify the material remains of piracy in 'western Rough Cilicia.' Since 1996 the author has directed a systematic archaeological survey of the region where ancient literary sources located the principal 'Cilician' pirate bases – Korakesion and the Kragos Mountain, presumably identical to the later Roman site Antiochia ad Cragum (modern Güney village). The purpose of the survey is to collect and record surface data capable of reconstructing all phases of settlement within the survey zone from the earliest survivals through to Ottoman times (**colour plate 28**). The survey team's ultimate objective is to provide a detailed archaeological history of this region as revealed by its evolving record of human landscape ecology.[19]

In peripheral areas such as western Rough Cilicia, evidence of native adoption of imported modes of economic production furnish a unique opportunity to view the development of an imperial world system through the lens of local societies. Visible remains of Graeco-Roman features (such as bath complexes and municipal buildings), the use of Greek in epigraphical records, not to mention evidence for local, ethnically Luwian, adaptation of Graeco-Roman political and religious forms such as annually elected magistrates, councils, assemblies and religious cults (including priesthoods for the imperial cult of Roman emperors), reveal that the inhabitants of Rough Cilicia adapted these attributes relatively late and somewhat discriminately. Equally likely is the possibility that local Luwian hierarchies behaved opportunistically when confronted by external powers seeking to exploit available local resources. Anthropological studies of modern, post-colonial behaviour in regions such as central Africa demonstrate for example that, when confronted by 'technologically advanced' European colonial powers, native hierachies selectively incorporated external economic mechanisms, including monetarised, market-based economic practices and specialised modes of production, without ever relinquishing local ascendancy or the underlying cognitive and ideological bases to the same.[20] In many instances native hierarchies were able to exploit the imported modes of economic development to insulate and reinforce their long-standing positions. To determine the appropriateness of these theoretical constructs for economic conditions in ancient Rough Cilicia, the Rough Cilicia research team is utilising multiple strands of evidence to calibrate the relative scale of regional resource production, particularly timber production. In western Rough Cilicia shipbuilding products (especially timber) and shipbuilding expertise itself can be viewed, in the context of the sea-based economies and polities of the ancient Mediterranean world, as a strategic resource, the control of which, historically, was actively sought by multiple competing core polities.[21] Team members rely on textual, archaeological and palaeo-environmental data in western Rough Cilicia as a means to evaluate changes in the region's patterns of settlement, environment, and resource development over a sustained period of time. To determine how best to describe incipient economic development in western Rough Cilicia, the survey team is attempting to establish both the timing and mode of deforestation and the degree of Roman involvement in various spheres of Luwian society. To assess the timing and the mode of regional deforestation, the team employs a number of strategies, including geomorphology, palynology and analysis of phytolith and macrobotanical assemblages from natural deposits.

During the period in question, the remote, narrowly hemmed-in coastal lands of western coast of Rough Cilicia were minimally populated by pastoral elements. The region harboured a dozen small settlements, including Hamaxia, Korakesion, Laertes, Syedra, Selinus, Nephelion, Lamos (**63**) and Charadros. At the time, however, most of these were little more than fortified way-stations garrisoned by Ptolemaic and Seleucid mercenaries to provide safe havens for coastal traffic and to exploit the mountainous region's natural abundance of timber and naval supplies.[22] Thus far, survey efforts in and around the Gazipasha basin have identified pre-Roman fortification walls, structures and/or ceramic remains at three coastal sites, Iotape, Selinus and Nephelion. Hellenistic finds at Iotape seem particularly significant because prior to its founding by Antiochus IV of Commagene around AD 52, no surviving testimony can confirm the existence of a community at this location (**colour plate 26**). Situated on a rock promontory with a beach cove on each side, Iotape's topography presents in miniature the same characteristics as Korakesion, thus, advancing itself as a likely pirate base. Further inland in the narrow canyon of the Hasdere, survey efforts have revealed pre-Roman remains at a number of sites, including Lamos, Asar Tepe, Tomak Asari (**65 & 66**) and Govan Asari, all of which are situated high above precipices 600m or more in altitude. At Lamos in particular, the survey team has identified remains of Hellenistic defensive installations, located inside the later, third-century AD curtain walls of the acropolis (**colour plate 27 & 28**). The ashlar construction of these remains points to a significant offshore commitment to the development of this relative backwater, probably in connection with the canyon's abundant forestry resources. Together with Hellenistic hilltop settlements discovered along the coast, including a fortified site situated high up on the coastal ridge between Kestros and Nephelion and a massive Hellenistic press complex recently discovered at Kale Tepe on the Delice River, these settlements call to mind Plutarch's (*Pomp.* 28.1) assertion that the pirates maintained fortresses and citadels in nearby mountains to conceal the whereabouts of their women, children, and 'a large disabled element of warriors' (**64**).

Nothing about the remains so far examined by the survey team allows for direct association with pirates, however. The fortification walls at Lamos could be Ptolemaic, and much of the Hellenistic ceramic remains appear to predate the period of the pirates, in fact. More significantly, ceramic materials that team specialists had hoped to exploit for purposes of controlling this aspect of the research agenda, namely, identifiable remains of Italian amphorae of the Roman Republican era commonly found at Delos, have for the most part failed to materialise in surface collections anywhere in the survey area, including Antiochia ad Cragum.[23] The accumulating evidence of Hellenistic settlement in this region may just as well reflect a more typical process of development by native Luwian inhabitants.

The difficulties posed by the absence of pre-Roman material remains at Antiochia ad Cragum seem particularly acute in this regard. Featural remains at Antioch date predominantly to the period of resettlement by Antiochus IV of Commagene, *c.* AD 52. Their relatively undisturbed character seemed at first to offer a prime opportunity to test theoretical assumptions about piracy. However, several weeks of investigation at Antioch revealed practically no pre-

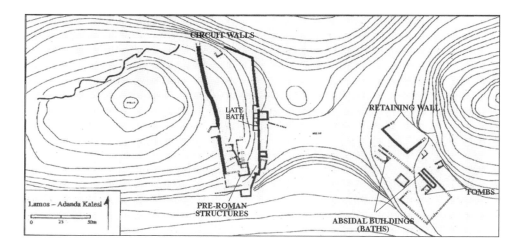

63 (Above) *Plan of Lamos acropolis by Michael Hoff and Rhys Townsend*

64 (Left) *IKONOS Satellite view of the acropolis of Lamos*

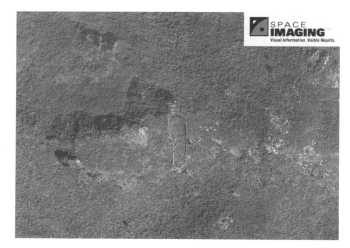

65 *Hellenistic ceramic remains at Tomak Asari. 'Whitish' slipped body sherd (upper right) is tentatively identified as a Will type 10 Italian amphora*

66 *View of Tomak Asari in the Hasdere Canyon*

Roman ceramic remains, not to mention any vestiges of Roman republican amphorae from Italy. Ceramic collections conducted in the vicinity of the Byzantine castle and hidden cove of the lower city produced an overwhelming mass of Byzantine ceramics dating from the tenth to twelfth centuries AD, with little if any material from preceding eras. Although the team produced a modicum of evidence to suggest pre-Roman habitation at the site's 'upper city', essentially nothing has survived at the so-called 'Pirate's Cove' or at the fortress of the Antikragos below. From an architectural standpoint, moreover, none of the surviving structures investigated thus far exhibits any obvious pre-Roman phase of construction.

As noted in an earlier publication (Rauh *et al.* 2000: 164), the survey team's analysis of Antiochia ad Cragum has been complicated by evidence of terracing, both modern and ancient. Perhaps as much as 3m of early Roman fill was employed to create the earthen foundation for the Roman gymnastic complex that survives at the Upper City. Likewise, contemporary inhabitants of the village (Güney) located on the site have for decades moved large quantities of earth from unknown locations to construct terracing for their homes and gardens. This realisation forced team members to abandon a number of ceramic collections deemed immaterial because of their likely movement from points unknown. The massive extent of artificial terracing for contemporary banana plantations obscures the archaeological record of the lower city as well. In other words, pre-Roman remains conceivably lie below various areas of post-occupational land disturbance at the site, leaving efforts on the part of team members to identify a potential context for the pirates at an impasse. Short of discovery of fragments of Republican era amphorae from Italy, team specialists would be hard pressed to demonstrate in any convincing manner that pre-Roman remains recovered at Antioch on the Kragos bore directly on the question of piracy, as opposed to that of native Luwian occupation.

Employing means of landscape ecology, the project's best hope is to analyse patterns of resource exploitation over time through a careful assessment of landscape alterations. Since the region was celebrated in Antiquity for its shipbuilding and maritime supplies, it stands to reason that these resources would have attracted the attention of sea-borne pirates (**67**). What is needed, ultimately, is the means to demonstrate a propensity on the part of the west Cilician natives to promote, suborn or otherwise participate in piracy.

Most of the results of the survey pertain, of course, to periods subsequent to the emergence of piracy in this area when remains of Early and Late Roman settlement are more abundant. Nevertheless, they appear to reflect a consistent pattern of behaviour on the part of the Luwian natives of this region sustained from earlier times. Although the results of the geo-archaeological component of the survey stand at a preliminary phase, significant indications of erosion of river basins, sedimentary deposits and declining pollen counts of native cedar, pine and juniper, obtained from geomorphological test trenches in the coastal plain around Selinus, are emerging from the field work. The pattern of erosion is particularly evident in the Biçkici River basin, where team specialists have identified steep terrace deposits, accelerated erosion, and related thick coarse-grained sedimentation throughout its valley. These reflect repeated events of catastrophic flooding that appear correlative with continuous deforestation. The results thus far conform to a general pattern of forest clearance and conversion to agriculture during Antiquity.[24]

The archaeological record of the Gazipasha basin appears, meanwhile, to present three distinct landscapes – the dispersed, relatively stratified settlement pattern of the coast; a shallow settlement pattern of small, nucleated settlements in the Hasdere Canyon (**68**); and a non-stratified pattern of non-architectural, comparatively impoverished situations and deeply eroded river basins in the northern area of the Delice and the Biçkici Rivers. The record also indicates that as urban settlements expanded and forestland yielded

67 *View of Çokele Kalesi, mountain bastion behind Alanya. View of a presumably Isaurian bastion of Late Roman era standing approximately 1500m. above the Dim Çay canyon. Rubble piles in the photograph are building remains. Cedar trees amid remains. The cedar zone in Cilicia is 1,400-1,800m*

to agro-pastoral landscapes, elite elements of the native population asserted increasing control over the terrain, its resources, and its production. Luwian elites of western Rough Cilicia clearly prospered and to some degree assimilated aspects of the predominant Graeco-Roman culture of the eastern Mediterranean. However, to a remarkable degree the native hierarchies appear to have selectively filtered imported attributes with an eye towards preserving their social ascendancy. The architectural research of the survey indicates, for example, a predilection for small Roman-era bath complexes (some with aqueducts) even at hinterland sites such as Asar Tepe and Gocuk Asari (**colour plate 24**). Other architectural attributes of mainstream Mediterranean culture, such as theatres, basilicas and stadia, are decidedly absent. The absence of such democratically oriented building complexes suggests that the importance of the wider populations in Luwian society was less than that of its 'elders'. The

68 *View of Hasdere Canyon looking north*

existence of elder hierarchies is not only suggested by Hellenistic literary testimony to the existence of '*tyrannoi*', therefore, but it can also be securely demonstrated by epigraphical references to councils, councillors and chief priests during the Roman era.

The region's inscriptions, particularly inscribed tombs and honorary statue bases, demonstrate, furthermore, the important place assigned to lineage in the native Luwian culture.[25] To be sure, lineage ties were important throughout the Graeco-Roman world, but the Luwian memorials reflect an extraordinary sensitivity toward lineage connections even by ancient standards. Descent from prominent elders is carefully preserved in dedications. Particularly noteworthy was the tendency to assign multiple sons the same name.[26] Female descent in the inscriptions is nearly as prominent as male (e.g. Bean and Mitford 1970: 87), indicating the importance placed on women in the lineage system despite their lack of political and civic status. Most significant of all are the numerous tomb dedications designated as 'heroons'; more than twenty such records survive in the survey area. To honour a deceased family elder as a 'hero' reflects an archaism during the Roman era and indicates the survival of a pre-Roman mindset capable of 'reproducing' itself even when submerged within a Roman world system. The veneration of elders is further supported by the team's architectural research at Lamos and Asar Tepe, where advanced Graeco-Roman temple design was used by inhabitants to construct tombs for the elders invariably situated at the centre of the urban community. Regional temple designs appear, in fact, to have been utilised more with 'heroons' than with cults of deities. Although decidedly taboo in Graeco-Roman culture, the presence of 'hero tombs' within urban precincts is increasingly recognised as a salient vestige of pre-Roman Anatolian cultures.[27] In addition, these 'hero tombs' are just as common in coastal cities such as Selinus as they are in the hinterland sites, indicating that there was no separation during the Roman era between the inhabitants of the hinterland and those of the shore. Very few Greek names, and slightly more Roman names are recorded in the region's inscriptions during the Early Roman era; the overwhelming majority of recorded nomenclature remained staunchly Luwian. This would indicate that native hierarchies were able to maintain their control over the 'port facilities' and hinterland resources of the region through the pirate era and beyond.

Much like the elder hierarchies in early modern Africa, the Luwian elites of Rough Cilicia appear to have reproduced the authority of their mode of production even while incorporating Graeco-Roman systems of taxation, monetarisation, specialised production (wine, oil and timber) for export purposes and cultural amenities such as the Roman ruler cult, roads, bath complexes and monumental building techniques. The labour issue remains less well delineated, but a number of 'corporate' tomb dedications at hinterland sites such as Lamos and Direvli indicate that junior elements of Luwian lineage groups were possibly dispatched by their elders to areas of hinterland production (particularly timber production) for such long durations that they were compelled to arrange for corporate burial societies (*koinon*) with wholly unrelated associates. The presence of freeborn, unrelated inhabitants in common tombs marks a striking development in a region whose inscriptions otherwise testify to the supremacy of lineage ties (Bean and Mitford 1970: 176f.). Combined with this is the complete absence of references to manumitted Luwians, and hence to slavery, in the region's inscriptions, something quite commonplace among burial associations in other regions harbouring large concentrations of slaves.[28] The absence of epigraphical references to local slavery would appear to indicate, therefore, that the Luwian elder hierarchies adapted their resource base to specialised levels of export production by dispatching their own 'juniors' to the production areas, and that they quite possibly exported captured slaves from the mountainous hinterland, not to mention their own disgruntled juniors, alongside wine, oil and timber. Luwian elders appear successfully to have transformed their social status as the living embodiments of Luwian ancestry into symbolic power, achieving a euphemisation that enabled them to transfigure relations of force by getting the violence they objectively contain misrecognised/recognised, and thereby producing their desired effect without having to expend energy (Raatgever 1985: 272). By accommodating off-shore Roman 'colonialists', entering willingly into the imperial ruler cult, co-operating with military officials, and opening their resource areas to Roman modes of taxation, surplus production, monetarisation and commercialisation, Luwian elders joined forces with the authorities of the world-system while reproducing and preserving the importance of their pre-Roman (lineage) mode of production.

Arguing backwards, one can posit a similar pattern of behaviour with respect to their dealings with immigrant bands of pirates. If pirate bands obtained external 'luxury goods' otherwise unavailable to the local elder hierarchies or 'tyrants', it is easy to see how the latter would have come to accept their presence and to attempt to accommodate this, in fact, by assigning elements of their 'junior' population to the work efforts of timbering operations, shipbuilding and seamanship required by the pirates themselves. A relationship of mutual co-operation could easily have resulted as more and more maritime refugees found asylum in these remote shores, bringing with them essential maritime skills and technologies. Despite the inability of the Rough Cilicia Archaeological Survey team to locate and to identify pirate remains in the narrow coastal stretch of western Rough Cilicia surveyed to date, there is no reason to reject the regional tradition for piracy. At Olympos, as noted above, recent Turkish survey work has revealed preliminarily the existence of a Hellenistic era fortress (Goktas Kalesi) on a narrow peak above the flaming vents of the 'Chimaera', as well as the remains of a stone-cut shrine near the harbour that possibly functioned as a Mithraeum (Atvur 1999: 27). This suggests that remains of Zenicetes' pirate enclave at this location not only survive on the landscape, but that the native inhabitants made an effort to preserve its memory.

At the same time it needs to be stressed that the recovered survey data for western Rough Cilicia suggests that the settlements along this coast were extremely small and frequently hidden from view. Some are situated at fortified hill sites high above the coastal ridges, others like Selinus possibly settled on the less visible landward flanks of coastal promontories, and still others such as 'the Kragos' and Iotape nestled amid rock precipices and hidden sea coves. Topographically, Hellenistic-era settlement in western Rough Cilicia presents itself as a series of small, fortified and extremely well-camouflaged sites along the coast. Rather than assimilate external cultural attributes or externally produced wares seemingly available from passing mercantile traffic, their inhabitants appear to have relied more on vernacular modes of construction and locally produced coarsewares. The settlements along this coast appear to have looked to the urban centres of Pamphylia for cultural, economic and political leadership and possibly serviced these centres as small satellite communities.

It remains difficult to determine at what point before 67 BC the Romans were adequately informed of the threat posed by the pirate settlements in western Rough Cilicia. Sites such as Korakesion and the Kragos were small, well hidden, and perhaps frequently relocated. With the entire Bay of Pamphylia at their disposal, pirate bands conceivably relocated several times from one end of the bay to the other during the course of the pirate menace's sixty-year lifespan. In time, the members of the Rough Cilicia Archaeological

Survey team hope to produce effective means to answer these questions. The evidence collected so far reminds us of the importance of furnishing an accurate regional context to a phenomenon such as the Cilician pirates and of the need to inform oneself of the sociological mainsprings to piracy before proceeding to identify pirate remains on the ground.

Maritime piracy

The other source of Cilician piracy arose from the natural antagonism that resulted from harsh labouring conditions at sea and the tendency, as noted above, of ancient seamen to assert their place within hierarchic society at large.[29] As bold and rebellious as the sailors of the maritime world may appear, they remained within the limits of ordered Mediterranean society, albeit as an underclass or subterranean element, divorced from, antagonistic to, but confined within that society. They provided the muscle, the technical knowledge and the experience that powered ancient merchantmen and conveyed the region's luxuries, raw materials and agricultural goods across the seas. However abused, despised and neglected, they remained essential cogs to a system of primitive accumulation; Mediterranean society itself could hardly have functioned without their participation.

Although it recruited its manpower from the same sources, Mediterranean piracy presented a wholly separate phenomenon. Pirates stood apart from land-dwelling society by positioning themselves to challenge the emerging hierarchy. As such they were recognised as outlaws and subjected to harsher punishments than those handed down to ordinary criminal elements. For unlike petty crime on land, maritime piracy had the capacity to disrupt the flow of foodstuffs to the urban centres of the world. Piracy used maritime lines of communication to subvert Mediterranean commerce and to threaten the very survival of its participating communities. As such pirates were not merely criminals, but as Cicero explains (*Verr.* 2.5.76), they were 'the most bitter, most dangerous adversaries of the Roman people, and what is more, a common foe to peoples and nations everywhere throughout the world'. At best pirates annoyingly co-existed with land-dwelling society, lurking about the choke points of the maritime sea-lanes and parasitically expropriating some small portion of the goods and materials that passed through their vicinity. At worst, as in the period under consideration, they forged a genuine maritime rebellion with the capacity to generate powerful armadas and to shut down the lines of trade. Although the origins of Cilician piracy were complex, its function as a release valve for the underlying social tensions of maritime society and, hence, as an expression of rebellion and reform, remain palpable.

Ancient piracy arose from several sources (**69**). At the local level, small-scale piracy occurred as a form of banditry at sea. Harsh treatment, scant livelihoods and rebellious attitudes in maritime centres throughout the Mediterranean invariably pushed some portion of the sailing population across the line into overt acts of crime. Once a seaman's instincts toward desertion or mutiny gave way to piracy, it ceased to be a redressive and defensive posture and assumed a far more aggressive stance. Local pirates in small, sleek, heavily-armed galleys perpetrated assaults indiscriminately on exposed sailing vessels after gathering intelligence about their cargoes in port. Plautus describes the process through a slave relating to an Athenian merchant how his voyage to recover the merchant's gold from Ephesus had gone awry (*Bacchidae* 286):

> — After we got the gold we embarked, eager for home. I was sitting on deck and while looking around my eye just happened to fall on a long, staunch, wicked looking galley being fitted out for sea . . . this galley was lying in wait for our ship. So I began to keep an eye on their operations aboard her. Meanwhile our ship weighed anchor and moved out of the harbour. As we left the harbour, they began to row after us fast as a bird, fast as the wind. Recognising what was up, we brought to at once. But they suddenly saw us lying to and began to slow down right there in the harbour.
> — What did you do then?
> — We put back to the harbour.
> — What did they do?
> — Towards evening they went ashore.

69 *Sixthy-century BC black figure kylix portraying a pirate craft attacking a merchant ship. Athenian cup in the British Museum, Arch. 85*

The eavesdropping ability of pirates in ancient harbours forms one of the staples of plot construction in Graeco-Roman fiction, and according to Strabo (14.1.32 (645)) posed a very real threat along the shores of Asia Minor, 'Sailors say the waters along the coast of Mount Korykos were everywhere the haunt of pirates. According to reports, the pirates would scatter themselves among the harbours of this coast, follow up the merchants whose vessels lay at anchor in them, and overhear what cargoes they had on board and their intended destination. Regrouping later, the pirates would attack the merchants after they had put to sea and plunder their vessels.' Much of this eavesdropping would occur where sailors and pirates naturally collected – in the bars and taverns of the harbours. In Chariton's *Chaereas and Callirhoe* (1.7–8), for example, a pirate chief named Theron at Syracuse composed his pirate crews from 'thugs handily stationed with boats in harbours posing as ferrymen'. Learning of a suitably lucrative opportunity, Theron hurried one morning to the harbour to assemble his band: 'some of them he found in brothels, others in taverns – an army fit for such a commander. Saying he had something important to discuss with them he took them "behind the harbour" to explain.'

The very decision to embark on the path of maritime crime meant, of course, that pirates were prepared to assault any and all voyagers sailing onboard a targeted vessel – merchants, entrepreneurs, land-dwelling passengers and labouring seamen alike. Assaults on maritime shipping necessitated that pirates potentially turn their backs on their own kind and be prepared to victimise sailors alongside other passengers of a merchant vessel, at the very least by plundering its cargoes and thereby denying the ordinary seaman his eventual wages. Pirates had little choice but to be ruthless: if captured, they were crucified. As Cicero demonstrates (*Verr.* 2.5.65–67), people of all social orders derived satisfaction from the sight of their executions: 'the *homines maritimi* of Syracuse, who had often heard and often trembled at the name of this pirate chief, longed to feast their eyes and satisfy their souls with the spectacle of his torture and execution . . . Crowds gathering to see the spectacle came from every quarter to greet his captor, not only from the towns through which the prisoners passed, but from neighbouring towns as well.'

While the indiscriminate character of pirate assaults made the pirate universally despised, the gravity of a pirate menace functioned, at the same time, as a crucial barometer of the intensity of maritime working-class frustration. Seamen as pirates were, in essence, labourers expropriating the workplace and arranging it anew. As a social world, the crew of a pirate vessel separated itself from the ways of the merchant and the captain to engage in a form of class war.

Beyond piracy as a local form of maritime crime, Mediterranean piracy frequently assumed a larger pattern of warfare and naval hegemony, particularly when conducted by less advantaged populations that resided in barren coastal regions bordering crucial sea-lanes. With its mountains, its jagged shores and inlets, its numerous islands, and its inordinate dependence on

maritime commerce, the Mediterranean basin fostered several regional populations, such as the Ligurians, the Illyrians, the Aetolians, the Black Sea
Thracians, the Cretans and the Cilicians, notorious for their tendencies
toward piracy.[1] In most cases, piratical endeavours were supplemented by shipbuilding capacities made available by abundant forestry resources in their
home regions. Luxuries, agricultural and finished goods, and raw materials
necessarily had to pass through these 'choke points' in search of suitable
markets. To seemingly 'antisocial elements', such as the Illyrians and the
Cretans, piracy offered a means by which to impose their authority over self-
declared 'territorial waters', providing a legitimate means by which to exact
'transit dues' in exchange for guarantees of safe passage. Accordingly, the
ruling elements of these regions employed piracy as a means to intimidate
distant, more prosperous commercial powers, causing the function of piracy
in these instances to assume larger significance. Established mercantile powers
attempting to construct viable trade routes across the Mediterranean
contemptuously described the aggressive behaviour of these remotely situated
polities as maritime crime. The perpetrators tended, however, to regard their
seizures as 'legitimate acts of war'.

Although regionally based piracy ships were generally manned by elements
drawn from the native warrior elites, the manpower and technical requirements of warships inevitably required the recruitment of skilled seamen from
further abroad. Many sailors eager to escape harsh conditions elsewhere
enlisted in regional pirate bands in exchange for portions of booty. In addition,
the capacity of regional pirate elements was greatly augmented during periods
of wider Mediterranean conflict when they could sell their services as privateers to competing regional empires. During the third and second centuries
BC, for example, the Carthaginians suborned the Ligurians, Philip V of
Macedonia the Illyrians, and Antiochus III of Syria the Aetolians, in their
efforts to oppose Rome. The piratical elements of Crete, Cyprus and Cilicia
so regularly bolstered the warring fleets of the Seleucids and the Ptolemies that
the ruling elements of these regional powers came quite naturally to regard
themselves as legitimate naval arms. With payment in 'coin of the realm', it
was substantially easier for them to recruit essential manpower, with the
frequent result that regional piracy tended to emerge from major conflicts
stronger than it began.

Towards the end of the second century BC, a new phase of piracy, referred
to universally as Cilician piracy, combined locally and regionally situated
outlaw behaviour with Mediterranean-wide maritime discontent to form a
more serious, complex menace. As repeated conflicts and the quickening
economic pace drove more and more young men onto the sea, working conditions worsened, driving more and more seamen into piracy. By the late second
century BC, the numbers engaged in piracy swelled to unprecedented levels to
pose a genuine threat to cities, empires and the international mercantile order.

The so-called Cilician pirates reflected a genuine attempt to challenge social authority on the seas, fomenting not merely rebellion but an underclass programme of reform.

The Cilician pirates emerged from a prolonged sequence of dynastic disputes in Seleucid Syria. During one such contest in the late 140s BC, a pretender named Diodotus Tryphon managed to install 'naval forces' at a number of impregnable fortresses along the eastern Mediterranean corridor – most particularly at Coracesium (Korakesion) and high above the inaccessible cliffs of 'the Kragos Mountain' in western Rough Cilicia. Although it straddled one of the main sea-lanes of the Mediterranean, the western corner of Rough Cilicia was otherwise remote, and minimally populated – a perfect environment for pirate habitation. As noted above, the dozen or so small settlements in this region were at this time little more than fortified way-stations for coasting traffic and for gaining access to region's natural abundance of ship-building materials and naval supplies. This combined with the fact that it straddled the main sea-lane to and from Egypt made it an attractive and relatively easy 'backwater' to inhabit.

Despite the death of Tryphon himself in 138 BC, his naval contingents continued to launch assaults throughout the region, apparently acting as independent, autonomous pirate bands. At first their marauding was tolerated by regional military powers – the republic of Rhodes, the Attalid kings of Pergamum, the Ptolemies of Egypt and Cyprus, and Roman commercial elements active in the Aegean. The pirates not only directed the thrust of their assaults against Seleucid assets, but they enhanced the illicit commerce of the region by generating sales of captured pirate booty (slaves and luxuries) at notorious harbours such as Aegean Delos, Lycian Phaselis and Pamphylian Side. As noted above, the role of independent cities in Pamphylia and eastern Lycia seems particularly significant in this regard because the region had endured centuries of oppression as a buffer zone between Aegean and Near Eastern hegemonies. At the eastern end of the Bay of Pamphylia, native Luwian elder hierarchies or 'tyrants' appear to have welcomed pirate bands into their coastal settlements as a way to add new maritime dimensions to their long-standing supremacy on shore. Military setbacks to several regional powers, combined with a solid dose of intimidation by Rome, temporarily converted the Bay of Pamphylia into a hegemonic 'no-man's-land', enabling its inhabitants to pursue an independent course with relative impunity. To some degree, therefore, Cilician piracy furnished a 'extra-legal' naval arm to the aspirations of various regional elites, and pirate enclaves soon emerged throughout the Bay of Pamphylia. As noted above, one pirate chief named Zenicetes carved out an independent territory for himself in eastern Lycia, centred in a castle near the eternal fires of the 'Chimera' and dominating the harbours of Olympos, Korykos and Phaselis. Further east the successors to Diotodus Tryphon constructed impregnable fortresses at Korakesion and the

'Kragos mountain', complete with well-stocked harbours, warehouses, ship sheds, and skilled artisans and labourers chained to their stations.

With minimal risk of reprisals by regional powers, a host population willing to fence their contraband, abundant resources for shipbuilding, adequate food resources, fortified positions along an imposing mountainous coast, and the close proximity of the most important maritime sea-lane in the world, the pirates of Cilicia began to conduct their ambuscades with greater audacity. By 102 BC, their depredations sufficiently outweighed the benefits of their illegal traffic to compel the Romans to take action against them, employing a combined programme of diplomatic pressure, legal prohibition and main force. These efforts proved minimally effective: the pirates survived a naval assault by M. Antonius, the grandfather of Mark Antony, who apparently got as far as Side, and soon gained new-found support from Rome's greatest adversary in the region, King Mithradates VI of Pontus. By aligning themselves with Mithradates at the outset of his war against Rome (88–84 BC), the pirates greatly enhanced their naval capacities and expanded their sway to new, more distant territories.

Although the commander of the Roman war effort, L. Cornelius Sulla, ultimately compelled Mithradates to withdraw from Asia, he was unable to address the pirate menace itself. Sulla's pressing need to return to Italy to defeat internal Roman adversaries obliged him to accept a half-finished peace in the region, a peace that left the pirates not only untouched but in a better position than they had been prior to the war. The sources uniformly stress the importance of the pirates' transition from a regional menace to one of wider proportions at this time. 'Piracy had always existed in certain locals', explains Cassius Dio (36.20.1), 'but at this time, ever since war had been carried on continuously in many different places at once, and many cities had been overthrown, sentences hung over the heads of all the fugitives. Since there was no freedom from fear for anyone anywhere, large numbers took to plundering.' Commenting specifically about the harsh conditions resulting from Sulla's settlement in the province of Asia (western Anatolia), Plutarch (*Pomp.* 24) concludes that 'some men of wealth, of good family, and of exceptional intelligence began to join the pirate fleets and to share in their enterprises, regarding piracy as a profession by which honour could be attained and ambition satisfied'.

As the Cilician pirates gained strength and sophistication, they exploited Roman preoccupations with civil war to extend their operations across the Mediterranean sea. 'For while the Romans were occupied with their opponents,' continues Dio (36.20.4), 'the pirates made great headway, sailing about to many quarters, and adding to their band all of like condition, until a small number of them, in the manner of allies, were able to assist many others.' As Appian observes (*Mith.* 92), the pirates offered genuine asylum to destitute seamen throughout the eastern maritime waters, 'sailors from Cilicia, Syria,

Cyprus, Pamphylia and Pontus, and those of almost all the eastern nations, who, on account of the severity and the length of the Mithradatic War, preferred to do wrong rather than to suffer it, chose the sea instead of the land.' Once the possibilities of strength in numbers, relative security, and profitable shares of booty began to present themselves, naval mercenaries and mobile seamen increasingly flocked to the pirate enclaves of the Bay of Pamphylia, finding there the very things unavailable to themselves in 'ordered' maritime society – a decent livelihood, a stable residence, and freedom from land-dwelling oppression. The Cilician pirates quickly came to represent an elite breed of seamen, recruited from the best crews of merchant ships, privateers and war fleets. As Plutarch explains (*Pomp.* 24.3), 'the fleets which put in at the Cilician pirate bases were admirably equipped for their own work with fine crews, expert pilots and light fast ships.'

The pirates gradually expanded their range of operations throughout the seas, selecting hidden locales, seizing control of promontories, desert islands and road-steads along crucial Mediterranean shipping lanes. Pirate chiefs roving in separate theatres of the sea employed the available conspiracy networks of maritime taverns to communicate with one another and to support one another militarily and financially. 'The pirates showed such friendship for one another,' explains Dio (36.22.4–5), 'as to send money and assistance even to those with whom they were wholly unacquainted, as if they were their nearest of kin. In fact, this was one of the chief sources of their strength – that those who paid court to any of them were honoured by all, and those who challenged any of them were plundered by all.' According to Plutarch and Appian, the pirates eventually wielded a combined armament of several hundred warships (including 90 decked ships of standard military class) and 30,000 naval combatants.[31]

The sudden cohesiveness of the Cilician pirates caught land-dwelling aris-tocracies everywhere by surprise. Instead of intermittent hit-and-run assaults on merchantmen, by the 70s BC the Cilician pirates displayed a capacity to shut down sea-lanes altogether, even during the quiet winter months. They mounted mainland assaults as well, allegedly storming more than 400 cities and twelve sanctuaries of the Hellenistic world. By relying on their knowledge of the trade routes, they roved into the western Mediterranean, aiding and abetting Sulla's recalcitrant enemy, Q. Sertorius, in Spain, and marauding commerce in and around Sicily, Sardinia and Corsica. Exploiting the sailor's advantages of expertise, experience and mobility, the Cilician pirates soon mounted a full-fledged maritime rebellion.

Cognisant of the seriousness of this threat, the Romans dispatched a number of pro-magistrates against them. The most successful prior to Cn. Pompeius Magnus was unquestionably P. Servilius Vatia (Isauricus), consul in 79 BC, who in a three-year campaign stormed the pirate empire of Zenicetes, restored Roman rule in Pamphylia, and conquered the Isaurians and other bandit tribesmen in the mountainous interior of Cilicia (Ormerod 1922). The effectiveness of Isauricus' campaign, combined with the likelihood of further assaults, did probably convince the Cilician pirates to redirect the force of their campaigns toward the West, hoping in this manner to draw Roman attention as far from the bases in Cilicia as possible. As a component of this strategy, they entered into closer diplomatic relations with Mithradates and Sertorius, an arrangement culminating in an 'unholy alliance' that converged on Rome from all points of the Mediterranean in 75–74 BC (Rauh 1997: 267). Piratical assaults on Italy proper were highlighted by inland raids and scorched-earth campaigns in southern Italy, by firings of fleets (military and commercial) in Ostia and Caieta, and by a series of sensational kidnappings of Roman dignitaries and very important persons. As Appian observes (*Mith.* 93), their dispersion, their knowledge and experience with the sea, their surreptitious movement, their effective communications, and their unity of purpose furnished the Cilician pirates a momentary advantage over their more heavily armed, better organised adversaries:

> It appeared to the Romans to be a huge and difficult task to destroy so large a force of seafaring men scattered every which way on land and sea, with no fixed possession to encumber their flight, sallying out from no particular country or any known places, having no property or anything to call their own, but only what they might chance to light upon. Thus the unexampled nature of this war, which was subject to no laws and had nothing tangible or visible about it, caused perplexity and fear.

Piracy at this scale can no longer be described as an incidence of maritime crime, or as the violent extension of some newly-formed hegemony in Pamphylia. Rather, it assumed the guise of a maritime rebellion. Cilician piracy articulated both the Mediterranean maritime labourer's frustration with his working conditions and his desire for a better life. As more and more Mediterranean seamen sought refuge in their bands, the Cilician pirates came to form a unique social order, a way of life voluntarily chosen, for the most part, by large numbers of men who directly challenged the ways of the society from which they excepted themselves. Vengeance against land-dwelling aristocracies played a large part in their motivation, but their purposes were not simply destructive. The Cilician pirates constructed their society in defiant opposition to the ways of the world they left behind. Though viewed as outcasts and criminals by established social orders, they themselves acted as revolutionary traditionalists, searching for a world in which men were justly dealt with, and the rich and the oppressors avenged. Through fair, egalitarian treatment and just behaviour within pirate bands and active efforts at co-operation externally between bands, pirates formed their own unique social order, with a sense of maritime ethos and a consciousness of kind (Rediker 1987: 254–280).

In place of the harsh realities of established maritime society, the Cilician pirates appear to have governed themselves according to a strict code of egalitarianism and social brotherhood. Pirate egalitarianism emerged, at least in part, as a reaction against the hierarchy of the merchant ship and its attendant privileges and abuses. Seamen were always more content when everyone shared equally in the toil and danger of maritime labour. In many areas of shipboard life – food, wages, and discipline – these burdens were inequitably distributed, provoking the rise of a levelling sentiment in opposition. An emphasis on equality also grew from the very scarcity of necessities aboard ship, from the fact that all too often the seamen faced poverty and deprivation. In other words, the pirates' egalitarianism both grew from and was nourished by the manifold vulnerabilities of life at sea (Rediker 1987: 261–7).

Pirate crews elected their captains and expected them to act as bold leaders in combat and fair administrators of justice. Crews organised themselves through written articles of agreement and cemented the loyalty of all new members by swearing them to the most dreadful sacred oaths. By these means they were able to form counter cultural communities socially isolated from mainstream Mediterranean hierarchies. 'Are not bands of robbers themselves like small realms?' asks St Augustine (*Civ. Dei* 4.4 and 6), 'Are they not groups of men commanded by a chief and drawn together by a social contract or by written agreements that determine their distributions of booty?' Discipline in work and in battle was tightly regulated; booty was distributed according to an archaic method of maritime shares; and some portions of the booty were set aside as a common fund for the needs of the permanently disabled. In contrast to their treatment under normal maritime conditions, pirates distributed the benefits as well as the risks of their labour fairly and equitably and attended to, rather than abandoned, the needs of their disabled and dependents. As Cicero observes (*De Off.* 2.40), 'the importance of justice is so great that not even those who engage in crime for a livelihood can survive without some canons of justice among themselves. If a pirate chief, for example, failed to distribute booty equitably among his crew, he would be abandoned or even killed by his comrades. Hence the rule 'honour among thieves' which they are all obliged to observe.'

Ensconced in their impregnable Cilician fortresses, the pirates sustained their communities generationally, supporting women, children and disabled pirates in a manner wholly inconceivable during their previous existence as seamen. When the Romans finally assaulted Korakesion, for example, Plutarch (*Pomp.* 28) reveals that the pirates had concealed 'their families, their property, and a large crowd of disabled warriors' in mountain forts and castles scattered behind this settlement. The internal discipline of the Cilicians is possibly revealed by the 'strange sacrifices' and 'secret rites' of the god Mithras that Zenicetes conducted for his pirate band at Olympos (Plut. *Pomp.* 24). The ascetic character of this religious cult made it popular among the pirates, and its magical aura of invincibility possibly steeled their resolve to withstand the military superiority of Rome. By these and other means the Cilician pirates consistently expressed a highly developed consciousness of kind that acted as a strategy of survival and formed a collectivist ethos. Cilician piracy was not simply an economic crime – the theft of private property. It was a movement in social reform, with thousands of armed seamen organising themselves into anarchic, yet highly motivated democracies, seeking to provide themselves with more tolerable living conditions, more stable communities, and a fair and more equitable social system. It was also a political act – a protest against the obvious use of state institutions to defend property and discipline labour. From here it was a small step to retaliate against the established hierarchy and to punish it for its years of indifference and neglect.

As compassionate and just as pirates were in their treatment of their own community, they behaved harshly and vengefully toward the oppressive elements of established society that hunted them down (Rediker 1987: 273f.). To the pirates vengeance was justice, and an extremely violent form at that. By engaging in a system of reciprocal terror, the pirates attempted to turn the tables on the social orders responsible for maritime oppression by making them the victims and the pirates themselves the arbiters of justice. During the peak of their military effectiveness the pirates engaged in successive waves of terrorist-style kidnappings of prominent Roman political and social figures, striking fear into the hearts of the Roman elite. Landward roving pirates kidnapped Julius Caesar, Publius Clodius, the aunt of Mark Antony, and two Roman praetors marching in full regalia along the Appian Way (Rauh 1997: 267). Aristocrats, generals and senators were not the only persons victimised by pirate justice, however; the superior social status of any Roman prisoner could leave him exposed to potentially brutal treatment, as Plutarch starkly explains (*Pomp.* 24):

> But the way in which they treated their prisoners was the most outrageous thing of all. If a prisoner cried out that he was a Roman and gave his name, they would pretend to be absolutely terrified; the pirates would smite their thighs and hands and fall down at his feet begging him to forgive them. The prisoner, seeing them so humbled and hearing their entreaties, would believe that they meant what they said. They would dress him in Roman boots and a Roman toga in order, they said, that there should be no mistake about his identity in the future. And so they would play with him for a time, getting all the amusement possible out of him until, in the end, they would let down a ship's ladder when they were far out to sea and tell him that he was quite free to go, wishing him a pleasant journey. If he attempted to resist, they threw him overboard and drowned him.

In this manner pirates reduced the institutions of the society they warred with to mere caricatures. By doing so they also diminished the lingering fears that they, as rebels against, but products of, that society, still bore in their hearts (Sherry 1986: 141). Other evidence suggest that the pirates were discriminating in their vengeance, punishing and assaulting some nobles, yet distinguishing others for instances of past kindness toward ordinary working men. In one example a number of pirate chiefs in warships beached near the seaside villa of the Roman general, P. Scipio Aemilianus, in Italy, allegedly to demonstrate notions of justice and fair play (Val. Max. 2.10.2), 'for they shouted to him from outside that they had not come to plunder his household or seize his person, but simply to gaze upon his countenance, to shake his hand, and to honour the man they so universally admired as a divine gift to humanity.' Incidents such as this reveal how pirates attempted to intervene against – and to modify – the standard brutalities that characterised social relations aboard ancient sailing vessels.

Beyond this, Cilician pirates flaunted their escape from the norms of established society by assuming, and thus mocking, the material trappings of land-dwelling status designation. Cilician pirate chiefs dressed in outlandish, colourful clothing and, according to Plutarch (*Pomp.* 24.3), ornamented their ships with 'gilded sails, purple awnings, and silvered oars.' In the popular consciousness pirates assumed stature larger than life, assuming flamboyant *nommes de guerre*, such as Agamemnon, Seleucus, Heracleo, and Pyrganio, and addressing themselves as tyrants, kings, and admirals (Cassius Dio 36.21.1; App. *Mith.* 92).

Apart from dress and behaviour deliberately intended to mock the established authorities, several of the most notorious behavioural patterns of the Cilician pirates reflected their momentous urge to celebrate hard-fought freedom. The social contours of piracy, although fully congruent with the labour process at sea, were often formed in violent antipathy to that world of work from which many seamen gladly escaped. From their hidden ports pirate crews celebrated their naval victories with endless rounds of drinking bouts and 'wenching'. It was the freedom to drink as much and as often as he liked that the ordinary sea outlaw prized above all others, as it furnished the undeniable proof that he was genuinely free. Sexual indulgence was a similarly cherished liberty, while music provided by talented members of the crew added a third important component to their revels. Cicero (*Verr.* 2.5.63, 71, 73) complains that the crew of a pirate ship seized in Sicily in 73 BC included 'several handsome youths' and 'six musicians' whom the Roman governor kept for his own purposes. Elsewhere he accuses P. Clodius, during his ransom by the Cilician pirates, of having submitted to their insults and sexual gratification (*Har. Resp.* 42; cf. *Div. in Caec.* 55). As Plutarch observes (*Pomp.* 24.3-4), it was the pirates' open and unbridled expression of freedom and escape from aristocratic dominance that most painfully offended Roman authorities:

[The Cilician pirates] were certainly formidable enough; but what excited the most indignation was the odious arrogance of it all – the gilded sails, the purple awnings, the silvered oars – the general impression that they were delighting in this way of life and priding themselves on their evil deeds. Roman supremacy was brought into contempt by their flute-playing, their stringed instruments, their drunken revels along every coast, their seizures of high ranking officials, and the ransoms they demanded from captured cities.

The Cilician pirates displayed a recurrent willingness to join forces at sea and in port, thereby expanding the basis of their movement to one of international scope. As Dio noted above, wholly unacquainted pirate crews exchanged greetings and invoked an unwritten code of hospitality to forge spontaneous alliances. 'The Cilician pirate chiefs', records Appian (*Mith.* 92), 'thought that if they should all unite they would be invincible.' Like the everyday common seamen that they were, the Cilician pirates transcended cultural and ethnic boundaries to forge vast maritime brotherhoods, implementing a psychological solidarity against a common foe. Organised into a broad confederacy, an ethnically diverse array of naval warriors cruised a 'pirate round' from Korakesion in Cilicia to Dianium in Spain, plundering sanctuaries and maritime cities, foraging inland, effectively shutting down the sea-lanes, and nearly starving the far-flung territories of the Roman Republic into submission.

Through decades of maritime violence the Cilician pirates effectively brought the evolving process of primitive accumulation in the Mediterranean region to a grinding, if temporary, halt. As with most rebellions, however, the size and scope of this maritime movement eventually surpassed the available manpower and resources necessary to sustain it. Seamen were, after all, a highly specialised wage-labouring force, one of several required in a complex society. Without a sustained and stable flow of goods and services from mainland agricultural regions, maritime society itself quickly fell into jeopardy. From the outset Cilician pirates had forged a fragile social world, dependent on foodstuffs and surplus resources generated by the very inhabitants they themselves imperilled by their raids. Apart from weapons and warships, the inhabitants of the pirate enclaves at Korakesion and the Kragos Mountain produced nothing and had no secure place in the economic order. Enclosed by towering mountains and narrowly bordering the sea, the agricultural pockets of western Rough Cilicia could hardly sustain an expanding population short of plunder. Owing to the pirates' own successes, the availability of outside resources must gradually have diminished. Pirates dwelling outside Cilicia were even more exposed, with no sustainable agricultural hinterlands, no cities, and, for purposes of security, exceedingly dispersed. Try as they might, they were unable to create reliable mechanisms through which to replenish their ranks or to mobilize their collective strength. These deficiencies of social organisation made them, in the long run, easy prey. As the Roman aristocracy gradually focused its attention on this menace, the pirates' very strengths – independence, diversity, dispersal and decentralisation – became double-edged weapons used to their own disadvantage.

In 67 BC the Roman popular assembly commissioned a proven young general, Cn. Pompeius Magnus, with extraordinary powers to eradicate piracy once and for all throughout the seas (**70**). With some twenty-four legates, 270 'ships of the line', and the authority to draw upon a complement of 120,000 infantry, 4,000 cavalry and 8,000 talents of revenue, Pompey swept the Mediterranean from west to east in a three-month campaign, cornering the last holdouts in their bases in Cilicia and defeating them, ultimately, in the waters off Korakesion (Rauh 1997: 267). The speed with which Pompey suppressed the pirates would seem remarkable, were it not for the fact that it resulted as much from his efforts at conciliation as it did from his reliance on main force (Plut. *Pomp.* 27). After crushing the last holdouts at Korakesion and apprehending some 20,000 renegades in all, Pompey allegedly contemplated that the majority of these seamen 'were poor and used to war; so he did not think it would be wise to let them go or to allow them to disperse and to reorganise themselves as bands' (Plut. *Pomp.* 28). According to Plutarch, Pompey resettled the pirates in 'the small and half-populated cities of Cilicia', at Tarentum in Italy, and at Dyme in Achaia, 'which was at that time very underpopulated and had a lot of good

70 *Pompey the Great – as a young man, based on a bust in the Uffizi Museum, Florence*

land'. In the final analysis, Pompey succeeded at suppressing this rebellion by furnishing captured pirates with the opportunity to return to the land.

With this solution a momentous phase in Mediterranean maritime history came to an end. The cycle of primitive accumulation had come around full circle. The survivors of this rebellion quickly assumed newfound status as the settled agricultural supporters of Pompey the Great. When summoned, their progeny would enlist in Pompey's armadas to fight against Caesar, not to mention the armadas of Pompey's son, Sextus, against the triumvirs, or those of Antony and Cleopatra against Octavian.[32] In these final conflicts, however, it was not so much the seamen who were renegades as their commanders. Incessant warfare had gradually converted marine employment into a seller's market; the dynasts at the end of the Hellenistic era had little choice but to recruit droves of landless seamen into their armadas. The experience of Cilician piracy undoubtedly touched the lives of numerous ordinary seamen, but more importantly it provoked a change in attitudes within the ruling class itself. Wave after wave of civil war and social chaos enabled rebellious maritime elements effectively to merge with the wider Mediterranean labouring population. For a brief time at least, pirates and ordinary seamen obtained for themselves a more legitimate place in Mediterranean society.

Conclusion

In his *Res Gestae*, Augustus claims as one of his greatest accomplishments his success at having 'cleared the seas of pirates', a feat that appears to have struck a universal chord. 'Given the widespread peace that prevails nowadays and the total absence of piracy,' remarks Strabo (3.2.5 (144)), 'all sailors feel wholly at ease.' Later orators such as Aelius Aristides would boast: (*To Rome* 10–13) 'we have no fear now either of the Cilician pass or of the narrow tracks through the Arabian sands into Egypt.' Likewise the early Christian writer Irenaeus acknowledges, 'because the world has been brought to peace by the Romans, we can travel the highways without fear and sail to any destination we may choose.'

No illusion should persist regarding the extent of maritime peace during the period that followed. Urban communities such as Alexandria, Athens, refounded Carthage and Rome and continued to demonstrate tendencies toward protest, demonstration and rioting during the imperial era. Many of the sources that describe the lowly plight of sailors date to the imperial era as well, showing little evidence of improvement in their situation. Reduced levels of military violence during the *pax romana* may have rendered sailors' existence somewhat safer, but the extension of Roman *imperium* throughout the seas also precluded the possibility of sailors seeking refuge in remote regions such as Rough Cilicia. In short, the satisfaction with the *pax romana* expressed by the sources in the previous paragraph was largely the satisfaction of landlubbers.

What the present study has attempted to demonstrate is that the volume of trade that occurred in the Mediterranean between 167 and 67 BC was the largest ever experienced in the ancient world. Converging forms of evidence indicates that this trade trended eastwards across the Mediterranean to the Indian Ocean, raising important questions about the extent to which macroregional trade stimulated rising productivity in the Mediterranean basin. This study has also attempted to demonstrate that Roman trade expanded in the wake of Roman military imperialism. Emerging amphora evidence indicates that Roman goods expelled Greek goods from the western Mediterranean and the Aegean in much the same manner that Roman armies crushed the maritime populations in their path. Evidence of Roman Republican amphora finds above the destruction levels at Carthage and Corinth indicate, once again, that Roman private traders continued to utilise these strategic harbours following the expulsion of their maritime populations. What changed was the disappearance at these places of once-thriving communities offering livelihoods for thousands of people. Accordingly, the evidence suggests that maritime communities, representative of a broader maritime culture throughout the Mediterranean, resisted Roman expansion at every step. To be sure, maritime labourers were not the only social element to oppose Rome at this juncture. However, more than any other cultural group maritime labourers communicated their forms of resistance to others, acting as a conduit for more general lower-class discontent.

Despite evidence of the ordinary seaman's continuing exposure to hardship, poverty and abuse, his experience during the violent years of the first century BC had taught land-dwelling aristocracies of the Mediterranean the crucial lessons of a complex society. In the bars and taverns of Mediterranean ports the anger of the maritime mob persisted, but its most aggressive energies appear to have been tempered by the sheer abundance of labouring opportunities as well as the attentiveness of the newly formed Roman imperial administration. However much land dwellers continued to revile the weather-beaten seaman, no one denied his importance. In the first century AD Pliny the Elder (*NH* 2.118, 125) complains that 'a universal multitude now sails the seas in search of profit', words seemingly corroborated by Juvenal's contemporary scorn (*Sat.* 14.276), 'gaze at our sea and our harbours now filled with mighty ships. Most of the population has now gone to sea. A fleet will sail anywhere your hopes for profits beckon – beyond the Carpathian waters, past the Gaetulian seas, beyond the straits of Gibraltar, sailing westwards to hear the sun hissing in Hercules' ocean. It is a noble return for all this trouble to sail home proud, with purse stretched tight and bags full of money.' The degree to which the survival and prosperity of Mediterranean society depended upon the smooth functioning of the maritime highways and of the workmen who sailed them was lost on very few. The disciplined work habits, collectivist mentality and egalitarian impulses of common seamen had left their impact on Rome, helping to ensure the Mediterranean world's prosperity for centuries to come.

Notes

1 Historical Introduction

1. Morton 2001: 37; Bradford 1971: 33. The specific gravity of the Mediterranean (1.028 in the west to 1.03 in the Levant) is higher than the Atlantic on the west (1.026) and the Black Sea in the east (1.102).
2. Its strength varies from 6 knots noted above at the Straits of Gibraltar to 2 to 6 through the channel between Sicily and North Africa, 2 to 3 knots off the coasts of Egypt, Palestine and Syria, about 4 through the Hellespont, about 2 around Crete, up to 6 or more through the Straits of Messina and about 0.5 to 1.5 knots along coasts of Italy and southern Gaul (Pryor 1988: 13).
3. Bradford 1971: 33; Morton 2001: 44.
4. Depending on the season an Atlantic subtropical high-pressure system over the Azores contends in the west with a North Atlantic sub-polar low-pressure system circulating between Iceland and Greenland. In the east a Mongolian high pressure system over Central Asia confronts an Indo-Persian monsoonal low pressure above Pakistan: Pryor 1988 14f.; Morton 2001: 46f.
5. For sailing speeds, see Casson 1971: 282f.
6. Frost 1973; Blackman 1982.
7. Strabo 14.3.2 (664). Knoblauch 1977: 43.
8. For the harbour of Phaselis, Blackman 1973.
9. See below, chapter 3.
10. See Boren 1957; Yavetz 1958; Brunt 1966; Frier 1982; Scobie 1986.
11. See Dyson 1995.

2 Cities

1. App. *Lib.* 69, 117; Lancel 1995: 415, 422.
2. App. *Lyb.* 128. The Byrsa area was levelled by Roman contractors in the Augustan era to create a flattened area for massive monumental construction. However, the *insulae* downslope have survived and been excavated. Lancel 1995: 156f.
3. App. *Lib.* 93; Strabo 17.3.15 (833); Lancel 1995: 414.
4. Lancel 1995: 176-7; Hurst 1979.
5. Hurst 1979: 27–8; Lancel 1995: 177. The chronology for the construction of this edifice is confused by the ceramic remains of Campanian A pottery, Dressel 1A and African Dressel 18 amphorae, all of which post-date its destruction in 146 BC.
6. Lancel 1995: 179, 189, named after the archaeologist who first mapped it.
7. Cicero described the place as heavily defended by walls and surrounded by harbours: Cic. *De Leg. Agr.* 2.32.87; Lancel 1995: 190.
8. Strabo 8.6.21–2 (379) (85 stadia); a very rough estimate.
9. Paris 1915; Rothaus 1995.
10. See Bruneau 1979: 99–104.
11. Xen. *Hell.* 4.4.12; Paus. 2.2.3; Plut. *Mor.* 146D; cf. Rothaus 1995.
12. See Engels 1990: 58f.; MacDonald 1986.
13. Scranton and Shaw 1978.
14. Ibrahim 1976; the panels were intended to be mounted as the decorative facing of the walls of some building but had never been installed. They were found in shipping crates, presumably delivered but abandoned because of some catastrophe.
15. Polyb. 40.7; Paus. 2.1.2; 7.16.7; 5.16.5; 17.15–16; Liv. *Per.* 52; Flor. 2.16; Oros. 5.3; Vell. Pat. 1.13; Plin. *NH* 24.6 and 12; 35.151; Val. Max. 7.5.4; cf. 2.7.1; Gell. *NA* 16.16.17.
16. For evidence of post-settlement occupation at Corinth: Grace and Savvatianou-Petropoulakou 1970: 285; Grace 1956: 146 n. 19; Will 1997: 126.
17. Diod. 32.26.2–3; Polyb. 38.15; Colin 1905: 625 f., 406f.
18. Pollux *Onomast.* 9.34; Arist. *Pax* 165; Luc. *Dial. Meretr.* 11.2; Plaut. *Epid.* 182f.; Arist. *Pol.* 2.5; Garland 1987: 143; Bloch 1912: 316.

19. Initial report by Vanderpool 1960; cf. Harrison 1975: 127 n.149; Habicht 1997: 310. The figure of Athena's broken left foot indicates that it was removed from its pedestal by force. Another theory holds that the gold staters struck by Aristion in 87/6 were likewise made from Delian treasure.
20. Dem. 22.76, 23.207; *IG* 2² 1627–31.
21. *IG* 2² 1627–31; Gabrielsen 1997: 93.
22. Similar access was provided in the neighbourhood of the junction of the south Long Wall by means of a postern inside and a larger gate outside. Another important gate stood at the north end of the peninsula of Eetioneia, near the shrine of Aphrodite: Garland 1987: 166–9.
23. Both silver and bronze Athenian coins buried at this time are dated by symbols marking the moment of this siege. The coins struck in 87/6 BC, for example, all bear the star between two half moons, symbols used by the minting administration of King Mithradates of Pontus and Aristion the tyrant to commemorate their joint issue (Habicht 1997: 304, 309).
24. Roussel 1916: 99; Badian 1976; Tracy 1979; Habicht 1997: 287f.
25. See below, chapter 3.
26. Kroll 1964: 81–117; S. Sherwin White 1978: 135; Höghammar 1993: 36; Rauh 1993: 6; Habicht 1997: 291.
27. Habicht 1997: 301. As Habicht notes, several inscriptions indicate that circumstances were still quite normal during the mid-90s BC.
28. Having previously served in 101/100: Habicht 1997: 301–2. No details of what became of Medeios are known. Someone by that name is on Sulla's staff in 86, either himself or his son, see note 24.
29. Athen. 5.214; Habicht 1997: 302, Ferguson 1911: 440.
30. Athen. 5.212; Habicht 1997: 300; Ferguson 1911: 441.
31. When the priestess of Athena came to him desperate for grain, he offered her pepper; when an embassy of priests and council members of the Areopagus came pleading for an end to hostilities, he ordered his guards to disperse them with volleys of arrows: App. *Mith*. 39; Plut. *Sull*. 13.
32. App. *Mith*. 38; for physical damage in Athens, see Habicht 1997: 307.
33. Plut. *Publicola* 15.4; Plin. *NH* 36.54; Habicht 1997: 313.
34. See below, chapter 3.
35. Small finds include a graffito ending in the Latin letters, ...QELUS, a small lead foil inscribed with the name, LEUK[IOS], and an amphora handle stamped in Latin characters, ...CUNDI; Rauh 1993: 88.
36. As Cicero (*De imperio Cn. Pompei* 17–19) and other sources indicate, the Roman Republic derived enormous revenues from the newly organised province of Asia; Rauh 1993: 43.
37. See chapter 5.
38. Those at Delos are dated to *c*. 132/0 BC: Diod. Sic. 34.2.19; Oros. 5.19; Ferguson 1911: 383–4.
39. Rauh 1993: 45; cf. Patai 1998: 142–5, for Maccabean and Hasmonean violence at Ashkelon, Iamneia (Yabhneh), Azotus (Ashdod), and Anthedon. The Herakliastai of Tyre erected their dedication in 153/2 BC (*ID* 1519).
40. For the Roman Piracy Law of 101/100 BC, see Hassall, Crawford, and Reynolds 1974, 195–220; de Souza 1999: 108f.
41. A votive offering dedicated by Damon of Ascalon and found in the Agora of Theophrastos praises Zeus Ourios and Palestinian Astarte for saving him from pirates (*ID* 2305). A Roman merchant named L. Octavius at Rome likewise dedicated a temple to Heracles out of gratitude for the god's help in rescuing him and his crew from pirates (Rauh 1993: 118).
42. Casson 1971: 281f.; Gabrielsen 1997: 71.
43. Fraser and Bean 1954; Rice 1999; Funke 1999.
44. Thuc. 8.44; Diod. Sic. 20.81–8, 91–100; Polyb 5.88–90; Diod. Sic. 26.8.1; Strabo 13.2.5 (622); Plin. *NH* 34.41; Gabrielsen 1997: 75.
45. See below, chapter 3.
46. Gabrielsen 1997: 50: the gift most probably included Mylasa, Alabanda, Herakleia ad Latmum, Myndos and Iasos as well.
47. Extant inscriptions never list full naval complements, Gabrielsen 1997: 97.
48. Unlike the other maritime communities under consideration, Rhodes attempted throughout its history to remain a conservative, stable society: Strabo 14.2.5 (652); Gabrielsen 1997: 37.
49. For the anti-Roman faction at Rhodes, Polyb. 20.8.5–7; 27.7.4, 8–12, 14.2; 28.2.3, 17.14; 29.5.8, 11.2; 30..6.1, 7.9–10; Liv. 44.23.10, 29.7; 45.22.9; Berthold 1984: 184.
50. Polyb. 25.4.8–10; App. *Mac*. 13.2; Liv. 42.12.3–4; Berthold 1984: 174.

51. His colleague, C. Decimius, tried to soften the blow by indicating to the assembly that Roman anger might be assuaged by the arrest and punishment of certain 'agitators' responsible for the recent anti-Roman policies: Liv. 45.10.4–15; Cass. Dio 20.68.1; Berthold 1984: 195.
52. Bevan 1968: 91f.; Raschke 1978: 762.
53. Fraser 1972: 6.
54. Strabo 17.1.6 (792); Plin *NH* 5.10.62; Eunostos was possibly named after Ptolemy I's son in law, King Eunostus of Cyprus.
55. Morton 2001: 198; Höbl, 2001: 65.
56. For the tower: Plin *NH* 6.18; Steph. Byz. s.v. *Pharos*; Schol Luc ad *Icaromenippum* 12; Jos. *BJ* 4.10.5; Caes. *BC* 3.112; Bevan 1968: 95; Fraser 1972: 17f.
57. Fraser 1972: 27. A Greek dedication inscribed on its base records in fact that the monument was erected to honour the Roman Emperor Diocletian in AD 297.
58. Höbl 2001: 61f. They may even have replaced native emmer wheat, *Triticum dicoccum*, by *Triticum durum*, the standard naked bread-wheat of the Greek world, to make Egyptian grain exports more palatable to foreign importers: Rathbone 1983: 51.
59. See below, chapter 3.
60. Strabo 17.1.13 (798); Fraser 1972: 132f.
61. See below, chapter 3.
62. After 256 BC, the Ptolemaic navy declined from a high of perhaps 400 decked warships to the 30 that supported the army at the Battle of Raphia in 218: Athen. 5. 203d; App. *Proem.* 10; Polyb. 5.68; Theoc. 17.86–92; Preaux 1979: 40; Van 't Dack and Hauben 1978.
63. Bagnall 1976: 25–79; Höbl 2001:191.
64. See below, chapter 3 for Rough Cilicia.
65. Launey 1949: 34–35. For the Seleucid fleet and its heavy reliance on pirates: Bickerman 1938: 98–100, 100 n. 9. For the reliance of the Ptolemies on pirates and Cretan mercenaries, see Paus. 1.7.3; Launey 1949: 199, 248–86, 1068–72; Brulé 1978: 162–3.
66. Around 60 BC Diodorus Siculus asserted that it possessed 300,000 citizens; conceivably, this figure refers only to registered adult male 'citizens'. Scholarly estimates put the total resident population at 700,000 by this time and the overall population, when those in transit are taken into account, at close to one million: Bevan 1968: 97; Fraser 1972: 91.
67. Bevan 1968: 327; Fraser 1972: 93f., argues that the city was founded with normal institutions, an assembly, a *prytaneis* and a *Gerousia*, but that these were suppressed during the chaos of the mid-second century BC. Lack of reference to them in the source literature indicates that they had no apparent influence.
68. Höbl 2001: 77f. As Höbl notes, the high emphasis on brother-sister marriages was only slightly more extreme the marital alliances arranged by the Macedonian royal house in the past.
69. Owing to frequent marriage alliances with the Seleucids, meanwhile, queens and princesses frequently sought refuge at Antioch.
70. Bevan 1968: 100, the line is corrupt.
71. Höbl 2001: 201, 189–90; Fraser 1972: 54f.; for Jewish generals and soldiers: Bevan 1968: 111f.; Jewish traders, Patai 1998: 70 and below.
72. To cover their tracks they announced that king and queen had simultaneously passed away, while making sure that those most capable of spoiling their scheme were removed from town. Rumours persisted and rebellion soon emerged.
73. Diod. Sic. 31.15a; Bevan 1968: 289–91; Fraser 1972: 121f.; Höbl 2001: 194 f.
74. Athen. 12.549c. Despite this atrocity Cleopatra consented to produce a child with Physcon, a son who became known as Ptolemy Memphites. She had difficulty accepting Physcon's decision to marry her daughter, Cleopatra III, however, not to mention his decision to elevate the latter to official status as 'Queen Cleopatra the Wife', thereby distinguishing her from 'Queen Cleopatra the Sister'.
75. Justin 38.8; Polyb. Fraser 1972: 61; Bevan 1968: 306; Hobl 2001: 197 f.
76. Justin 38.8 clearly views this as a formally sanctioned and sustained immigration.
77. Cic. *De leg agr* 1.1, 2.41–2; Höbl 2001: 211. He had apparently taken out sizable loans from Romans and gave his estate to Rome as a form of surety.
78. Most of the initial party died amid the violence at Puteoli and those who managed to survive continued to be hunted down in Rome. The embassy's leading dignitary, the celebrated philosopher Dion of Alexandria, was actually poisoned at the house of his Roman host: Cass. Dio 39.13–14; Strabo 17.1.11 (796); Cic. *Cael.* 23; Höbl 2001: 228.

79. Now deeply in debt, the king had little choice but to hand over control of the state treasury to his creditor, Rabirius Postumus, who proceeded as official *dioiketes* to plunder the royal domain in an effort to recoup his loans. Ultimately, the mob compelled Postumus to flee. Both he and Gabinius and Rabirius returned to Rome to face prosecutions.

3 Material remains

1. Hackin and Hackin 1939, Hackin and Hackin 1954; Rashke 1978: 632–3: The ivory statues plaques and coffers are of Indian workmanship, possibly from the ivory workshops of Mathura.
2. For the date, Casson 1989: 6.
3. Casson 1989: 228; Wheeler 1954: 145f.; Begley *et al.* 1996; Begley *et al.* in press.
4. Will 1991; Will 1996; Will 1997; Will in press.
5. With significant concentrations during the later years of the reign of Augustus (27 BC – AD 14).
6. Will in press; Baldacci 1972.
7. Casson 1989: 289f.; Crosby 1986: 104f.
8. Casson 1989; Raschke 1978: 660.
9. Casson 1989: 164f., 179f.; Faller 2000: 141; Ritti 1988; Joshi 1988.
10. For Plocamus and the Latin inscription of his freedman Lysas at the Wadi Manih, see Rashke 1978: 644, 662; Faller 2000: 61f., 111f.
11. Crosby 1986: 104f.; Faller 2000: 127; Ritti 1988; Joshi 1988; Raman 1988; Devendra 1988; Rao and Gudigar 1988; Ardika 1999; Basa 1999; Mukherjee 1999; Soebadio 1999; Ray 1999.
12. Rashke 1978: 665; cf. Rajan 1988. Most of the ports mentioned by the Periplus writer, Muziris, Nelkynda, Kolchoi, Argaru, Kamara, and Sopatma, were located like Poduke/Arikamedu in this region (Casson 1989: 47).
13. The term appears to refer indiscriminately to traders from the western end of the Indian Ocean. Rashke 1978: 645; cf. Rajan 1988.
14. Rashke (1978: 630f., 675) notes, for example, that more Roman coins have been found in a single hoard in Poland than in all of India.
15. For the cost of pepper in the Mediterranean, see Plin. *NH* 12.14; Rashke 1978: 650f.; Gianfrotta and Pomey 1981: 135.
16. Best discussion, D'Arms 1981: 48f.
17. Gianfrotta 1981; Parker 1992: 29.
18. This is sometimes calculated from analysis of surviving cargoes, such as estimated quantities of amphorae stacked in cargo holds times the relative weight of a full amphora; and sometimes on the basis of surviving dimensions of the shipwreck itself: Parker 1992: 26: Casson 1971: 183f.; Pomey and Tchernia 1978; Gianfrotta and Pomey 1981: 282f; Hopkins 1983.
19. Parker 1992: 7. The team of Robert Ballard is currently conducting deep sea exploration of a Byzantine wreck in the Black Sea and of two Phoenician wrecks off Israel: Ballard and Stager 2002; Brody and McCann 2003: 33–4.
20. These are usually published first in regional archaeological journals such as *Gallia*; as well as in more specific, field-oriented journals such as the *International Journal of Nautical Archaeology*.
21. A recent conference on 'Transport Amphorae and Trade' at the Danish Institute in Athens (October 2002), focused on late Roman amphora production. Edited by Jonas Eiring and John Lund, contributions will appear in *JDAI*, forthcoming.
22. Parker 1992: 7, argues the reverse, noting for example that the wreck evidence points to periodic revivals of maritime activity in the years following events such as the destruction of Carthage and Corinth (as shown by his table 6), which in turn tends to confirm the possibility that wreck statistics bear some relationship to wider effects.
23. Steffy 1985; Parker 1992: 131–2.
24. Parker 1992: 232; Gianfrotta and Pomey 1981: 281. Excavators also recorded finding clusters of some 10,000 almonds (their sacks disintegrated) and other goods amid the remains. Post excavation analysis of the hull indicates that for the ship to be properly trimmed, something heavy, a sizable load of perishable goods such as cloth, must have sat in the forepart of the ship.
25. Benoit 1961; Parker 1992: 200–01, Gianfrotta and Pomey 1981: 151, 237f., 287f.; Long 1987.
26. Lamboglia 1964; Parker 1992: 49f.; Gianfrotta and Pomey 1981: 153f., 250, 282f.; Will 1987: 184.
27. Tchernia et al. 1978; Parker 1992: 249–50; Gianfrotta and Pomey 1981: 11f., 105f., 125f., 187f., 250f, 260f., 279f.

28. Parker 1992: 252–3; Gianfrotta and Pomey 1981: 199–203; Hellenkemper-Salies *et al.* 1994; for the date: Rotroff 1994: 143.

29. Weinberg *et al.* 1965; Parker 1992: 55–6; Gianfrotta and Pomey 1981: 195–9; cf. Frost 1963: 127 f. and figs. 17–19, for important photographs of the unpublished statuary.

30. Liv. 29.24; 29.26.3; 25.31; App. *Lib.* 13; Polyb. 1.52.6; Caes. *BC* 2.23; App. *BC* 5.97.

31. Polyb. 5.68; Liv. 35.43.3; App. *BC* 1.79; Cic. *Fam.* 12.14.1.

32. McCormick 2001: 106–08, based on estimates of subsidized and privating shipping and influenced by Oros. 7.42.12–13: the assemblage of some 4,700 transports by an African rebel to attack Italy in AD 413.

33. Cloth, wax and other materials were used as well.

34. The Chian seal the sphinx appears on both coins and amphora stamps: Grace 1979: figs. 48-49; Zemer 1977: 37, no. 31; Doger 1992: 86, type 6. Alpözen 1995: 82-5. For Chian luxury wines, see as well Salviat 1986: 160 f.; Tchernia 1986: 33, 64, 100–04.

35. Grace 1979, figs. 22–5; Grace 1934: 214–40; Grace 1970: 289–317; Alpözen 92; Doger 1992: 87–90; Finkielsztejn 2001.

36. During the peak period of production these stamps were dated by the month: Grace 1934: 199. Grace argues that the date applied primarily to the stamp itself or its die, which was then a licence, valid for a limited period, permitting a manufacturer to sell goods in return for a payment to the government which he in turn collected by raising the price of his commodity to cover the amount. See Finkielsztejn 2001.

37. Lund, unpublished paper delivered at Fuglsang in 1994 and personal communication; the point is disputed by Finkielsztejn 2001.

38. If this is correct the merchant's stamp may also have served to indicate that he had paid the necessary duties to export the wine.

39. Grace and Savvatianou-Petropoulakou 1970, 289–302, 317–24. See Finkielsztejn 2001 for revised chronology, modifying the periods slightly by five to ten years; cf. Lund 2002. Approximate chronology includes Rhodian Period I 400–240 BC, Period II 240–210 (stamps dated by months), Period III 210–175 (dated by a deposit at Pergamum), Period IV 175–146 (between the deposit of Pergamum and the destruction of Carthage and Corinth), Period V 146–108 (from the destruction of Carthage and Corinth to the destruction of Samaria in 108), Period VI 108–88/86 (deposits of the sack of Delos in 88 and the sack of Athens in 86), Period VII, first century BC.

40. For analysis of Rhodian distribution patterns, see Lund 1993; Lund 1995; Lund 1999; Lund 2000; Finkielsztejn 2001.

41. Grace 1934: 240–75; Grace and Savvatianou-Petropoulakou 1970: 317–53; Doger 1992: 91–5; Alpözen 1995: 86–91.

42. Proto-Knidian amphoras begin in Rhodian Period II. Grace argues that Period IV A Knidian jars (188–166 BC) were stamped by Rhodian *phrourarchoi* who administered the city at that time: Grace 1970: 318; Fraser and Bean 1954: 93–4. Period VI Knidian jars (108–78) are stamped by municipal magistrates referring to themselves as *androi*.

43. Grace and Savvatianou-Petropoulakou 1970: 363–4; Grace 1979: figs. 6–60; Alpözen 1995: 97; Doger 1992: 95; Zemer 1977: 43, no. 35 is a late third/early second-century version.

44. A process of wiping down and smoothing surviving uneven ridges on the external wall with a cloth dampened with seawater.

45. Finds at Delos suggest as little as 5 per cent of Koan jars were stamped: Empereur 1982: 233; S. Sherwin-White 1978: 240; Höghammar 1993: 35. Grace 1979: fig. 59 shows the crab and club symbol common to Koan coins.

46. Hesnard 1986: 75f. For the export of Koan wine and its good quality, Strabo 14.1.15 (637); 14.2.9 (654); S. Sherwin White 1978: 236–40; Höghammar 1993: 35; Tchernia 1986: 100–05.

47. A preliminary typology in her amphora report for the excavations at Cosa: Will 1987a; emended in Will 1987b and Will 2001. Equally important for the forms in question are Will 1979; Will 1982.

48. Will 1982; Will 1987a: 172, 177–8; Will 1987b: 25f.; Tchernia 1986: 49f. for discussion of the *Loisios* amphoras. Type 1a was most prevalent from late fourth to the first quarter of the third century BC; Will type 1b in the second half of the third century BC; Will type 1c, c. 200 BC; Will type 1d, second half third century to the 150s BC; Will type 2 (Greco-Italic form E) from first to third quarters of the second century BC.

49. Also manufactured near Pompeii and in the eastern Mediterranean: Will 1987a: 179.

50. As well as others in Manching, Germany: Will 1987b: 25f. Will type 1c was taller than 1a with a longer neck, and longer handles that attach at the rim. The rim itself is slightly higher than that of 1a and out flaring. The fabric is coarse pinkish buff clay.

51. Will 1987a: 172; Will 1987b: 30f. Will 2001.

52. Will 1987a: 183: Will 1987b: 33f.

53. Will 1987a: 175, the Cosa area accounts for 70% of all Sestius stamps found so far on land and Cosa is the only place where almost all known varieties of Sestius stamps occur. These facts render the existence of a Sestius wine production centre all but a certainty at this port. Cf. Peacock and Williams 1986: 86, class 3.

54. Cic. *Att.* 16.4.4; Will 1979; Will 1987a: 176; cf. D'Arms 1981: 56f.; with McCann and Will 1984.

55. Will 1987a: 174, 183, the size of the shipment of amphorae in the upper Grand Congloué wreck implies that Sestian wine was *vin ordinaire*.

56. Will 1987a: 183-4; Peacock and Williams 1986: 89, class 4 Will type 4b is second only to 4a in frequency at Cosa. Type 4b production centres have been identified at Tarracina and Brindisi. Archaeologists found hundreds of Type 4b jars in the Albenga and Spargi wrecks. For type 4b stamps: Will 1987a: 182.

57. Some are stamped with Sestius stamps: Will 1987a: 174; 201–02; cf. Peacock and Williams 1986: 91, class 5. Type 5 (c. 75–25 BC) has a large collar-like rim and a narrow mouth. Long ribbed handles, narrow in section and S-shaped in profile flank a long neck that widens at the bottom. The shoulder is unusually narrow and joins with the neck in an offset manner. The body is narrow and carrot-shaped, tapering to a solid toe. Stamps are infrequent. Will type 5 appears to have evolved from a garum jar originally produced in Spain (Will type 2), where many have been found. Type 5 totals at Cosa are greater than at any other site.

58. Will 1987a: 204; Will 1989: 302–05; cf. Peacock and Williams 1986: 98, class 8.

59. Will 1987a: 204; Hatzfeld 1912, 143; cf. Tchernia 1986: 53f., 129f., for the argument that they also carried wine.

60. Will 1987a: 205; cf. *CIL* 9.6079. Tchernia 1986: 54; Palazzo 1989; Cipriano and Carre 1989: 77f.

61. Its production was sustained by surviving Punic wine producers and perhaps by Roman colonists. See Rotroff 1994: 142–3; S. Wolff 1986; Peacock and Williams 1986: class 32, p. 151–2.

62. What follows is based on Rauh 1999, where detailed documentation is provided.

63. Specialists now recognize that even this figure is misleading because most of the Rhodian stamped handles found at the Athenian Agora date to the third century BC (while the Knidian do not), making the Knidian distribution of the late second century BC significantly greater.

64. Grace 1952: 518; 1985: 42. Cf. Lund 1999; Finkeilsztejn 2001.

65. Lund 1993; Lund 1999; Finkeilsztejn 2001.

66. Specialists point to unpublished finds of forms related to Will type 10 (Lamboglia 2) at Rhodes, Kos and Halikarnassos – as well as to a shipwreck bearing 3,000 jars of forms related to Will type 10 (Lamboglia 2) at Yalikavak near Myndos – as further evidence of increased exportation of Italian wines to the region. Tchernia 1986: 72f.; Sibella 2002: 8f.

67. Namely, eastern Lycia, Pamphylia, Cyprus and Syria. Thousands of Roman amphora finds in France confirm literary reports (Diod. Sic. 5.26.3) of significant exchanges of Roman wine and oil for Gallic slaves; Tchernia 1986: 73, 88.

68. For the Will type 1, see **colour plate 21**; for the Will type 10 in the George McGhee Collection in Alanya, see Sabella 2002: 8, fig. 10. Remains of a similar, stamped Italian amphora appears misidentified as a 'drain pipe' in Jones 1950: 149–296, 296, no. 1050, plate 169. For the Will type 5 at Issos (Kinet Hüyük), see figure **40**. For finds in Israel, see Rauh 1999: 183 n. 38.

69. Preliminary results at one Hellenistic site in the Hasdere Canyon, Tomak Asari, reveal tentatively identified Will type 10 body sherds. This was conceivably a native site; see figure **66**.

70. As noted above, Virginia Grace points to the appearance after 108 BC of amphoras stamped by Knidian *androi* as further proof of administrative changes in conformance with Roman provincial rule.

71. See below, chapter 5.

4 Roman trading society

1. See above, chapter 3.

2. Cic. *Rab. Post.*; Cic. *Fam.* 13.69.1; *ILLRP* 1026; *CIL* 1² 2340 a, c; 10.8041 no. 130, 8051 no. 26; Nicolet 1977: 860.

3. Liv. 22.28.3; 41.3.4; *BAfr.* 84.1.

4. Plaut. *Mil. Glor.* 1176–81, cf. 1283; *Asin.* 69; *Pers.* 154–7.

5. Diod. Sic. 35.25, 37.5; 36.3.1–2; Liv. *Per.* 70; Dio frg. 97; Val. Max. 2.10.5; Cic. *Att.* 5.21.10-12; 6.1.3–7, 16; 6.2.7–10; 6.3.5-7; Cic. *Fam.* 1.9.26; Cic. *Verr.* 2.1.73–4; Cic. *Flacc.* 71–2; ps. Ascon. 242 St.; Schol Bob. 157 St.; Plut. *Luc.* 7, 20; App. *Mith.* 83.

6. This chapter relies extensively on the model of Rediker 1987: 77f. For descriptions of ancient cargo ships, Casson 1971; Gianfrotta and Pomey 1981; Parker 1992.

7. Steffy 1985a; Parker 1992: 22, 231f.; Gianfrotta and Pomey 1981: 236f.

8. Parker 1992: 23; Gianfrotta and Pomey 1981: 276f. 'Shell-first' construction techniques were obviously known and to some degree utilised as well. Parker 1992: 23; Gianfrotta and Pomey 1981: 263–6. 'Stitched' boats require more maintenance, of course, but they can be cheaper to build and easier to disassemble for repair.

9. Parker 1992: 27; 243f.; Gianfrotta and Pomey 1981: 260f., 271f..

10. Casson 1971: 257; *P. Lond.* 1164 h = *Select Papyri*, no. 38, lines 7–11.

11. For the size of crews, Parker 1992: 29; Gianfrotta and Pomey 1981: 293f.

12. Parker 1992: 29; Gianfrotta and Pomey 1981: 294–5.

13. Gianfrotta and Pomey 1981: 289–90; Parker 1992: 28.

14. Casson 1971: 245; cf. Gianfrotta and Pomey 1981: 294.

15. Parker 1992: 31f.; Gianfrotta and Pomey 1981: 281f.; and above, chapter 3.

16. Parker 1992: 28; Gianfrotta and Pomey 1981: 224, 281f.

17. Similar evidence exists for Greece: Thuc. 2.90; Xen *Hell* 1.1.6; Patai 1998: 61.

18. Parker 1992: 232; Gianfrotta and Pomey 1981: 286f.

19. Or, as seems more likely, the number of the ship's officers. One plate bore the Greek graffito possibly indicating the name of the proprietor: Parker 1992: 232; Gianfrotta and Pomey 1981: 294.

20. See below, chapter 5.

21. Petronius 103. In a surviving papyrus Ptolemaic policemen guarding the Nile were enjoined by authorities to apprehend naval deserters and all sailors 'bearing the brand': Lewis 1986: 465.

22. For example, Cic. *De Rep.* 2.7.

23. For Syrian and Jewish barmaids and prostitutes in Italy, see Kleberg 1957: 70f.

5 Cilician Piracy

1. The following section is based on Rauh *et al.* 2000, where full documentation and bibliography can be found.

2. Strabo 14.3.2 (664). For Side's harbour, Mansel 1963: 27; Knoblauch 1977: 43; Brandt 1992: 49.

3. Note Sidetan naval participation in Rome's siege of Carthage in 149–146 BC: App. *Lib.* 123; and funeral stelae of two slaves claiming Sidetan origin at Delian cemeteries on Rhenea: Couilloud 1973: nos. 319, 418.6.

4. *ILLRP* 342; *IGRP* 4.1116; Cic. *De Orat.* 1.82; *Brut.* 168; Liv. *Per.* 68; *Obseq.* 44; *MRR* 1.568–70; Suppl. 19; P. de Souza 1999: 102–8, argues, however, that Side cooperated with Antonius against the pirates, despite Strabo.

5. Judging from Poseidonius' description of Q. Oppius' status as *strategos Pamphylias*: Athen. *Deip.* 5.213a; Jacoby *FGrH* 87 F. 36 (50); cf. App. *Mith.* 17, 20; Gran. Lician. 35B; Liv. *Per.* 78; *MRR* 2.42, Suppl. 152; A. Sherwin-White 1976: 9.

6. Cicero accuses Cn. Cornelius Dolabella and his legate C. Verres of wrongfully plundered these cities. His rhetoric conceivably masks a legitimate effort on their part to reassert authority in the region: *Verr.* 2.1.53–8; A. Sherwin-White 1976: 10–11; A. Sherwin-White 1984: 153–4; de Souza 1999: 124.

7. Cic. *Verr.* 2.1.53–8; Cic. *De Leg. Agr.* 1.5, 2.50; Alciphr. 1.8; with Marasco 1987a: 137 n. 70; *MRR* 2.80, A. Sherwin-White 1976: 10–11; A. Sherwin-White 1984: 153–4; de Souza 1999: 124. For the harbour of Attaleia, Lehmann-Hartleben 1923: 123, plan 18.

8. Flor. 1.41.5; Strabo 145.3.3 (665), 14.5.7 (671); Eutrop. 6.3; Flor 1.41. According to Plutarch *Pomp.* 24.5, the Mithraic cult at Olympos continued to his day. Strabo 14.5.7 (671) reports that when Roman forces commanded by the P. Servilius Vatia (Isauricus) stormed the heights in 77 BC, Zenicetes blocked himself within his castle along with his family and his treasure and set everything ablaze. For the Yanartas ('the flaming stone', slightly north and high on a slope above Olympos), the Mithraic cult, see Hani 1964; A. Diler 1991; O. Atvur 1999.

9. Thuc. 2.69; Cic. *Verr.* 2.4.21; Strabo 14.3.9 (667); 14.5.7 (671); Liv. 37.23.1; Bryce 1986: 206. Cicero (*ad loc.*) indicates that control of the town was wrested from its inhabitants by pirates. For the harbour at Phaselis, Blackman 1973.

10. See, for example, Strabo 14.3.9 (667); Dem. 35.1–2; Bryce 1986: 214. Lycia was traditionally identified

with settlements along the Xanthos, Arykandos and Limyros rivers.

11. Strabo 14.5.2 (668), Plut. *Pomp.* 28.1; Vell. Pat. 2.32.4; Fischer 1972.

12. See Rauh 1997: 265; Rauh et al. 2000: 167f.

13. On the crest above the cove stands another Late Roman church and a row of tombs: Rauh et al. 2000: 167f.

14. Shaw 1984: 3–52; Shaw 1990: 199–233; P. Desideri 1991: 299–304; Hopwood 1983: 173–88; Hopwood 1986: 343–56; Hopwood 1989: 191 f.; Hopwood 1990: 171–87; Hopwood 1991: 305–09; Lewin 1991: 167–84; Russell 1991: 283–97; Syme 1986: 159–64; C. Wolff 1999.

15. Bean and Mitford 1970: 109; cf. R.S. Bagnall 1976: 115–16; Brandt 1992: 50–1. By comparison, Lycian populations had adopted a written script based on Greek by the fifth century BC. While the written script employed in Pamphylian amphora stamps indicates a more delayed process of assimilation, the maritime cities of this region likewise established a solid record of involvement in Hellenistic affairs, furnishing mercenaries, warships, and educated dignitaries to competing Hellenistic powers.

16. Luwian was an Indo-European language related to Hittite, rooted in the Bronze Age. As a written language Luwian survives in a series of hieroglyphic texts, of which the latest, a bilingual inscription in Phoenician and Luwian found at Karatepe in Flat Cilicia, is datable to the 6th century BC. How late Luwian was still spoken is impossible to say, but there is considerable evidence for the continued viability of other native languages in Asia Minor even into the early centuries AD. See Houwink ten Caten 1961; Cambel 1999; Neumann 1980.

17. Their rebellion in AD 52 was resisted specifically by merchants and shippers: Tac. *Ann.* 6.41, 12.55; cf. Dio 55.28.3. Similar tensions emerged in the fourth century AD: Amm. Marc. 14.2.1–20; Lewin 1991: 171–77; Shaw 1990: 230–1; Mitchell 1993: 1:70–9; Magie 1950: 494, 1354–5; Lenski 1999: 414.

18. Many scholars point to a relationship between the two. Ormerod 1922: 36–41; Ormerod 1987: 205; Marasco 1987b: 129; Benabou 1985: 66; Garlan 1974: 2; Dell 1967: 357.

19. Annual reports, interactive GIS maps, video clips and an on-line manuscript about the team's discovery of ancient Juliosebaste are available at the project website: http://pasture.ecn.purdue.edu/~rauhn

20. Meillassoux 1960; Meillassoux 1981; Rey 1971; Rey 1975; Terray 1969; Terray 1975; van Binsbergen and Geschiere 1985.

21. Fulford 1992; Randsborg 1991; Rauh and Wandsnider 2001, Rauh *et al.* 2000: 155f., Rauh and Wandsnider 2002.

22. Liv. 33.20.4–5 (197 BC): 'Korakesion at that time resisted the siege efforts of Antiochus [III of Syria], Zephyrium, Soli, Aphrodisias, Korykos, Anemurium [the promontory that marks the very boundary of Cilicia] and Selinus having gone over to his side. All the other castles [*castellae*] along this shore either out of fear or desire surrendered to him without a fight. Only Coracesium despite overwhelming odds closed its gates and resisted.' All of the mentioned sites are situated on imposing promontories.

23. See Rauh *et al.*, 2000: 156. Since this publication the team found a few amphora body sherds preliminarily identified as Will type 10 at Tomak Asari. There is reason to believe that this was a native Luwian settlement: see the on-line manuscript at the website.

24. See the 2001 Annual Report at the project website.

25. For the region's inscriptions see Heberdey and Wilhelm 1896; Heberdey and Kalinka 1897; Peribeni and Romanelli 1914; Bean and Mitford 1962; Bean and Mitford 1965; Bean and Mitford 1970.

26. Preserving the grandfather's name while distinguishing between sons as 'elder' and 'junior': Bean and Mitford: 1970: 70.

27. Cormack 1997; cf. Antonnaccio 1995.

28. Waltzing 1895; Ziebarth 1896; Poland 1909.

29. What follows is based on Rauh 1997, where detailed documentation can be found. The argument is modeled closely on that of Rediker 1987: 254f.

30. Most recently, de Souza 1999: 70f.

31. Plut. *Pomp.* 28.2; App. *Mith.* 93; Rauh 1997: 266.

32. Cic. *Att.*16.1; App. *BC* 4.85; 5.78f.

Bibliography

Alpözen 1994
   T.O. Alpözen, A.H. Özdas, and B. Berkaya, 'Commercial Amphorae of the Bodrum Museum of Underwater Archaeology'. *Maritime trade of the Mediterranean in ancient times*. Ankara: Bodrum Museum of Underwater Archaeology.
Antonaccio 1995
   Carla M. Antonnaccio, *An Archaeology of Ancestors*. Lanham, MD: Rowman and Littlefield.
Ardika 1999
   W. Ardika, 'Ancient Trade Relations between India and Indonesia', in Behera 1999, 80–9.
Avtur 1999
   Orhan Atvur, 'Olympos Antik Kenti (1991–92 Çalismaları)', *Arkeoloji ve Sanat 88*, 13–31.
Badian 1976
   E. Badian, 'Rome, Athens and Mithradates', *AJAH 1*, 105–28.
Bagnall 1976
   Roger S. Bagnall, *The Administration of the Ptolemaic Possessions Outside Egypt*. Leiden: E.J. Brill.
Baldacci, 1972
   P. Baldacci, 'Le principali correnti del commercio di anfore romane nella Cisalpina. Importazione ed esportazione alimentari nella Pianura Pada centrale dall III sec. a.C. al II d.C.', in *I Problemi della ceramica romano di Ravenna della Valle Padana e dell'altro Adriatico. Atti del Convegno internazionale, Ravenna, 10–12 Maggio 1969*. Bologna: A. Forni, 103–31.
Ballard et al. 2002
   R.D. Ballard, E. Stager, D.Master, D. Yoenger, D. Mindell, L.L. Whitcomb, H. Sing and D. Piechota, 'Iron Age Shipwrecks in Deep Water off Ashkelon, Israel', *AJA 106* (2002), 151–68.
Basa 1999
   K.K. Basa, 'Early Trade in the Indian Ocean: Perspectives on Indo-Southeast Asian Maritime Contacts (c. 400 BC – AD 500)', in Behera 1999, 29–71.
BE
   Bulletin Epigraphique. Edited by L. and J. Robert. Published annually in *Revue des Etudes Grecques* since 1938, now collected in 8 volumes up to 1977.
Bean and Mitford 1962
   G.E. Bean and T.B. Mitford, 'Sites Old and New in Rough Cilicia', *Anatolian Studies 12*, 185–217.
Bean and Mitford 1965
   G.E. Bean and T.B. Mitford, *Journeys in Rough Cilicia in 1962 and 1963*. Vienna: Austrian Academy of Science.
Bean and Mitford 1970
   G.E. Bean and T.B. Mitford, *Journeys in Rough Cilicia 1964–1968*. Vienna: Austrian Academy of Science.
Begley 1996
   V. Begley, P. Francis, I. Mahadevan, K.V. Raman, S. Sidebotham, K.W. Slane, E.L. Will, *The Ancient Port of Arikamedu. New Excavations and Researches 1989–1992*. Volume One. Pondichéry: Ecole française d'extrême-orient.
Begley in press
   V. Begley, P. Francis, I. Mahadevan, K.V. Raman, S. Sidebotham, K.W. Slane, E.L. Will, *The Ancient Port of Arikamedu. New Excavations and Researches 1989–1992*. Volume Two. Pondichéry: Ecole française d'extrême-orient, in press.
Behera 1999
   K.S. Behera (ed.), *Maritime Heritage of India*. New Delhi: Aryan Books Int.

Benabou 1985

M. Benabou, 'Rome et la police des mers au 1er siècle avant J.C.: la répression de la piraterie cilicienne', pp. 60–9 in *L'Homme méditerranéan et la mer. Actes du Troisième Congrès International d'études des cultures de la Méditerranée Occidentale* (Jerba, Avril 1981), eds M. Galley and L. Ladjimi Sebai. Paris: Boccard.

Benoit 1961

F. Benoit, Fouilles sous-marines. *L'épave du Grand Congloué à Marseille. Gallia Supplément 14*. Paris: CNRS.

Berthold 1984

R.M. Berthold, *Rhodes in the Hellenistic Age*. Ithaca NY: Cornel U. Press.

Bevan 1968

E.R. Bevan, *The House of Ptolemy. A History of Hellenistic Egypt under the Ptolemaic Dynasty*. Chicago: Ares Press 1968, reprint of 1927 edition.

Blackman 1973

D.J. Blackman, 'The Harbours of Phaselis', *IJNA 2.2*: 355–364.

Blackman 1982

D.J. Blackman, 'Ancient harbours in the Mediterranean. Parts I and II', *IJNA* 11: 79–104; 185–211.

Bloch 1912

Ivan Bloch, *Die Prostitution*. Berlin: Louis Marcus Verlag.

Boren 1957

Henry C. Boren, 'The Urban Side of the Gracchan Economic Crisis', *AHR* 6, 890–902.

Bradford 1971

E. Bradford, *Mediterranean Portrait of a Sea*. New York: Harcourt Brace Jovanovich Inc.

Bradley 1989

Keith R. Bradley, *Slavery and Rebellion in the Roman World, 140 BC – 70 BC*. Bloomington and London: Indiana U. Press.

Brandt 1992

Hartwin Brandt, *Gesellschaft und Wirtschaft Pamphyliens und Pisidiens im Altertum*. Bonn: Habelt.

Brody and McCann 2003

A. Brody and A.M. McCann, 'Exploring the Deep', *Archaeology Odyssey 6.1*, 30–9.

Brulé 1978

P. Brulé, 'La piraterie crétoise hellénistique', *Annales littéraires de l'Université de Besançon, 223*. Paris: Les Belles Lettres.

Bruneau 1983

Philippe Bruneau, Guide de Délos. Paris: E. de Boccard.

Bruneau 1979

Philippe Bruneau, 'Deliaca III: 23: Le problème des phares', *BCH 103*, 82–187 (99–104).

Brunt 1966

P.A. Brunt, 'The Roman Mob', *Past and Present 35*, 3–27.

Brunt 1971

P.A. Brunt, *Italian Manpower, 225 BC – AD 14*. Oxford.

Bryce 1986

Trevor R. Bryce, The Lycians Vol. 1: *The Lycians in Literary and Epigraphic Sources*. Copenhagen: Museum Tusculanum Press.

Bickerman 1938

E. Bickerman, *Institutions des Séleucides*. Paris: Librairie orientaliste Paul Geuthner.

Cambel 1999

Halet Cambel, Corpus of Hieroglyphic Luwian Inscriptions, vol. 2: Karatepe-Aslantas. Berlin.

Casson 1971

Lionel Casson, *Ships and Seamanship in the Ancient World*. Princeton: Princeton U. Press.

Casson 1989

Lionel Casson, *The Periplus Maris Erythraei*. Princeton: Princeton U. Press.

CIG

Corpus Inscriptionum Graecarum, ed. A. Boeck. Berlin: G. Reimer, 1828–77.

CIL

Corpus Inscriptionum Latinarum, ed. Th. Mommsen et al., Berlin: G. Reimer, 1863–.

Cipriano and Carre 1989

M.T. Cipriano and M.-B. Carre, 'Production et typologie des amphores sur la côte adriatique de l'Italie', *EfR* 1989, 67–104.

Colin 1905

G. Colin, Rome et la Grèce 200–146 av. JC. Paris: BEFAR.

Cormack 1997

Sarah Cormack, 'Funerary Monuments and Mortuary Practice in Roman Asia Minor', in S. Alcock (ed.), *The Early Roman Empire in the East*. Oxford: Oxbow Monograph 95, 137–56.

Couilloud 1973

M.-Th. Couilloud, 'Les monuments funéraires de Rhénée', *Exploration Archéologique de Délos 30*. Paris: E. de Boccard.

Crosby 1986

Alfred Crosby, *Ecological Imperialism. The Biological Expansion of Europe, 900–1900*. Cambridge: Cambridge U. Press.

D'Arms 1981

John H. D'Arms, 'Commerce and Social Standing in Ancient Rome'. Cambridge, MA: Harvard U. Press.

Dell 1967

H.J. Dell, 'The Origin and Nature of Illyrian Piracy', *Historia 16*, 344–58.

de Souza 1999

Philip de Souza, *Piracy in the Graeco-Roman World*. Cambridge: Cambridge U. Press.

Devendra 1988

S. Devendra, 'Indian Oceanic Shipping and Southern Sri Lanka', in Rao (ed.), 1988, 143–4.

Diler 1991

Adnan Diler, 'Lykia Olympos Daginda Bir Ön Arastırma'. *Türk Arkeologiji Dergisi 29*, 161–76.

Doger 1992

E. Doger, *Antik Cagda Amphoralar*. Izmir: Sergi Yayin Evi.

Dyson 1995

Stephen L. Dyson, *The Creation of the Roman Frontier*. Princeton: Princeton U. Press.

EfR 1989

'Amphores romaines et histoire économique. Dix ans de recherche'. Actes du colloque de Sienne (22–24 mai 1986) organisé par l'Università degli Studi di Siena, l'Università degli Studi di Roma–La Sapienza, le Centre national de la recherche scientifique (RCP 403) et l'École française de Rome. Rome: École française de Rome.

Empereur 1982

J.-Y. Empereur, 'Les Anses d'Amphores Timbrées et les Amphores: Aspects Quantitatifs', *BCH 106*, 219–33.

Empereur and Garlan 1986

J.-Y. Empereur and Y. Garlan (eds), 'Recherches sur les Amphores Grecques'. *BCH Supplément 13*. Paris: Les Belles Lettres.

Engels 1990

Donald Engels, *Roman Corinth. An Alternative Model for the Classical City*. Chicago and London: U. Chicago Press.

Faller 2000

Stephan Faller, *Taprobane im Wandel der Zeit. Das Sri-Lanka Bild in griechischen und lateinischen quellen zwischen Alexanderzug und Spätantike*. Stuttgart: Franz Steiner Verlag.

FGH

Felix Jacoby, *Die Fragmente der griechischen Historiker*. Leyden, 1950.

Finkielsztejn 2001.

Gérald Finkielsztejn, 'Chronologie détaillée et révisée des éponymes amphoriques rhodiens, de 270 à 108 av. J.-C. environ. Premier bilan', *BAR International Series 990*. Oxford: Archaeopress.

Fischer 1972

T. Fischer, 'Zu Tryphon', *Chiron 2*, 201–13.

Fraser 1972

P.M. Fraser, *Ptolemaic Alexandria*. Oxford: Clarendon.

Fraser and Bean 1954

P.M. Fraser and G.E. Bean, *The Rhodian Peraea and Islands*. Oxford: Clarendon.

Frier 1982

Bruce W. Frier, 'Roman Life Expectancy: Ulpian's Evidence', *HSCP 86*, 213–51.

Frost 1973

Honor Frost, 'The offshore island harbour at Sidon and other Phoenician sites in the light of new dating evidence', *IJNA 2.11*, 75–94.

Frost 1963

Honor Frost, *Under the Mediterranean: Marine Antiquities*. Englewood Cliffs, NJ: Prentice-Hall.

Fulford 1992

M.G. Fulford, 'Territorial Expansion and the Roman Empire', *World Archaeology* 23(3), 294–305.

Funke 1999

P. Funke, 'Peraia: Einige Überlegungen zum Festlandbesitz griechischer Inselstaaten', in Gabrielsen et al. 1999, 55–75.

Gabrielsen 1997

V. Gabrielsen, *The Naval Aristocracy of Hellenistic Rhodes*. Århus: Århus U. Press.

Gabrielsen et al. 1999

V. Gabrielsen, P. Bilde, T. Engberg-Pedersen, L. Hannestad, J. Zahle (eds), *Hellenistic Rhodes: Politics, Culture, and Society*: Århus: Århus U. Press.

Garlan 1978

Y. Garlan, 'Signification historique de la piraterie grecque', *Dialogues d'histoire ancienne 4*, 1–16.

Garland 1987

R. Garland, *The Piraeus: from the fifth to the first centuries BC*. Ithaca NY: Cornell U. Press.

Garnsey and Whittaker 1983

P. Garnsey and C.R. Whittaker (eds), *Trade and Famine in Classical Antiquity*. Cambridge: Cambridge Philological Society.

Gianfrotta 1981

P.A. Gianfrotta, 'Commerci e pirateria: prime testimonianze archeologiche sottomarine', *MEFRA 93*, 227–42.

Gianfrotta and Pomey 1981

P.A. Gianfrotta and P. Pomey, L'archéologie sous la mer. Histoire, techniques, découvertes et épaves, avec la collaboration de F. Coarelli, French edition, Paris: Fernand Nathan, 1981; Italian edition, Milan: Arnoldo Aondadori.

Grace 1934

V. Grace, 'The Stamped Amphora Handles Found in the American Excavations in the Athenian Agora 1931–1932. A catalogue treated as a chronological study', Cambridge, MA: Harvard University dissertation, published in *Hesperia 3* (1934), 197–310.

Grace 1949

V. Grace, 'Standard Pottery Containers of the Ancient Greek World', in *Hesperia Supplement VIII*, Commemorative Studies in honor of Theodore Leslie Shear. Princeton U. Press, 1949, pp. 175–89.

Grace 1950

V. Grace, 'The Stamped Amphora Handles', in H. Goldman (ed.), Excavations at Gozlu Kule, Tarsus I: The Hellenistic and Roman Periods. Princeton U. Press, pp. 135–48.

Grace 1952

V. Grace, 'Timbres amphoriques trouvés à Délos', BCH 76, 514–40.

Grace 1956

V. Grace, 'Stamped Wine Jar Fragments', Hesperia, Supplement X. Small Objects from the Pnyx: II. Princeton: American School of Classical Studies, 113–89.

Grace 1965

V. Grace, 'The Commercial Amphorae', in G.D. Weinberg et al. 1965.

Grace 1979

V. Grace, *Amphorae and the Ancient Wine Trade*. Princeton: American School of Classical Studies in Athens.

Grace and Savvatianou-Petropoulakou 1970
    V. Grace and M. Savvatianou-Petropoulakou, 'Les timbres amphoriques grecs', in Ph. Bruneau, *L'Ilot de la Maison des Comédiens*. Paris: EAD 27, 277–374.
Grace 1985
    V. Grace, 'The Middle Stoa Dated by Amphora Stamps', *Hesperia 54*, 1–54.
Grainger 1990
    J.D. Grainger, *The Cities of Seleukid Syria*. Oxford: Clarendon.
Grainger 1991
    J.D. Grainger, *Hellenistic Phoenicia*. Oxford: Clarendon.
Habicht 1997
    Christian Habicht, 'Athens from Alexander to Antony', Cambridge, MA: Harvard U. Press.
Hackin and Hackin 1939
    J. Hackin and J.R. Hackin, 'Recherches archéologiques à Bagram', *Chantier no. 2* (1931), *MDAFA 9*, Paris.
Hackin and Hackin 1954
    J. Hackin and J.R. Hackin, 'Les fouilles de Bagram (1939)', in J. Hackin (ed.), Nouvelles recherches archéologiques à Bagram, *MDAFA 11* (Paris 1954), 11–16.
Hammond 1989
    N.G.L. Hammond, *The Macedonian State. Origins, Institutions, and History*. Oxford: Clarendon.
Hani 1964
    J. Hani, 'Plutarque en face du dualisme iranien', *Revue des Etudes Grecques 77*, 489–525.
Harrison 1975
    Eve Harrison, *Archaic and Archaistic Sculpture Agora XI*. Princeton: Princeton U. Press.
Heberdey and Wilhelm 1986
    Rudolf Heberdey and Adolf Wilhelm, 'Reisen in Kilikien', *Denkschriften des kaiserlichen Akademie der Wissenschaften*. Vienna: Gerold, 44, 1–169.
Heberdey and Kalinka 1897
    Rudolf Heberdey and Ernst Kalinka, 'Bericht über Zwei Reisen im südwestlichen Kleinasien', *Denkschriften des kaiserlichen Akademie der Wissenschaften*. Vienna: Gerold, 45, 1–57.
Hellenkemper-Salies 1994
    G. Hellenkemper-Salies, H.-H. von Prittwitz, and G. and G. Bauchhenss (eds), *Das Wrack. Der antike Schiffsfund von Mahdia Katalogue des Rheinischen Landesmuseums*, 1. Cologne.
Hesnard 1986
    A. Hesnard, 'Imitations et Raisonnement archéologique: A propos des amphores de Rhodes et de Cos', in Empereur and Garlan 1986, 69–79.
Hesnard and Gianfrotta 1989
    A. Hesnard and P.A. Gianfrotta, 'Les bouchons d'amphore en pouzzolane', in *EfR* 1989, 393–441.
Höbl 2001
    G. Höbl, *A History of the Ptolemaic Empire*. London and New York: Routledge.
Höghammar 1993
    K. Höghammar, 'Sculpture and Society. A Study of the Connection between Free-Standing Sculpture and Society on Kos in the Hellenistic and Augustan Periods'. Borea: *Uppsala Studies in Ancient Mediterranean and Near Eastern Societies 23*.
Hopkins 1983
    Keith Hopkins, 'Models, Ships and Staples', in Garnsey and Whittaker 1983, 84–109.
Hopwood 1983
    Keith Hopwood, 'Policing the Hinterland: Rough Cilicia and Isauria', pp. 173–88 in 'Armies and Frontiers in Roman and Byzantine Anatolia'. Proceedings of a colloquium held at University College, Swansea, in April 1981, S. Mitchell (ed.). Oxford: *BAR International Series 156*. Monograph (British Institute of Archaeology in Ankara) no. 5.
Hopwood 1986
    Keith Hopwood, 'Towers, Territory and Terror: How the East was Held', pp. 343–56 in The Defence of the Roman and Byzantine East. Proceedings of a colloquium held at the University of Sheffield in April 1986, P. Freeman and D. Kennedy (eds). Oxford: *BAR International Series 297. Monograph (British Institute of Archaeology in Ankara) no. 8.*

Hopwood 1989

Keith Hopwood, 'Consent and Control: How the Peace was Kept in Rough Cilicia', pp. 191–201 in 'The Eastern Frontier of the Roman Empire', D.H. French and C.S. Lightfoot (eds). Oxford: *BAR International Series 553*. Monograph (British Institute of Archaeology in Ankara) no. 11.

Hopwood 1990

Keith Hopwood, 'Bandits, Elites and Rural Order', pp. 171–87 in *Patronage In Ancient Society*, A. Wallace-Hadrill (ed.). London and New York: Routledge.

Hopwood 1991

Keith Hopwood, 'The Links between the Coastal Cities of Western Rough Cilicia and the Interior during the Roman Period', *De Anatolia Antiqua (Eski Anadolu) 1*, 305–09.

Houwink Ten Cate 1961

P.H.J. Houwink Ten Cate, *The Luwian Population Groups of Lycia and Cilicia Aspera during the Hellenistic Period*. Leiden: E.J. Brill.

Hurst 1979

Henry Hurst, 'Excavations at Carthage, 1977-1978, Fourth Interim Report', *Antiquaries' Journal 59*, 19–49.

Ibrahim 1976

L. Ibrahim, *Kenchreai, eastern port of Corinth: results of investigations by the University of Chicago and Indiana University for the American School of Classical Studies at Athens. II: The Panels of Opus Sectile in Glass*. Leiden: Brill.

ID

Inscriptions de Délos dédicaces postérieures à 166 av. J.-C, ed. P. Roussel and M. Launey. Paris: H. Champion, 1926.

IG

Inscriptiones Graecae. Berlin: G. Reimer, 1873–1927. Editio minor, 1913–.

ILLRP

Inscriptiones Latinae Liberae Rei Publicae, ed. A. Degrassi. Florence: La Nuova Italia, 1957.

Joshi 1988

J.P. Joshi, 'Archaeological Perspective of Marine Activities in Ancient India', in Rao (ed.) 1988, 99–103.

Jones 1950

F.F. Jones, 'VI. The Pottery' in H. Goldman (ed.), *Excavations at Gözlü Kule, Tarsus. Volume I. The Hellenistic and Roman Periods*. Princeton: Princeton U. Press.

Kleberg 1957

Tonnes Kleberg, *Hôtels, restaurants et cabarets dans l'antiquité romaine. Études historiques et philologiques*. Uppsala: Almquist and Wiksells.

Knoblauch 1977

P. Knoblauch, *Die Hafenanlagen und die anschliessenden Seemauern von Side*. Ankara: Türk Tarih Kurumu.

Koehler 1986.

C.G. Koehler, 'Handling of Greek Transport Amphorae', in Empereur and Garlan 1986, 49–67.

Kroll 1964

J.H. Kroll, 'The Late Hellenistic Tetrobols at Kos', *American Numismatic Society, Museum Notes 11*, 81–117.

Lancel 199

Serge Lancel, *Carthage: A History*. Oxford and Cambridge: Blackwell.

Lamboglia 1964

N. Lamboglia, 'Il primo saggio di scavo sulla nave romana di Albenga', *RSL 20 (1964)*, 219–29.

Launey 1949

M. Launey, *Recherches sur les armées hellénistiques*. Paris: Boccard.

Lehmann-Hartleben, K. 1923

K. Lehmann-Hartleben, *Die Antiken Hafenanlagen des Mittelmeeres. Klio Beiheft 14*, Leipzig.

Lenski 1999

Noel Lenski, 'Assimilation and Revolt in the Territory of Isauria, from the 1st Century BC to the 6th Century AD', *Jounal of the Economic and Social History of the Orient 42*, 413–65.

Lewin 1991
    A. Lewin, 'Banditismo e civiltas nella cilicia tracheia antica e tardoantica', *Quaderni di Storia* 76, 167–84.
Lewis 1986
    Naphtali Lewis, 'P. Hibeh, 198 on Recapturing Fugitive Sailors', *AJP 89*, 465–9.
Long 1987
    Luc Long, 'Appendix 1: the Grand Congloué Site: a Reassessment', in McCann et al. 1987, 164–6.
Lund 1993
    John Lund, 'Rhodian Amphorae as Evidence for the Relations between Late Punic Carthage and Rhodes', in P.A. Bilde, I. Nielsen and M. Nielsen (eds), *Aspects of Hellenism in Italy. Acta Hyperborea* 5. Copenhagen: Museum Tusculum Press, 359–75.
Lund 1995
    John Lund, 'Response to G. Finkielsztejn', in T. Fischer-Hansen (ed.), *Ancient Sicily. Acta Hyperborea* 6. Copenhagen: Museum Tusculanum Press, 297–302.
Lund 1999
    John Lund, 'Rhodian Amphorae in Rhodes and Alexandria as Evidence of Trade', in Gabrielsen et al. 1999, 187–204.
Lund 2000
    John Lund, 'Transport Amphorae as Evidence of Exportation of Italian Wine and Oil to the Eastern Mediterranean in the Hellenistic Period', in Lund and P. Pentz, *Between Orient and Occident*. Studies in Honor of P.J. Riis. Copenhagen: National Museum of Denmark, 77–100.
Lund 2002
    John Lund, 'Review of Gérald Finkielsztejn, Chronologie détaillée et révisée des éponymes amphoriques rhodiens, de 270 à 108 av. J.-C. environ. Premier bilan', *BAR International Series 990*. Oxford: Archaeopress, 2001. Bryn Mawr Classical Review 2002.11.23.
McCann 1987
    A.M. McCann, J. Bourgeois, E.K. Gazda, J.P. Oleson and E. L. Will, *The Roman Port and Fishery of Cosa*. Princeton: Princeton U. Press.
McCann and Will 1984
    A.M. McCann and E.L. Will, Review of J.H. D'Arms and E.C. Kopff (eds), 'The Seaborne Commerce of Ancient Rome. Studies in Archaeology and History'. *MAAR* 36 (1980), in *AJA 88 (1984)*, 92–95.
McCormick 2001
    M. McCormick, *Origins of the European Economy. Communications and Commerce, AD 300–900*. Cambridge: Cambridge U. Press.
MacDonald 1986
    B.R. MacDonald, 'The Diolkos', *JHS* 106, 191–5.
Magie 1950
    David Magie, *Roman Rule in Asia Minor to the End of the Third Century after Christ*. Princeton: Princeton U. Press.
Mansel 1963
    A.M. Mansel, *Die Ruinen von Side*. Berlin.
Marasco 1987a
    Gabriele Marasco, 'Roma e la pirateria cilicia', *Rivista Storica Italiana* 99, 122–46.
Marasco 1987b
    Gabriele Marasco, 'Aspetti della pirateria cilicia nel 1 secolo A.C.' *Giornale Filologico Ferrarese 10*: 129-145.
Maryon 1956
    H. Maryon, 'The Colossus of Rhodes', *JHS 76*, 68–86.
Meillassoux 1960
    Claude Meillassoux, 'Essai d'interprétation du phénomène économique dans les sociétés traditionelles d'auto-subsistance', *Cahiers d'études africaines,* 4, 38–67.
Meillassoux 1981
    Claude Meillassoux, *Maidens, Meal and Money. Capitalism and the domestic community*. Cambridge: Cambridge University Press. Originally published in French as *Femmes, greniers et capitaux*. Paris, 1975.

Mitchell 1993

Stephen Mitchell, *Anatolia: Land, Men and Gods in Asia Minor. Vol. 1, The Celts in Anatolia and the Impact of Roman Rule*. Oxford: Clarendon.

Morton 2001

J. Morton, *The Role of the Physical Environment in Ancient Greek Seafaring*. Leiden: Brill.

MRR

T.R.S. Broughton, *The Magistrates of the Roman Republic* (with Supplement). Cleveland, OH, 1951–3; reprint with Supplement, Atlanta, GA: Scholars Press, 1986.

Mukherjee 1999

B.N. Mukherjee, 'The Maritime Contacts between Eastern India and South-east Asia: New Epigraphic Data', in Behere 1999, 201–13.

Neumann 1980

Günter Neumann, 'Kleinasien' in Günter Neumann and Jurgen Untermann (eds), *Die Sprachen im Römischen Reich der Kaiserzeit*, Cologne: 167–85.

Nicolet 1977

Claude Nicolet, *L'Ordre équestre à l'époque républicaine*, 312–43 av. J.-C. Paris.

Oleston 2000

J.P. Oleston, 'Ancient sounding weights: a contribution to the history of Mediterranean navigation', *JRA* 13 (2000), 293-311.

Ormerod 1922

H.A. Ormerod, 'The Campaigns of Servilius Isauricus against the Pirates', *Journal of Roman Studies* 12, 35–56.

Ormerod 1987

H.A. Ormerod, *Piracy in the Ancient World*. Liverpool, 1928; Reprint, New York: Dorsett Press.

Palazzo 1989

P. Palazzo, 'Le anfore di Apani (Brindisi)', in *EfR* 1989, 548–53.

Paris 1915

J. Paris, 'Contributions à l'étude des ports antiques du monde grec', *BCH 39*, 5–16.

Paris 1916

J. Paris, 'Contributions à l'étude des ports antiques du monde grec: le port de Délos', *BCH 40*, 5–73.

Parker 1992

A.J. Parker, 'Ancient Shipwrecks of the Mediterranean and the Roman Provinces'. *BAR Int. Series 580*, Oxford: Tempus Reparatum.

Patai 1998

R. Patai, *The Children of Noah: Jewish Seafaring in Ancient Times*. Princeton: Princeton U. Press.

Peacock and Williams 1986

D.P.S. Peacock and D.F. Williams, *Amphorae and the Roman Economy. An introductory guide*. London and New York: Longman.

Peribeni and Romanelli 1914

R. Peribeni and P. Romanelli, 'Studii e ricerche archeologiche nell'Anatolia meridionale', *Monumenti Antichi* 23, 6–224.

Poland 1919

F. Poland, *Geschichte des griechischen Vereinswesens*, Leipzig.

Pomey and Tchernia 1978

P. Pomey and A. Tchernia, 'Le tonnage maximum des navires de commerce romains', *Archaeonautica* 2, 233–52.

Préaux 1939

Claire Préaux, *L'économie royale des lagides*. Chicago: Ares Press, 1979 reprint of Brussels 1939 edition, 40.

Pryor 1998

John H. Pryor, *Geography, Technology, and War. Studies in the Maritime History of the Mediterranean, 649–1571*. Cambridge: Cambridge U. Press.

Queyrel 1991

F. Queyrel, 'C. Ofellius Ferus', *BCH* 115, 389–464.

Raatgever 1985
    Reini Raatgever, 'Analytic tools, intellectual weapons: The discussion among French Marxist anthropologists about the identification of modes of production in Africa', in van Binsbergen and Geschiere 1985, 290–330.

Rajan 1988
    K. Rajan, 'Seafaring Activities of Tamil Nadu Coast', in Rao (ed.) 1988, 22–4.

Raman 1988
    K.V. Raman, 'Port Towns of Tamil Nadu – Some Field Data and the Prospects of Marine Archaeology', in Rao (ed.) 1988, 114–18.

Randsborg 1991
    K. Randsborg, *The First Millennium AD in Europe and the Mediterranean: An Archaeological Essay*. Cambridge: Cambridge University Press.

Rao 1988
    S.R. Rao (ed.), 'Archaeology of Indian Ocean Countries'. Proceedings of the first Indian Conference on Marine Archaeology of Indian Ocean Countries. October 1987. Dona Paula (Goa), India: National Institute of Oceanography.

Rao and Gudigar 1988
    S.R. Rao and P. Gudigar, 'Underwater Cultural Heritage of Indian Ocean Islands', in Rao (ed.) 1988, 153–5.

Raschke 1978
    M.G. Raschke, 'New Studies in Roman Commerce with the East', in H. Temporini (ed.), *Aufstieg und Niedergang der römischen Welt, II. 2*. Berlin and New York: Walter de Gruyter.

Rathbone 1983
    D. Rathbone, 'The Grain Trade and Grain Shortages in the Hellenistic East', in Garnsey and Whittaker 1983, 45–55.

Rauh 1986
    N.K. Rauh, 'Cicero's Business Friendships: Economics and Politics in the Late Roman Republic, *Aevum 60*, 1–30.

Rauh 1993
    N.K. Rauh, *The Sacred Bonds of Commerce: Religion, Economy, and Trade Society at Hellenistic Roman Delos, 166–87 BC*. Amsterdam: J.C. Gieben.

Rauh 1997
    N.K. Rauh, 'Who Were the Cilician Pirates?' in *Res Maritimae: Cyprus and the Eastern Mediterranean from Prehistory to Late Antiquity*, ed. S. Swiny, R. L. Hohlfelder, and H. Wylde Swiny, pp. 263–83. *American Schools of Oriental Research, Archaeological Reports No. 4*. Atlanta, Georgia: Scholars Press.

Rauh 1999
    N.K. Rauh, 'Rhodes, Rome, and the Eastern Mediterranean Wine Trade', in Gabrielsen et al. 1999, 162–86.

Rauh et al. 2000
    N.K. Rauh, R.F. Townsend, M. Hoff and L. Wandsnider, 'Pirates in the bay of Pamphylia: an archaeological inquiry', in G.J. Oliver, R. Brock, T.J. Cornell, and S. Hodkinson (eds), *The Sea in Antiquity, British Archaeological Reports International Series 899*. Oxford: 151–180.

Rauh 2001
    N.K. Rauh, Website, Rough Cilicia Arcaeological Survey Project. http://pasture.ecn.purdue.edu/~rauhn/

Rauh and Wandsnider 2001
    N.K. Rauh and L. Wandsnider, 'Dağlık Kilikiya Yüzey Araştırma Projesi: 1998 ve 1999 Raporları', *Araştırma Sonuçları Toplantısı 2. Cilt*' (22–26 Mayis 2000, Izmir). T.C. Kültür Bakanlığı, Anıtlar ve Müzeler Genel Müdürlügü, Ankara, 2001, pp. 259–72 (in Turkish). English version posted at project website: http://pasture.ecn.purdue.edu/~rauhn/ : Project Archive, 1998 and 1999 Reports.

Rauh and Wandsnider 2002
    N.K. Rauh and L. Wandsnider, Dağlık Kilikiya Yüzey Araştırma Projesi: 2000 Sezon Raporı. Araştırma Sonuçları Toplantısı 2. Cilt (28 Mayis – 01 Haziran 2001, Ankara). T.C. Kültür Bakanlığı,

Anıtlar ve Müzeler Genel Müdürlügü, Ankara, pp. 45–56. English version posted at project website: http://pasture.ecn.purdue.edu/~rauhn/ : Project Archive, 2000 Report.

Ray 1999

H.P. Ray (ed.), *Archaeology of Seafaring. The Indian Ocean in the Ancient Period*. Delhi: Pragati Publications.

Rediker 1987

Marcus Rediker, *Between the Devil and the Deep Blue Sea: Merchants, Seamen, Pirates, and the Anglo-American Maritime World 1700–1750*. Cambridge: Cambridge U. Press.

Reger 1994

Gary Reger, *Regionalism and Change in the Economy of Independent Delos*. Berkeley: U. California Press.

Rey 1971

P.P. Rey, *Colonialisme, néo-colonialisme et transition au capitalisme: exemple du 'Comilog' au Congo-Brazzaville*. Paris: Maspero.

Rey 1975

P.P. Rey, 'The Lineage Mode of Production', *Critique of Anthropology 3*, 27–79.

Rice 1999

E.E. Rice, 'Relations between Rhodes and the Rhodian Peraea,' in Gabrielsen et al. 1999, 45–54.

Ritti 1998

S. Ritti, 'Shipping in Ancient India', in Rao (ed.), 1988, 5–7.

Rostovtzeff 1932

Michael Rostovtzeff, *Caravan Cities*. Oxford: Clarendon.

Rothaus 1995

Richard Rothaus, 'Lechaion, Western Port of Corinth: a Preliminary Archaeology and History', *Oxford Journal of Archaeology 14 (3)*, 293–306.

Rotroff 1994

Susan I. Rotroff, 'The Pottery', in Hellenkemper-Salies *et al.* 1994, 133–52.

Roussel 1916

P. Roussel, *Délos, Colonie Athénienne*. Paris; reprinted with annotations and bibliographical revisions by Ph. Bruneau, M.-T. Couilloud-Ledinahet, R. Étienne, 1987.

Russell 1991

James Russell, 'Cilicia – Nutrix Vivorum: Cilicians Abroad in Peace and War during Hellenistic and Roman Times', *De Anatolia Antiqua (Eski Anadolu) 1*, 283–97.

Salviat 1986

Françoise Salviat, 'Le vin de Thasos. Amphores, vin et sources écrites', in Empereur and Garlan 1986, 145–95.

Scobie 1986

A. Scobie, 'Slums, Sanitation, and Morality in the Roman World', *Klio 68*, 399–433.

Scranton and Shaw 1978

R. Scranton and J. Shaw, *Kenchrea, Eastern port of Corinth: results of investigations by the University of Chicago and Indiana University for the American School of Classical Studies at Athens I, Topography and Architecture*. Leiden: Brill.

SEG

Supplementum Epigraphicarum Graecarum. Volumes 1–25 (1923–71) ed. J.J. Hondius, A.G. Woodhead et al. Volume 27 (1976–7) ed. H.W. Pleket and R.S. Stroud. Amsterdam: Gieben, 1976–.

Shaw 1984

B.D. Shaw, 'Bandits in the Roman Empire', *Past and Present* 105, 3–52.

Shaw 1990

B.D. Shaw, 'Bandit Highlands and Lowland Peace: The Mountains of Isauria-Cilicia', *Journal of the Economic and Social History of the Orient* 33, 199–233.

Shenouda 1976

S. Shenouda, 'Alexandria', *Princeton Encyclopedia of Classical Sites*. Princeton: Princeton U. Press, 36–8.

Sherry 1986

F. Sherry, *Raiders and Rebels: The Golden Age of Piracy*. New York: Hearst Marine Books.

A. Sherwin-White 1976

A.N. Sherwin-White, 'Rome, Pamphylia and Cilicia 133–70 BC', *Journal of Roman Studies 66*, 1–14.

A. Sherwin-White 1984

A.N. Sherwin-White, *Roman Foreign Policy in the East 168 BC to AD 1*. London.

S. Sherwin-White 1978

Susan Sherwin-White, 'Ancient Cos. An Historical Study from the Dorian Settlement to the Imperial Period'. *Hypomnemata* 51, Göttingen.

SIG³

Sylloge Inscriptionum Graecarum, 3rd edition. W. Dittenberger. Lipsiae: S. Hirzel, 1903.

Steffy 1985

R. Steffy, 'The Kyrenia ship: an interim report on its hull construction', *AJA* 89, 71–101.

Sibella 2002

P. Sibella, 'The George McGhee Amphora Collection at the Alanya Museum, Turkey', *The INA Quarterly* Vol. 29 Suppl. 1. College Station: Institute of Nautical Archaeology.

Soebadio 1999

H. Soebadio, 'Indian-Indonesian Cultural Relations', in Behera 1999, 72–9.

Syme 1986

Ronald Syme, Isauria in Pliny. *Anatolian Studies 36*, 159–64.

Syme 1995

Ronald Syme, *Anatolica. Studies in Strabo* (posthumously edited by A. Birley). Oxford: Clarendon.

Tchernia et al. 1978

A. Tchernia, P. Pomey, A. Hesnard, M. Couvert, M.-F. Giacobbi, M. Girard, E. Hamon, F. Laubenheimer, F. Lécaille, A. Carrier-Guillomet, A. Chéné, J.-M. Gassend, G. Réveillac, M. Rival, 'L'épave romaine de la Madrague de Giens (Var). Fouilles de l'Institut d'archéologie méditerranéenne'. *Gallia supplément 34*. Paris: CNRS.

Tchernia 1986

André Tchernia, *Le vin de l'Italie romaine – essai d'histoire économique d'après les amphores*. Rome: Ecole française de Rome.

A. Tchernia 1992

André Tchernia, 'Le dromadaire des Peticii et le commerce oriental', *MEFRA 104*, 293–301.

Terray 1969

E. Terray, *Le Marxisme devant les sociétés 'primitives'*. Paris: Maspero.

Terray 1975

E. Terray, 'Classes and class consciousness in the Abron kingdom of Gyaman', in Bloch (ed.), *Marxist Analyses and Social Anthropology*. London: Malaby Press, 85–137.

Tracey 1979

Stephen V. Tracey, 'Athens in 100 BC', *HSCP 83*, 211–35.

Vanderpool 1960

Eugene Vanderpool, 'News Letter from Greece', *AJA 64*, 265–7.

Van 't Dack and Hauben 1978

E. Van 't Dack and H. Hauben, 'L'Apport égyptien à l'armée navale lagide', in H. Maehler and V.M. Strocka (eds), *Das ptolemäische Ägypten. Akten des internationalen Symposions 27.–29. September 1976 in Berlin*. Mainz am Rhein: Philipp Von Zabern, 60–93.

Waltzing 1895

J.P. Waltzing, *Etude historique sur les corporations professionnelles chez les Romains*. Louvain.

Binsbergen and Geschiere 1985

Wim van Binsbergen and Peter Geschiere (eds), *Old modes of production and capitalist encroachment. Anthropological explorations in Africa*. London: KPI Limited.

Weinberg 1965

G.D. Weinberg, V.R. Grace, G.R. Edwards, H.S. Robinson, P. Throckmorton, E.K. Ralph, 'The Antikythera Shipwreck Reconsidered', *Transactions of the American Philosophical Society*. N.S. Vol. 55, Part 3. Philadelphia: APS.

Wheeler 1954

Mortimer Wheeler, *Rome Beyond the Imperial Frontiers*. London.

Will in press

E. Lyding Will, 'The Mediterranean Shipping Amphorae from the 1989-92 Excavations', in V. Begley et al., *The Ancient Port of Arikamedu. New Excavations and Researches 1989–1992. Vol. 2*, in press.

Will 2001

E. Lyding Will, 'Defining the Regna Vini of the Sestii', in N.W. Goldman (ed.), *New Light From Ancient Cosa. Classical Mediterranean Studies in Honor of Cleo Rickman Fitch*. New York: Peter Lang, 35–47.

Will 1997

E. Lyding Will, 'Shipping Amphorae as Indicators of Economic Romanisation in Athens', in M.C. Hoff and S.I. Rotroff, *The Romanisation of Athens*. Oxford: Oxbow, 117–33.

Will 1996

E. Lyding Will, 'Mediterranean shipping amphorae from the 1941-50 Excavations', in V. Begley et al., *The Ancient Port of Arikamedu. New Excavations and Researches 1989–1992. Vol. 1*. Pondichéry: Ecole française d'extrême-orient, 317–20.

Will 1991

E. Lyding Will, 'The Roman Shipping Amphorae from Arikamedu', in V. Begley and R. De Puma (eds), *Rome and India: The Ancient Sea Trade*. Madison: U. Wisconsin Press, 151–6.

Will 1989

E. Lyding Will, 'Relazioni mutue tra le anfore romane. I ritrovamenti in oriente, alla luce dei dati ottenuti nell'occidente', in *EfR* 1989, 297–309.

Will 1987a

E. Lyding Will, 'The Roman Amphorae', in McCann et al. 1987, 171–222.

Will 1987b

E. Lyding Will, 'The Roman Amphorae from Manching: a Reappraisal', *Bayerische Vorgeschichtsblätter* 52, 21–36.

Will 1982

E. Lyding Will, 'Graeco-Italic Amphorae', *Hesperia* 51, 338–56.

Will 1979

E. Lyding Will, 'The Sestius Amphorae: a Reappraisal', *JFA 6*, 339–50.

Wolff 1999

C. Wolff, 'Comment devient-on Brigand?' *REA* 101, 393–403.

Wolff 1986

Samuel R. Wolff, *Maritime Trade at Punic Carthage*. Chicago: University of Chicago dissertation.

Zemer 1977

Avshalom Zemer, *Storage Jars in Ancient Sea Trade*. Haifa: National Maritime Museum Foundation.

Ziebarth 1896

E. Ziebarth, *Das griechische Vereinswesen*, Leipzig.

Index